Complexities of Teaching:
Child-centred Perspectives

Ciaran Sugrue

The Falmer Press

(A member of the Taylor & Francis Group)
London • Washington, D.C.

UK   The Falmer Press, 1 Gunpowder Square, London, EC4A 3DE
USA   The Falmer Press, Taylor & Francis Inc., 1900 Frost Road, Suite 101,
         Bristol, PA 19007

First published in 1997

**A catalogue record for this book is available from the British
Library**

**Library of Congress Cataloging-in-Publication Data are
available on request**

ISBN 0 7507 0479 9 cased
ISBN 0 7507 0480 2 paper

Jacket design by Caroline Archer

Typeset in 10/12pt Times by
Graphicraft Typesetters Ltd., Hong Kong.

*Printed in Great Britain by Biddles Ltd, Guildford and King's Lynn
on paper which has a specified pH value on final paper
manufacture of not less than 7.5 and is therefore 'acid free'.*

Contents

This book is dedicated to my first teachers: my father and mother. My late father communicated an infectious curiosity about the world, which he combined successfully with the storyteller's art. My mother continues to delight in the art of conversation: a talent that she deploys along with her considerable capacity for framing penetrating questions. I am very grateful to them both for these (and many other) invaluable influences.

Acknowledgments

There are numerous individuals to whom I owe a debt of gratitude for their assistance in the completion of this work. My thanks to the sixteen teachers who participated in the study, and in particular the teacher whom I call 'Helen' who took the considerable risk of having me in her classroom for several weeks. Nick and Bernadette MacAuliffe who adopted my family from the time of our arrival in Toronto and whose assistance, during our stay and my repeated journeys across the Atlantic as I completed my PhD thesis, was generous and invaluable. Brent Kilbourn, the Chair of my thesis committee, was unfailingly enthusiastic, supportive, and unstinting with his time, advice and feedback while I continue to value his friendship. Andy Hargreaves was a valued and vital member of the thesis committee also and his ideas had a significant shaping influence on the work. David Hunt, who completed the committee's triumvirate, was supportive, good humoured and constructively critical throughout. Colleagues at home, Andy Burke, Martin Carney, Mark Morgan and Hugh Gash provided practical support, while in Toronto Rita O'Brien, Mary Beattie, Vepe Percival and Helen Harper offered advice and provided assistance in reaching various goals and deadlines.

I am particularly grateful to Andy Hargreaves for initial encouragement to reshape the thesis into its current form. His colleague and friend Ivor Goodson took primary responsibility for this task but between them, at various stages throughout the process, they have been generous with their time and advice. I have come to value their capacity to provide constructive criticism and practical advice while being careful not to dictate. Their company, friendship, wit and willingness to 'have a laugh' along the way are valued and appreciated. At Falmer Press, Anna Clarkson, Jackie Day and all the others who contribute to the editorial and production process were a pleasure to work with and never tired of making suggestions for improvement!

The contributions of Siobhán Nolan and Clíona Uí Thuama have been particularly significant and invaluable throughout this process and without their support and skill it would have been impossible to complete the work on schedule. Finally, words are inadequate to express my gratitude to my partner Joan whose support has been generous to a fault and she has borne the inevitable domestic and other burdens with a steely stoicism. Thanks to our daughters Dervla and Caragh whose patience, good humour and sometimes loaded questions were important and often timely reminders to engage with important dimensions of the human condition other than writing!

Introduction

This book sets out to understand, recover and reinvent child-centred teaching. In recent years, child-centred teaching has come under vicious and virulent attacks from entrepreneurs, mass media, politicians, and, in some instances, the educational establishment itself. Child-centred teaching has been pilloried and parodied as the source of all that is economically unproductive and morally degenerate in the closing years of this century. Child-centred teaching has been compared to traditional teaching or class teaching like vice is to virtue or weakness is to strength. In this widespread assault on child-centred teaching, few have cared to understand what it is really like in practice, for understanding is not their purpose. Yet many others, parents and teachers among them, have let their perceptions of child-centred teaching be strongly influenced by the caricatures that abound in the media.

This book sets out a rather different understanding of child-centred teaching. It is an understanding that is grounded neither in naïve defensiveness, nor in peremptory dismissal. Rather, it is grounded in close encounters with the words and practices of child-centred teachers themselves. These close encounters reveal that the world of child-centred teaching is a highly complex, and in many respects a surprising one. It includes a complex cocktail of competing and sometimes contradictory images of teaching that are frequently categorized rather arbitrarily as traditional or progressive for the purpose of demonization or valorization. For example, child-centred teaching may often include class teaching rather than being unremittingly opposed to it. Yet class teaching, or whole class instruction, far from being a panacea, emerges as a pedagogical device with strengths and limitations like any other. Child-centred teaching pushes children to the limits of their learning rather than merely allowing them to follow their own interests or 'rest on their laurels', if that is what they choose. And amid accusations of pupil licence and lack of direction, it is a world in which structure is everywhere, sometimes in a supportive, guiding and framing manner, but with potential also to stifle and to snuff out individual flair and initiative, where conformity and uniformity can become highly prized and privileged. Though structure is pervasive, practitioners find time also to care for learners, to be attentive to their personal and emotional needs, so that teaching emerges as a complex and sophisticated mélange of cognitive and pastoral concerns.

While other investigations of child-centred teaching have neatly categorized, frequently in overly simplistic ways, classroom routines and rituals as traditional or progressive in a mutually exclusive, oppositional, and adversarial manner, the present study seeks to celebrate the complexity, uncertainty, and multi-faceted nature of primary classrooms, and to make sense of teaching traditions, and child-centred teaching in particular, from the perspective of those who daily dice, frequently against the odds, with its inherent tensions and dilemmas. These tensions, dilemmas and complexities in teachers' lives and work are compounded by the uncertainties and paradoxes of late twentieth-century societies where the sometimes contradictory messages of educational change literature and research on effective schooling serve to undermine and to destabilize the often fragile ecology of classrooms that teachers struggle to achieve and maintain. Finding stability amid such uncertainty and complexity is further exacerbated by being encouraged and sometimes coerced into committing to lifelong learning and continuous improvement when survival in dealing with the immediacy and intensity of engagement with learners leaves teachers physically, mentally and emotionally drained, to the extent that some seek refuge in alternative careers, if such are available, in disability pensions and early retirement packages.

This growing complexity and uncertainty is heightened when teachers, to an unprecedented and accelerating degree, are faced with new and more varied curricula — including sexuality and relationships, civic and social education, greater emphasis on information technology and science — which they are expected to graft on to the more traditional fare of basic literacy and numeracy without any diminution in standards or increase in available time. Fragmentation, overload and burnout are typical consequences of these agendas as teachers seek to be both rigorous and relevant in their programmes and teaching. Still further complexity, uncertainty and insecurity exist when child-centred policies have been shrouded in a climate that is increasingly dominated by accountability, transparency, national testing, league tables, and performance indicators, and where teaching methods are reappraised and interrogated also. The same methodological recipes, finely honed on the anvils of classroom practice, are no longer guaranteed to enable hard-pressed practitioners to navigate towards predetermined educational shores. As traditional family structures and values become more fragile and fractured, parenting styles more diverse, learners' behaviours and expectations more unpredictable and unstable, where the intensity and complexity of classroom engagements resemble 'black holes', the emotional labour of teaching has increased dramatically as teachers are obliged to care for and nurture learners as well as providing cognitive challenge.

Within the emotional maelstrom of contemporary classrooms, some practitioners seek to reduce complexity and uncertainty by clinging to established pedagogical recipes, and are encouraged to do so by policy-makers and researchers who seek to stem the tide of change by reinscribing more formal teaching strategies, greater emphasis on structuring and whole class instruction, with less emphasis on more informal teaching strategies such as individualization, group and project work. In these complex and uncertain times, caring for and challenging learners create serious moral and practical dilemmas for teachers, the intensity of which vary significantly depending on the social context of their work. Demands for greater cognitive challenge and higher standards appear to contradict and conflict with the need to create classroom climates which are warm, friendly and supportive; where there is time and space for adult–child relationships to be formed and sustained, opportunities for independent learning created and creative endeavour encouraged and rewarded. Classrooms, therefore, are sites of struggle where teachers, on a daily basis, grapple with these complexities as they seek to give meaning and coherence to contemporary versions of teaching traditions: where back-to-basics in its various guises is pitted against more humane, just and equitable versions of classroom practice which is frequently located within a progressive ideology of schooling. Out of this complex, competing and conflicting set of circumstances, this study, through close collaboration with experienced practitioners, seeks to reinvent child-centred teaching. By grounding it in the multiple realities of teachers' work, as they live out these tensions and dilemmas in classrooms, some situated certainty is restored to an important educational enterprise.

In seeking to acknowledge the complexities of classroom life as outlined above, this study assumes that policy issues, practitioners' intentions and actions, as well as the contexts of their work, are intimately and inextricably linked. Consequently, the process in which teachers engage when constructing teaching is not merely the putting into practice of official policy, but a complex amalgam of these various competing and often conflicting factors. It is critical that the voices of practitioners be heard in the ongoing debate on restructuring teaching, learning and schooling in ways that reflect these changing times, their ambiguities and uncertainties without privileging teachers' perspectives or being sentimental about a lost golden age in teaching characterized by certainty, security and continuity. It is this complexity that gives rise to the three-phased, emergent design of the study which is reported in this book. It was conducted in Irish primary schools where there has been a policy of child-centred education since 1971. The study is based on three levels of data: interviews with sixteen primary teachers to elicit their teaching intentions in relation to official child-centred policy; classroom mini case studies of six of the interviewees to document these interests in practice; and an intensive case study of one of these teachers to get to grips with the complexity and coherence of child-centred teaching from the perspective of those who practice it.

These three phases recognize the multi-faceted nature of practitioner's teaching intentions and actions while being attentive to the role played by contextual constraints and biography in shaping individual's practice. Analysis of data generated during phases one and two of the inquiry provides three cultural themes: *Structure, Communication* and *Balance*. These are the lens through which a major case study of one practitioner's teaching is analysed, interpreted and reconstructed. The interpretive comments of the major case study connect the particulars of this teacher's practice with aspects of extant literature on traditional and progressive teaching. In this way, the inquiry's detail becomes a conduit for grounding a more inclusive, complex, reconstructed vision of child-centred teaching.

This study, though situated within the socio-historical traditions and particularities of primary education in Ireland, speaks to audiences in the antipodes, as well as Britain, Europe, and North America. Information flux and flows, which characterize contemporary societies, diminish more established distinctions between centre and periphery so that voices (which have been silent, silenced, and margin-alized) enter and illuminate mainstream discourses in education. From a substantive perspective, the pendulum swings of educational reforms in Ireland move to inter-nal rhythms and traditions while being informed and influenced, to varying degrees, by international discourses. These reforms have been more recent and rapid than elsewhere, thus creating a different dynamic in a traditionally conservative system. In these circumstances, precisely because a system occupies a different space on the reform continuum, and responds differently to outside influences, it has the potential to speak to, shape and influence, discourses on teaching traditions in other con-texts. The recurring dilemmas and tensions in primary classrooms in Ireland, there-fore, situated as they are amid this growing complexity and uncertainty, inform and illuminate international discourses around versions of traditional and progressive teaching, where these are reconstructed in, and shaped by, teaching practices.

Chapter 1 begins by invoking the uncertainties and complexities of the postmod-ern condition, and seeks to situate the study within this larger social framework. It discusses key terms such as teaching and learning, as well as traditional and child-centred teaching. Traditional teaching is dealt with briefly and the chapter's major focus is theoretical and empirical literature on progressivism: its fundamental prin-ciples are analysed and relevant survey, observational, and case-study research is discussed also from substantive and methodological perspectives. Finally, I situate myself within discourses on the grand narratives — traditional and progressive — through brief reference to my apprenticeship of observation, my experiences as class-room teacher, school inspector, teacher educator and researcher.

Chapter 2 revisits the substantive focus of the study and contextualizes the prob-lem by providing a succinct account of the significant shaping influences on primary schooling in Ireland. The chapter's major focus is the three-phased research design of the study, its elaboration, and justification, selection of participants, negotiation of entry, and ethical considerations, as well as some comment on how the text is intended to function.

Chapter 3, the first of five empirical chapters in the study, reports on the six-teen interviewees' teaching intentions, how they interpret child-centred policy, and how they approach their practice. These intentions are reported under three organ-izing cultural themes: Images of Teaching, Planning Intentions and Pedagogical Intentions. Their reconstructed accounts are analysed against the backdrop of the previous chapter, while similarities, complexities and variations between intentions and teaching traditions are carefully scrutinized. It becomes apparent that practi-tioners' intentions are januform — influenced by both traditions — and it emerges also that context and biography have a significant shaping influence on their inter-pretations of policy as manifest in their teaching intentions.

Chapter 4 seeks to narrow the study's focus through a series of mini case studies: to identify common cultural themes of practice. There is some preliminary methodological discussion on the selection of participants and the purpose of this second phase of the inquiry. The three emergent cultural themes are Structure, Communication and Balance, and a pastiche of practice is reconstructed through them in an instrumental fashion to reveal their complexity, presence and pervasiveness in each practitioner's classroom despite contextual and biographical variations. Each cultural theme becomes a lens for in-depth investigation of one practitioner's teaching constructions.

Chapter 5 sets the scene for the major case study. It does so by providing a comprehensive contextualization of the case, beginning with a biographical sketch of the participant, a description of the study's context, the community, its school and socio-economic circumstances. A typical day in the classroom of the collaborating teacher is described and the substantive themes of the inquiry are renamed and reoriented to reflect the idiosyncrasies of this teacher's practice and to orient the reader towards the content and structure of the major case study: phase three of the inquiry.

Chapter 6 is the first of three chapters each of which provides detailed interpretive accounts of the study's substantive themes. This opening chapter of the major case study provides a brief but succinct reconstruction of the essential structure of this teacher's practice that reveals a finely differentiated framework, a series of cognitive steps through which the various elements of the curriculum are structured with varying degrees of flexibility and rigidity.

Chapter 7 continues the in-depth investigation of practice through the cultural lens of communication. The conversational style of the practitioner reveals a complex mix of informal and formal pedagogical rules and routines with enormous implications for classroom climate, and the nature and quality of classroom relationships in ways that synergize teaching traditions. Informal routines, which cultivate, develop and sustain relationships between teacher and learners, impact significantly on more formal pedagogical routines that bring to life the underlying structures identified in the first theme.

Chapter 8 investigates practice through the cultural lens of balance. Contextual influences are particularly significant as the practitioner seeks to balance the social and cognitive needs of learners. This more widely focused theme indicates how classroom tensions and dilemmas are shaped by school, community and system-wide policies and structures. Collectively the three themes reveal the essential unity of practice and their rich detail provide many opportunities for regrounding and revisioning a more inclusive account of child-centred teaching.

Chapter 9 moves beyond the boundaries of the study and, in so doing, seeks to set a partial agenda for a more inclusive reconstructed vision of child-centred teaching that is grounded in the multiple realities of practice. It appropriates the multi-headed Hydra as a more complex metaphor for dealing with the complexities of teaching and learning. The discussion is focused primarily on classrooms, but the importance of the school, community and system-wide policies is commented on too. Reconstructing child-centred teaching, it is argued, necessitates paying attention to a complex web of interacting issues such as planning and structuring of content, class teaching, group teaching and group work, and social as well as cognitive development in an inclusive manner. This reconstruction process is not something that practitioners can undertake alone: collaboration and collegiality within schools are vital and policies and structures need to be created which facilitate this necessity to keep practice under review in ways that respect, support and renew the voices of practitioners. The chapter seeks to avoid prescription and attempts to set an agenda for debate where child-centred teaching in particular, and traditions of teaching in general, are being revisioned, revitalized and reconstructed.

The interpretive accounts that this book provides are intended to function at a number of levels. First, they provide detailed descriptions of actual practice, which will be of particular interest to practitioners in a variety of settings. The thick descriptions and interpretive comments invite them to reflect critically on practice in general and their own in particular. Though my primary motivation for undertaking this study is to understand the complexity of child-centred teaching and to illuminate and to reconstruct teaching traditions from a child-centred perspective, there is, in Wolcott's (1992, p. 15) terms, an 'underlying commitment to change . . .', a realization that 'things are not right as they are or, most certainly, are not as good as they might be'.

Second, teacher educators who engage with student teachers, beginning teachers and experienced practitioners will find this book of relevance to their work. Educational researchers with an interest in interpretive inquiry will find its substance meaningful also. Some policy-makers will be engaged by its detail and find its concluding discussion apposite to policy formulation. Those with an interest in comparative education should gain insight and understanding from this text also. This is particularly so in the context of European Union (EU) where free movement of teacher educators, researchers, and teacher and student exchanges, are growing and welcome phenomena. In this context, the text will make a modest contribution to celebrating the multiple realities of primary schooling in ways that respect diversity while contributing to identification of common problems and dilemmas.

Third, one of the significant issues that has emerged from recent research in Britain is a new found interest in the strengths of 'class' teaching and this has been mirrored by a North American focus on 'time on task' and 'cognitive structuring'. Because of the persistence of class teaching in the Irish setting, this text has the potential to highlight its weaknesses as well as its strengths. In this sense, through the details of the present study, issues of policy and practice, in other contexts, may be illuminated also. The text has the capacity to reinforce a point that is increasingly incontestable: that the dedication, energy, imagination *and expertise* (both subject matter and pedagogical) of class teachers is critical to the quality of teaching and learning in schools (Hargreaves and Fullan, 1992; Hargreaves, 1993). Consequently, the details surrounding the emergent themes speak to professional development issues and the process of educational change.

Chapter 1

Complexities of Teaching: Child-centred Perspectives

Introduction

The two grand narratives of teaching — traditional and progressive — entered this century like ideological cyclops. Their fortunes have subsequently waxed and waned as they were buffeted by economic, socio-political and ideological seismic shifts and social tremors. These grand narratives are usually described as being in opposition: each emphasizing and attempting to compensate for what the other allegedly does not possess, and, therefore, cannot provide. Grand narratives themselves can be regarded as the products of modernity and, it is claimed, in a postmodern age such cyclopic and myopic ideological perspectives are no longer sustainable: grand narratives are increasingly regarded as anachronistic (Boyne and Rattansi, 1990). It becomes necessary, therefore, to situate traditions of teaching within this wider milieu.

in the past

Modernity and Postmodernity

Distinctions between modernity and postmodernity are problematic and contested. By situating discussion and analysis of teaching traditions within a postmodern (rather than a modern) framework new possibilities for interpretation, synthesis and synergy emerge.

Modernity is essentially a European enlightenment concept and its central characteristics are generally agreed to be

> ... that nature can be transformed and social progress achieved by the systematic development of scientific and technological understanding, and by its rational application to social and economic life. (Hargreaves, 1994, p. 25)

There have been obvious and well-documented implications of this modernistic paradigm for curricula and teaching. Essentially the factory model was imposed on schools so that pupils were organized into age cohorts (classes or standards) and taught a set programme which was teacher driven and systematically tested at regular intervals to measure progress (Goodson and Ball, 1984; Hargreaves, 1994). This model of teaching has its roots in the industrial revolution, and it gave credence to the monitorial system inspired by Lancaster and Bell. Additional consequences were homogenization of curricula, the creation of a reward system and the meritocracy as well as the feminization of teaching (Erickson and Shultz, 1992; Katz, 1987). This system was also about the development and perpetuation of social élites, it was oppressive to many, it exacerbated existing social divisions through the provision of educational tracks (academic, technical and vocational), and through these various mechanisms promoted and exercised social control (Eggleston, 1977; Willis, 1977; McLaren, 1986; Aronowitz and Giroux, 1985).

Lest the reader form the impression that the characteristics of modernity apply to traditional teaching only, progressive teaching is very definitely a product of European Enlightenment also. Rousseau, frequently referred to as the father of progressivism, has been followed by a succession of like-minded individuals who sought to bring about educational reforms; Pestalozzi, Froebel, Herbart, and Montessori are usually cited in this context while John Dewey has attained the status of academic folk-hero in North America. Surrounded by the characteristics of modernity, proponents of traditional and progressive teaching ideologies have been able to insulate and isolate themselves within their own paradigms. These ideologies have been espoused by politically conservative and liberal groups respectively. This has been a recipe for confrontation and as these two great power blocks have sought supremacy in terms of educational policy and practice, the minds and hearts of teachers and children have been pawns in a kind of educational super league. Inevitably, the educational research community has entered the fray also. Consequently (as will be evident later in this chapter) a succession of reports have been selectively appropriated to vindicate or to demonize traditional or progressive teaching, depending on the camp (paradigm) being espoused.

Great power blocks, which were built on the axioms of modernity, have suffered irreparable damage in recent years and the crumbling of such certainties are symbolized in the fall of the Berlin Wall and the dismantling of apartheid in South Africa (Sparks, 1994). These particular moments have become a collective metaphor for the crisis of modernity where the certainties, apparent permanence, and self-assurance of a pervasive 'Technical Rationality' have yielded to persistent criticism (Schön, 1983). Hegemonic control, domination, and influence of key ideologies have been eroded, at least within the academy. This has come about because, as Lyotard suggests, postmodernity is 'incredulous towards metanarratives' (quoted by Rorty, 1994, p. 160). Hargreaves (1994, p. 43) suggests that the postmodern condition is at once full of 'potency and precariousness'. Le Rider (1993, p. 296) warns that it has the potential for 'an anarchy of individualist values which coexist but are unaware of one another, or even mutually exclusive'. Nevertheless, he, and many other writers, readily recognize that the very 'indeterminacy' of the postmodern 'can be extremely fruitful, allowing for recombinations of unbelievable variety and richness . . .' (p. 301). My preference in this chapter (and throughout the text) is to investigate child-centred teaching through a postmodern rather than a modern lens. Such an approach implicitly recognizes that 'no tradition . . . can speak with authority and certainty for all of humanity' (Aronowitz and Giroux, 1991, p. 116).

As part of this approach, the chapter reconstructs traditional and progressive teaching ideologies in terms of their sentiments, assets and liabilities. However, as the focus of this study is child-centred teaching, analysis of this grand narrative is more extensive and in-depth. Research on progressive teaching is analysed and discussed in terms of substantive content and methodological design. A focus on these studies' research methods has important implications for the conduct of the present inquiry. Finally, through very brief biographical details, I situate myself within discourses on teaching traditions and indicate my interest in the problem. However, to begin with, as a means of situating traditional and progressive teaching traditions within a wider context, it is necessary to identify common meanings attaching to teaching and learning, as these are central to understanding both traditions.

Teaching

What is called teaching in Britain and Australia is called instruction in the United States and in Canada (Hargreaves, 1994, p. ix). In my cultural context, instruction typically carries vocational overtones. For example, students, apprentices and others receive instruction while horses and greyhounds are trained. When my parents reprimanded me, wagging an index finger in my direction, they commonly stated, 'you were under strict instructions' to do such and such. Instructions left no room for ambiguity; they were highly prescriptive and no discretionary interpretations were permitted. Giving instructions was tantamount to rule by dictat. Receiving instruction in a particular subject, therefore, suggested mirroring as closely as possible, both in form and content, the information being transmitted by the instructor. Memorization, verbatim internalization rather than understanding was required so that appropriate amounts of information could be regurgitated in response to examination question.

Teaching in comparison with training and instruction seemed qualitatively different without being able to say why very clearly. The common elements in teaching, instruction and training appear to be a teacher, a student and some content. This common-sense evidence, which is circumscribed by cultural and class issues, seems to imply that in training and instruction there is greater expectation on the part of teachers that directions will be followed with accuracy, to the letter, slavishly. Teaching, on the other hand, seems to allow for some initiative or interpretation on the part of learners. Teaching and learning are intimately connected and it is difficult to come to terms with one without reference to the other.

An Etymology of Teaching and Learning

The majority of words that we use in everyday speech in relation to teaching and learning are derived primarily from Latin. These Latin roots appear to carry many of the culturally shaded meanings identified above. *Chambers English Dictionary*

(Macdonald, 1981) defines teaching as 'the act, practice or profession of giving instruction' thus putting instruction and teaching on a par. The same source describes training in apparently narrower terms when it says: 'to instruct and discipline: to cause to grow in the desired manner: to prepare for performance by instruction, practice, diet, exercise, or otherwise'. Training, therefore, appears to have an end in view that is non-negotiable; it remains faithful to and consistent with the Latin words *exerceo* — to exercise, or *disciplina* — training. The role of the learner in these circumstances is to follow instructions to the letter and/or to subject one's self unconditionally to the wisdom of the instructor. Polanyi (1958, p. 207) has described such a process as the 'transmission of ... [the] aggregate of intellectual artifacts from one generation to another'. This requires a 'process of communication' so that one person places 'an exceptional degree of confidence in another, ... the student in the teacher ...' A teacher is one 'whose profession is, or whose talent is the ability to impart knowledge, practical skill, or understanding' (Macdonald, 1981). Within these parameters, good students, those who are teachable (*docilis*) are those who adopt a passive, docile attitude towards the teacher. Significantly the Latin word used to describe this kind of learning is *accipio*: to accept as true and to be receptive to the pronouncements of the teacher. Learners are teachers' disciples (*disciplinus*) suggesting a relationship of trust and an investment of authority in the teacher. The language commonly used around teaching and learning is imbued with these shaded meanings. Its general import suggests passivity and acceptance and a lack of questioning on the part of learners. Despite popular misconceptions, the Socratic method is not premised on the term *educare* — to nurture or to care for — but rather on the term *educe* — to lead out or to adduce. It is rather ironic that, despite this misunderstanding, educators have recently identified care as an important dimension of teaching (Noddings, 1992; Hargreaves and Tucker, 1991; Ben-Peretz, 1996). To be educated by means of the Socratic method is to be liberated and empowered rather than enslaved or controlled. Small wonder, perhaps, that Socrates was perceived as subversive: a threat to society that warranted his elimination!

In contrast with passivity, docility and trust implicit in commonplace notions of teaching, the concept of learning suggests more active participation on the part of learners. Cognitive dissonance, which is central to conceptual development, is an active process carefully contrived by practitioners and entered into by learners. To access and acquire information, to become aware and to ascertain is derived from the Latin word *cognosco* (cognition), while *disco* (to learn) suggests that without some cerebral turbulence conceptual development is unlikely to occur. Teaching and learning, therefore, appear to be at odds. The former requires the learner to be attentive, and passive while the latter encourages active engagement on the part of the learner. Without delving any further into the etymology of these key terms, what has been identified so far supports the contention that one of the primary functions of schools, schooling and curricula is principally concerned with transmission of information and this has been privileged over creating opportunities for learning: a process which necessitates active participation and engagement of learners. A more adequate conception of schooling, therefore, seems to suggest that a synergic mix or productive tension between the social requirement of cultural continuity needs to be balanced with active and critical engagement of learners' faculties: continuity with transformation. This fundamental tension has immediate and profound implications for the purposes of schooling and the nature of pedagogy and curricula. Further explorations of these tensions can be achieved through an exposé of the grand narratives of teaching: traditional and progressive.

Traditional Teaching

The axioms of traditional teaching have been variously labelled didacticism, transmission, teaching as telling, teacher-centred, rigid, uniform, narrow and content driven (Bullough, 1992; Samuelowicz and Bain, 1992). It is said to include centrally prescribed text and syllabi which allow for very little discretion on the part of teachers. Further circumscription is typical in the form of terminal examinations. Such examinations impose a particular standard on all pupils regardless of ability or social circumstance. The payment by results system which operated throughout the British Empire ensured that, by fair means or foul, teachers attempted to increase their annual salaries by maximizing the grades of their students (Coolahan, 1981; O'Buachalla, 1988; Holmes, 1911). This frequently resulted in less able pupils being ignored or discouraged from school attendance or sitting public examinations, while more able learners were rigidly streamed with 'scholarship' classes being formed for the brightest and the best. Within this tradition there were two strands: the narrowly academic curriculum pursued with rigour, which was primarily preparatory to becoming a 'clerk of the empire' and 'an educated gentleman', and the elementary strand, which leaned towards relevant schooling for hewers of wood and drawers of water. In different respects, both strands were vocational and utilitarian and rooted in social divisions and hierarchies. Such leanings are present in contemporary educational discourse in the guise of promoting 'enterprise', thus making school relevant to working life, while others' clamour for greater rigour by advocating a return to 'basics'. Traditional teaching, as the term is used in this text, is cognizant of both strands as played out in primary classrooms.

Class teaching was the dominant pedagogy of traditional schooling and regarded by its critics as inimical to differing abilities, interests and capacities of learners. Its general *raison d'être* was to teach a programme, to cover a course or prescribed curriculum content. It was typically packaged in notes that were tailored to examination questions. This content-driven approach to curriculum also had a significant impact on the use of time. Timetables were constructed, slavishly followed and typically reflected the dominance of the 3Rs in the curriculum, with little or no attention being paid to a subject area that was not examined. Emerson summarizes this tradition as follows:

> The so-called 'traditional' method of teaching by rote, in class, through rigid subject definition and with emphasis on the '3Rs', was dominant for much of this century. It both remains a regular practice in some schools

and provides something of a flagship for moral rearmament in the 1980s and 1990s. (1993, p. 14)

The role of pupils in such circumstances was to be 'actively passive and industri-ously receptive' while in every other respect leaving themselves 'in the teacher's hands' (Holmes, 1911, p. 67). Child-centred teaching, by contrast, was intended as a counter-blast to this stifling rigidity and uniformity: 'at its apparent opposite is the so-called "progressive" method' (Emerson, 1993, p. 14).

Child-centred Teaching

Progressive teaching has been variously labelled as 'developmental' (Blyth, 1965) 'craftsman teaching' (Gracey, 1974), 'individualistic' (Ashton, 1975), 'informal' teaching (Bennett, 1976), 'process' teaching (Blenkin and Kelly, 1981, 1983) and, of course, child-centred (Entwistle, 1970). The term progressive itself tends to be used in a generic manner to include all of the above. Throughout this text, the terms progressive and child-centred are used interchangeably. As the term progressive sug-gests its earliest advocates were reformist and thus perceived as liberal. In the early stages of the Progressive Education Association in America, (founded in 1919), its agenda was 'liberal-minded' and the preserve of the 'upper middle class' (Counts, 1932, pp. 7–8). Counts, a founding member of the association, suggests that many of these people were 'romantic sentimentalists' who could probably not 'be trusted to write our educational theories and shape our educational programs . . .' (1932, p. 8). Polarization of educational debate into liberal and conservative, progressive and traditional frequently cloaked and minimized internal disagreements. For example, Dewey was critical of the espousal of freedom as the absence of restraint only and went on to say: 'All new and reforming movements pass through a stage in which what is most evident is a negative phase, one of protest, of deviation, and innovation' (Cobb, 1929, p. 67). If, as Dewey suggests, paradigms begin by being defined in terms of what they are not rather than what they purport to be, this negative starting point is entirely modernist as it seeks to oppose and to dominate; yet it needs the very thing it opposes as part of its own identity. Consequently, after a period of protest, the parent ideology may become moribund through lack of commitment.

There is a seductive and seamless attractiveness to the rhetoric of child-centred teaching. Adherents argue that process is more important than product, understanding more important than acquisition of information, and originality and creativity more prized than regurgitation of 'the facts'. Acquisition of information is deemed to be less important as knowledge is assumed to be constructed rather than god-given so that emphasis is on meaning-making on the part of learners. Critics suggest that this tradition of teaching lacks rigour and is more interested in social engineering than the promotion of high academic standards (Cox and Dyson, 1969, 1970, 1971; Cox and Boyson, 1975; Bantock, 1980). Though frequently not very visible within the rhetoric of progressive teaching, many of its leading advocates believed passionately in an approach to teaching that contributed towards a more equitable and just society and in the capacity of teachers through mass schooling to contribute towards that end (Dewey, 1916; Cunningham, 1988). Liberal economic policies assumed that all boats would rise with the tide so that progressive education policies were expected to promote interalia, greater fraternity and equality.

The basic sentiment of progressive teaching stands in opposition to the axioms of its traditional counterpart: it seeks to give a more central role to learners. It may be said to favour learning more than teaching. However, this is to assume that teaching can only be didactic, formal and teacher centred. Potter (1967, p. 459) suggests that 'much of the methodology and attitude toward education commonly accepted in contemporary schools is due largely to the influence of progressive education.' Dewey summarized the distinctive contribution of progressive thinking as follows:

> Respect for individual capacities, interests and experience, enough external freedom and informality at least to enable teachers to become acquainted with children as they really are; respect for self-initiated and self-conducted learning; respect for activity as the stimulus and centre of learning and perhaps above all belief in social contact, communication, and cooperation upon normal human plane as all-enveloping medium. (1928, p. 198)

Principles of Child-centred Teaching

In the Irish context, official policy documents and reports regularly assert that there are five basic principles of child-centred teaching (Ireland, 1990a), while earlier publications suggest that there are seven, thus illustrating a degree of arbitrariness and disagreement in this regard (Ireland, 1985; Sugrue, 1990). At its inception, the American Progressive Education Association identified seven as a 'minimum set of principles'[1] (Potter, 1967, p. 455). In the Irish context, identification of principles has been primarily a form of retrospective rationalization: an attempt to separate sentiment from a more rational basis for classroom practice. Dictionary definitions suggest principles are 'a source of action' or 'a settled rule of action' (Macdonald, 1981). Principles can be regarded as either 'weak' or 'strong' to the extent that they provide necessary and sufficient conditions for classroom action (Hirst and Peters, 1970). The analysis of principles of child-centredness that follows suggests that, because these principles serve as weak guides to action in classrooms only, it is necessary to have recourse to actual practice as a more adequate means of illuminating their understanding. Through the particulars of grounded case studies the parent ideology is reviewed, revised, revitalized and revisioned.

While the basic sentiment of progressive education is opposed to the perceived rigidities and uniformities of traditional education, what does it propose? In an introductory chapter, it is not possible to deal comprehensively with progressive ideology internationally. Consequently, I begin with Irish policy documents and connect analysis of them with relevant international literature. This circumscribed and selective review of literature serves two purposes. It helps to separate sentiment of progressive ideology from its general import for classroom practice and substantively it provides a frame of reference that situates the grounded study of child-centred teaching: the primary focus of this text.

The five principles that are said to underpin primary practice in the Irish context are:

1   full and harmonious development of the child;
2   respect for individual difference;
3   activity and discovery;
4   environment-based learning;
5   integration of subject matter.

These principles are said to be implicit in *The Primary Teacher's Handbooks* (Ireland, 1971) that marked the introduction of a child-centred policy in the setting (Ireland, 1990). Subsequent reports and policy statements have quoted selectively from these handbooks as evidence that these principles, though not clearly enunciated at the time, were, nevertheless, what provided the essential thrust and springboard for progressive practice and reform.

Full and Harmonious Development

Because children 'are complex human beings . . . with physical, emotional, intellectual and spiritual needs . . .', the handbooks state, it is necessary to 'cater for . . . [their] full and harmonious development . . .' (Ireland, 1971, p. 13). The basic sentiment of this statement implicitly stands in opposition to the rigidity, uniformity, and lock-step approach of a narrow academic or vocational approach to teaching and curriculum (Eggleston, 1977). It would seem churlish in the extreme to oppose the full and harmonious development of any child. Yet, sentiment can be a poor guide to action. Alexander (1984, p. 12) identifies 'whole child' and 'whole curriculum' as 'two imperatives' of progressivism. In relation to the former, he suggests that intimate knowledge of the child in a classroom context is difficult to achieve. Primary teachers, he continues, particularly at the upper end of such schools, would need extraordinary breadth and depth of subject matter knowledge to match the whole child with an equally whole curriculum. This perspective recognizes the importance of a whole curriculum, which is assumed to be a very broad range of options so as to maximize the variety and development of human potential. Perhaps the idea of full and harmonious development is not a principle at all but the outcome of a broadly based curricular provision (Sugrue, 1990). Sentiment, therefore, must not preclude the question: What would such provision look like in practice?

It is relatively uncontentious that a broadly based curriculum is desirable, particularly when considered against the rigid tradition of elementary schooling. Consequently, there is little difficulty embracing the sentiment of 'whole child/whole curriculum'. The inclusion of subjects such as physical and health education, music, art, craft, drama, science, information technology, and social studies in the primary curriculum is generally taken to be a significant improvement on the restricted diet traditionally provided by the 3Rs. However, the simple seduction of such an approach needs to be resisted. Grafting the compulsion of a range of subjects to reading, writing and 'rithmetic can also become equally rigid in ways that are inimical to individual bent and interests. Noddings (1992, p. 30) states that 'it is high time we stopped regarding liberal education as the highest form of education, next to which all others seem inferior' as this leads to waste of 'public resources and individual talents . . .'. Curriculum provision, as we have come to know it, is invariably a very restricted selection from culture, and making it compulsory for all learners when it is 'designed for the capacities of a few' is wasteful and inimical to equality (Noddings, 1992, p. 31).

The promotion of social reform, which was part of the agenda of the pioneers of progressive teaching in North America, was unsuccessful as there was a general neglect 'of power relationships' (Zilversmit, 1993, p. 176). As Sarason (1990, p. xiv) correctly points out, 'change will not occur unless there is an alteration of power relationships among those in the system and within the classroom.' His comment suggests that merely altering the content of the curriculum is unlikely to improve the opportunities of the socially disadvantaged or marginalized. Promoting a more broadly based curriculum, a liberal education once reserved for the few, does little to improve the life-chances of the many. It may be suggested, therefore, that broadly based curricular provision, commonly believed to be an improvement on traditional fare and therefore one of its significant assets, can also be a liability, as it is selective and can become restrictive and prescriptive also.

Those who address this dilemma usually have recourse to arguments about a 'balanced' curriculum. But curriculum balance is a culturally loaded device that concentrates decisions in the hands of an influential élite. For example, balance may be interpreted as the acquisition of a second language in school, be it the compulsion to learn Irish, provision of mother tongue in multicultural Toronto or in many English inner-cities, Welsh among our Celtic neighbours, Spanish in a growing number of American States, Catalan in Catalonia, or Africans in pre-apartheid South Africa. Even if there were universal agreement (which there is not) that a broadly based liberal curriculum was in the best interests of all learners, it could be delivered in a manner that did not excite or engage learners.

It is not clear, therefore, what an appropriate balance might look like in practice. Prescribing an appropriate amount of time to be devoted to music or drama might correspond with some learners' needs and interests but be tedious in the extreme for those whose talents and abilities lay elsewhere. In the case of students who have interests in, and aptitudes for, these disciplines, they could be delivered in a pedagogical style that frustrated rather than enhanced their skills and understanding. If a broadly based curriculum is an asset, the methodological repertoire of teachers is critical to ensure adequate involvement of learners and their engagement with different subject matter areas. However, the more broadly based a programme, the less time there is available for all subjects. Some critics suggest that this is a significant liability as students' engagement remains superficial and there is little meaningful interaction with the rigour inherent in particular subjects (Bantock,

1980). While a broadly based curriculum is ostensibly intended to serve the talents and interests of learners, in many instances it is the talents of teachers and their interests (and competencies) in particular subject areas that determine to a significant degree the nature and extent of learners' engagement with aspects of a prescribed programme. Too much is left to chance or it is unrealistic to expect primary teachers, particularly at the senior end of the school, to have subject matter expertise and pedagogical skills across the entire curriculum (Alexander, 1984, 1992).

The basic sentiment of learners' full and harmonious development may be sound, but its content and delivery are highly problematic. Consequently, it is necessary to consider the principle as informing practice, though mere consideration is not sufficient to determine classroom action. Therefore, in a weak sense only can the principle be said to guide action. To the extent that it is against rigidity, uniformity and narrowness of programme content, the principle indirectly indicates appropriate action. Without reference to actual practice, the rhetoric of child-centred ideology is imprecise in its implications for teaching. Full and harmonious development may be an important rallying cry or slogan for progressive educators, but its implications for classrooms will vary significantly depending on social and cultural context.

Individual Difference: Needs, Interests and 'Readiness'

The *Plowden Report* (Report of the Central Advisory Council for Education (CACE) 1967, p. 9) declares: 'at the heart of the educational process lies the child' and this has become a slogan for progressives. *The Primary Teacher's Handbooks* (Ireland, 1971, p. 13) assert, in similar vein, that 'because each child is an individual' he or she must 'be valued' for themselves and this necessitates provision of 'variety of opportunities', thus enabling learners to develop at their 'own rate' and to their 'fullest capacity'. Individual autonomy and liberty understood against the backdrop of European Enlightenment, its struggle with feudalism, with absolute authority over peoples' lives and the goal of individual perfection through reason, are noble sentiments that are difficult to resist (Darling, 1994). Developing the 'full capacity' or potential of learners resonates with the basic sentiment of the first principle also. Because there is significant overlap between the principles, an uncritical response recognizes a seamless ideology only. Assets implicit in the exhortation are a shift in emphasis from a teacher-centred approach to putting the child centre-stage: treating learners as individuals shifts the focus from whole class teaching to tailoring content to individual needs and interests. Such an approach expresses a preference for a pedagogy that includes individualization, project work and group work in the form of mixed ability and ability grouping depending on the nature of learning activities. Progress, it is suggested, will be tempered by acknowledgment of individual difference and a recognition that readiness varies from one learner to the next. Piagetian constructivism and stage theory have been invoked in support of this general thesis (Plowden, 1967). It is necessary, therefore to ask: How can these sentiments be converted into guides to action for teaching and learning? Typical responses address this question with reference to individuality and individual's needs, interests and readiness.

Individual Needs

In the social context in which Rousseau and Froebel wrote, they quite appropriately championed the rights and freedoms of the individual (Boyd, 1975; Froebel, 1887). The latter argued that education should 'be passive' so that interference and pre-scription should be avoided, thus maximizing learners' autonomy (Froebel, 1887, p. 7). However, this is *freedom from* constraint and repression more so than *freedom* to exercise individual judgment (Sartre, 1966). This freedom from has been pursued in the present century through the development of the welfare state to the extent that there is a growing consensus that the 'discourse on rights' needs to be tempered with 'the discourse of duties . . .' (Roche, 1992, p. 246). Watt (1989) is aware of the tension between rights and duties when he identifies egocentrism and altruism as two strains of individualism. Similarly, Dewey (1902, 1916) sought to balance the needs of the individual with those of society. In a school system that promotes unbridled competition, egocentric development is championed at the ex-pense of a more caring society. Contemporary examples in the form of Reaganomics and Thatcherism illustrate how social cohesion and the fabric of civil society can become a thing of shreds and patches when marketplace ideology champions indi-vidual rights more than the collective responsibility to care, with profound implica-tions for teachers' classroom actions (Noddings, 1992; Lawton, 1992). Respect for individual difference must be protected and promoted, needs and interests recognized, while wider social interests and responsibilities cannot be ignored (Entwistle, 1970). It may be suggested, therefore, that an important asset of progressive ideology is its promotion of respect for individuals, while recognizing that its implications for teaching are problematic.

The editor's prologue to *Émile* warns that Rousseau intended the story by way of 'illustration' only; it is incumbent on all educators, he suggests, to 'work out methods appropriate to their own conditions' (Boyd, 1975, p. 1). This stricture accords with Goodson's (1994, p. 111) perspective that we must 'move away from decontextualised modes of analysis' to an understanding of curriculum and teach-ing as '*social construction*'. Within the rubric of child-centred teaching, therefore, learners' needs and interests must be tempered by social requirements.

Nurturing and Moulding

Rousseau, Froebel, Dewey and others, to varying degrees, espouse the state of na-ture argument which is typically transformed into the 'horticultural metaphor' (King, 1978). This metaphor suggests a peripheral role for the teacher where learners are allowed to pursue their own interests at their own pace. For example, an elementary student in a state school in Ontario, Canada, is to become, according to policy docu-ments, 'a lifelong learner . . . self-motivated, self-directed problem-solver' (Ontario

Ministry of Education, 1990, p. 7). An almost identical rhetoric is invoked for a Catholic education in Ireland where, according to Lane (1991, p. 16), 'one of the principle roles of the school is to initiate pupils into an experience of life-long, self-directed learning'. When rhetoric of this nature becomes global and decontextualized, its implications for classroom actions become correspondingly imprecise. Those who are critical of an open-ended agenda of 'growth', facilitated but unimpeded by teachers, frequently suggest a moulding metaphor as a means of balancing individual's needs with attention to the greater good. If, as Dewey (1916, p. 116) suggests, 'each individual is born with *distinctive* temperament', too much uniformity of curricular and pedagogical provision may result 'in stunting the true gifts of nature'. In seeking to leave the coercive force of authoritarian classrooms behind, there is seductive appeal in the concept of beginning with learners' needs, as it assumes that this will solve the problem of motivation.

In terms of the growth metaphor, close observation would reveal learners' needs, and these could then be husbanded by the teacher. Nevertheless, the practitioner has responsibilities to society also, which imply moulding learners for good citizenship and initiating them into cultural traditions. Consequently, the practitioner is expected to mediate between the conflicting demands of the growth and moulding metaphors. Many adults, however, are aware of just how tyrannical even a 2-year-old can be in its demands: in pursuit of its own needs and interests without reference to the needs and interests of others. Aristotle suggests that it is necessary to cultivate good habits of an intellectual and moral kind because we possess neither by 'nature'. Consequently, it is necessary that they be 'made perfect by habit' (Thompson, 1955, 1102, pp. 15–25). Similarly, interests are cultivated by the process of engaging with them. This cultivation of interests goes through a series of stages from habituation to knowing, understanding to appropriation, in a self-interested, enlightened fashion. This perspective is in agreement with a perception of schooling which suggests that part of its function is to broaden the horizons of learners through the cultivation of additional interests (Dearden, 1984; Peters, 1969; Hirst and Peters, 1970; Hirst, 1974).

Learners' Interests

Callan (1988, pp. 61–2) makes a particularly important distinction between 'pursuing an interest' and 'developing an interest'. Interests can be pursued in a mentally moribund manner where the individual does so to fuel existing prejudices rather than to enlighten. Only if there is an openness to being changed, to arriving at a different perspective, can an interest be regarded as genuinely developmental, and therefore educative. Consequently, if there is an onus on the educator to cultivate additional interests in learners, there is a concomitant obligation to engage them with subject matter in ways that are genuinely developmental. A reasonable interpretation of this perspective, from the practitioner's point of view, would be to suggest that not only is it necessary to be an authority in one's subject specialism, it is also necessary to have a variety of pedagogical and interpersonal skills which are necessary to cultivate developmental interests in learners (Alexander, 1992).

While nurturing existing needs as well as cultivating additional interests is part of practitioners' responsibility, the growth metaphor is incapable of identifying particular interests as having more educative value than others. It is limited also because it does not indicate when the practitioner should intervene, either to extend existing interests or cultivate new ones. Barrow (1984, p. 82) distinguishes between teaching content that is 'based on' learners' interests as opposed to 'taking some account' of them. Similarly, Entwistle (1970, p. 27) indicates that 'interests develop whilst one is being educated, as well as being a point of departure for the educational enterprise.' It has been suggested already that one means that practitioners have at their disposal in resolving some of these tensions is to strike while the iron is hot: when readiness is manifest in the learner.

Readiness

Readiness is a concept that can be accommodated easily within the growth metaphor. It suggests that it is futile to present a child with a task that is beyond his or her maturational stage of development: intervention ought to take place when readiness is observed in the learner. However, early intervention may force the child and create a hot-house flower that will fade all too soon. Nevertheless, the metaphor implies that percipient intervention can hasten growth without distorting development. It is at this point that the analogy breaks down again. There is no indication as to the direction in which growth should be encouraged. Value judgments are also required which cannot be supplied by nature. Alexander (1984, p. 93) suggests that a difficulty with the 'ideological potential' of child-centredness is its need for simplification: it may even be distorted in an effort to achieve its potential. Consequently, 'Piagetian theory may be interpreted as confirming a doctrine of readiness rather than as challenging teachers' ingenuity to provide children with appropriately structured and sequenced learning experiences', such as when a teacher emphasizes the importance of pre-reading activities and postpones formal reading for as long as possible (Alexander, 1984, p. 93). Apart altogether from individual differences among children, the appropriateness of this kind of delay might be questionable because of the stimulation which many children receive at home and/or in pre-school. In such situations, there is a real tension between the need for development and the need to be sure that a learner is ready to take a developmental step. Perhaps the influence of psychology in the field of teacher education and the concomitant focus on the negative effects of 'failure' (Holt, 1970) have encouraged practitioners to be particularly cautious so that many classroom activities lack the degree of challenge that is necessary for development.

Barrow (1984, p. 123) argues that the concept of readiness tells 'us when we must not do things' until some maturational point has been reached. However, it does not follow that 'we should do things as soon as somebody is ready' (p. 123). In the meantime, of course, it is necessary to be doing something to keep all those bundles of energy gainfully employed. The *Report of the Review Body on the Primary Curriculum* (Ireland, 1990a, p. 16) is quite explicit: 'it is essential to emphasise the importance of teaching as a means of developing readiness.' However, the principle does not provide any simplistic recipes for curricular action. It may be concluded, therefore, that in a weak sense only does the principle of individuality provide a necessary but insufficient condition for action. Practitioners are condemned to resolving tensions between learners' existing needs and the cultivation of additional interests through teaching routines. Once more, the proof of this particular principle is in the actions of practitioners rather than in any *a priori* prescription.

Activity and Discovery

The Primary Teacher's Handbooks[2] state that: '. . . children now play a much more active role in their own education . . .' while it may be more accurate to say that they are permitted and encouraged to be active agents rather than passive recipients (Ireland, 1971, p. 134). It is asserted in the handbooks that 'the principles of investigation, observation and discovery should be applied to as many situations as possible' (p. 134). However, how such a pedagogical approach will actually function in classrooms, 'will depend greatly on the intelligent guidance by the teacher who will advise, direct and help pupils along the road to discovery when assistance is considered necessary' (p. 134), echoing a point previously articulated in the Hadow (1931) and Plowden (1976) reports. More recently, there have been calls for greater differentiation between 'free' and 'directed' discovery but such an approach should not 'involve the teacher only minimally' (Ireland, 1990a, p. 17). Rather, learning requires 'a high level of teacher skill and preparation' which is a coded means of advocating a more interventionist role on the part of the teacher than envisaged in earlier documentation (p. 17). Plowden (1967) and Hadow (1931) articulate similar caveats around the twin issues of activity and discovery, while the former report states: 'the curriculum is to be thought of in terms of activity and experience rather than of knowledge to be acquired and facts to be stored', and cautions that discovery is a term that 'can be loosely interpreted and misunderstood' (Central Advisory Council for Education, 1967, p. 529). The report's endorsement of discovery receives strong qualification with the need for 'astringent intellectual scrutiny' and 'intellectual stiffening' (CACE, 1967, p. 201). The basic sentiment, yet again, appears sound as it stands in opposition to an emphasis on memorization of facts in a repetitive, passive, rote manner. Collectively these reports signal a growing acceptance that a combination of teaching as telling and learning as memorization, though it had some appeal, was (and continues to be) extremely tedious, dull, repetitive and soul destroying for many. However, as the caveats above suggest, there was awareness from the outset that, while consideration be given to the learner when shaping content and pedagogy, the teacher has ultimate responsibility for getting the balance right between these competing concerns. It may be said, therefore, that what this principle is against is one of its central assets, but what it is for is its 'Achilles heel!'

'Play' Methods

The general perspective, derived from the importance and apparent success of play methods in kindergarten, suggest that well-structured, sequenced materials enable learners to take initiatives with and responsibilities for their own learning, thus figuring things out or making discoveries for themselves. As an antidote to the passivity and rigidity associated with traditional curricula, activity and discovery proved to be something of an irresistible cocktail. Though Piaget wrote extremely little that relates directly to schooling, his 'constructivist epistemology'[3] found favour with advocates of progressive methods (Forman and Twomey Fosnot, 1982). His theory provided academic respectability for play methods and their potential for all ages of the primary school, at a time when primary teachers were being awarded degrees for the first time and the general climate favoured further pro-fessionalization of teaching (Cunningham, 1988; Alexander, 1984; Goodson and Hargreaves, 1996). Piaget appears to give unqualified support to the perceived need for activity and discovery in the following:

> I do not believe that new concepts even at school level are always ac-quired through adult didactic intervention. This may occur but there is a much more productive form of instruction: the so called 'activity schools' endeavour to create situations that, whilst not spontaneous in themselves, evoke spontaneous elaboration on the part of the child, if one manages both to spark his interests and to present the problem in such a way that it corresponds to the structures he has already formed himself. (1959, p. 11)

Critics, such as Bantock, (1980, p. 47), and the authors of the Black Papers (Cox and Dyson, 1969, 1970, 1971; Cox and Boyson, 1975), suggest that 'the dangers of progressivism' are 'fragmentation and trivialization' resulting in a privileging of process over content.

Discovery Learning

Superficially there is a degree of continuity between the innocent, unfettered rompings of the young Émile in natural surroundings, free from the corruption of European society, and the busy pupils in an activity-based infant classroom. However, in the first instance, learning is significantly influenced by chance, while remaining un-structured and unsystematic. In the second, it may be highly structured and sequenced and, although the teacher may not be engaged directly in instructing the learners, the planned activities are designed to develop their conceptual frameworks by stretching them through the 'factor of equilibration' thus leading to development rather than learning (Forman and Twomey Fosnot, 1982, p. 187; Furth and Wachs, 1975, p. 14). The assumption of this approach is that discoveries arrived at through engagement with problem-solving activities, independently of the teacher, are more likely to ensure 'proper understanding', and insights gained through such problem-solving are more likely to remain with learners (Barrow, 1984, p. 132). However, it would be a mistake to conclude that, as a consequence, discovery learning is either the best or the only valuable method of learning. The Socratic method may be regarded as a sophisticated form of guided discovery, while there is nothing to suggest that direct instruction is less valuable or inimical to developing understanding. Nevertheless, popular interpretations of Piagetian developmentalism suggest that the learners are primarily interested in pursuing answers to their 'own self-generated and self-regulated questions' which tends to place less value on instruction and teacher intervention (Forman and Twomey Fosnot, 1982, p. 191). Consequently, it is alleged by anti-progressives that Piagetian psychology (though this may be no more than a convenient scapegoat) has undermined the verities of more didactic forms of teaching by being labelled traditional, and, thus also, inimical to the best interests of the learners. The oppositional nature of grand narratives tends to perpetuate intellectual skirmishing rather than seeking common ground.

Discovery methods are frequently criticized for their assumptions in relation to the intrinsic motivation of learners (Peters, 1969; Dearden, 1984). Emphasis on individual development, the fountainhead of which is the child's innate curiosity, militates, it is argued, against children from lower socio-economic backgrounds who lack the support and motivation enjoyed by middle-class learners. Being a self-motivated problem-solver requires a level of self-discipline which many adults do not possess, let alone their school-going off-spring! Consequently, Dearden (1984, p. 156) suggests that in an active, problem-solving environment it is tempting for some 'to wander off out of sight somewhere or to become what Bruner has memorably called a "cruiser" '. However, these shortcomings of activity and discovery are not insurmountable, though they do suggest that for some pupils a more directed, structured interactive (rather than didactic) environment may be appropriate, for much or some of the time.

A Vygotskian Perspective

A significant alternative to the rather isolated, egocentric, self-motivated problem-solver, which also provides an alternative to the lack of intrinsic motivation in some learners, is the Vygotskian 'zone of proximal development' ('zo-ped'). This zone is described as:

> ... the distance between the actual developmental level as determined by independent problem solving and the level of potential development as determined by independent problem solving under adult guidance or in collaboration with more capable peers. (quoted by Bruner, 1989, p. 24)

Within this framework, teacher and learner enjoy a 'dialogical' (Vygotsky, 1989, p. xxxiv; Cole, John-Steiner, Scribner, and Souberman, 1978) relationship, and through the 'zo-ped' the 'child's empirically rich but disorganised spontaneous concepts "meet" the systemasticity and logic of adult reasoning' (Vygotsky, 1989, p. xxxv). In these circumstances, there is a more definite pedagogical role for practitioners who mediate the internal logic of subjects and disciplines through their conceptual frameworks. Consequently, learners, who are scaffolded by teachers, are expected to appropriate the latter's more sophisticated conceptual structures. This Vygotskian perspective has the virtue of bringing the growth and moulding metaphors into productive tension. It is possible to conclude, therefore, that 'there is undoubtedly an important place for discovery learning . . . in the curriculum' as 'varying degrees of unstructured problem-solving', but it should only be part of an extensive pedagogical repertoire that needs to be varied depending on context and relative maturity of learners (Barrow, 1984, p. 133). It is apparent that activity and discovery, when deployed with appropriate structure and rigour, have an important contribution to make to teaching and learning. However, they make greater demands than more conventional methods on practitioners' pedagogical and organizational expertise. Consequently, stories of their inept, time-wasting execution abound in the folklore of more conservative primary teachers and certainly amongst critics and opponents of progressivism. Add to this a lack of resources, large classes and pressure to complete a prescribed curriculum, and small wonder that exemplary evidence of activity and discovery is in relatively short supply. However, there is nothing intrinsic to these methods that suggest they should fill the pedagogical repertoire of practitioners to the exclusion of other teaching skills. Once more, it is necessary to turn to actual practice to seek further illumination of the issues.

Curriculum Integration

Both *The Primary Teacher's Handbooks* and the Plowden Report advocate an integrated curriculum. The former asserts that 'the young child is not conscious of subject barriers' to the extent that 'the curriculum should reflect this attitude of the child and be seen more as an integral whole rather than as a logical structure containing conveniently differentiated parts' (Ireland, 1971, p. 19). The latter states that 'children's learning does not fit into subject categories' (p. 203). More recently the Ontario Ministry asserted that 'children learn in a holistic and integrated fashion based on personal perceptions of the world' (Ontario Ministry of Education, 1990, p. 5). This principle suggests that there is merit in being flexible when mediating content to learners, especially younger students. Organizationally this requires 'blocks of time' rather than 'half-hour periods' (Ireland, 1971, p. 22). The principle has been sloganized as, 'we teach children not subjects': a sentiment which revolts against the tyranny of rigid subject boundaries with correspondingly rigid timetabling which had scant regard for the interests or abilities of learners. However, as an ideology, child-centredness is often clearer about what it is against rather than what it is for. It is necessary, therefore, to identify more solid ground than sentiment for acceptance and promotion of integration as a principle which guides classroom actions.

It is relatively easy to understand and to support the argument in favour of integration at kindergarten level and Plowden supports this perspective in the phrase 'the younger the children, the more undifferentiated their curriculum will be' (CACE, 1967, p. 203). This distinction suggests that as the child gets older, there is a need for greater differentiation into subject disciplines (Whitehead, 1962). It is surprising, therefore, and perhaps a little disingenuous, to discover that for reasons of 'convenience' the Plowden Report as well as *The Primary Teacher's Handbooks* structure content under conventional subject-matter headings. Barrow (1984) advocates a similarly pragmatic stance because, he says, there is no conclusive proof for or against the integration of subject matter in the curriculum. However, it is necessary to examine some of the issues involved before the merits of his pragmatism and the assets of the principle can be assessed.

From an epistemological perspective, much of the debate on integration is underpinned by an espousal of knowledge as God-given, out there (a rationalist perspective), whose advocates suggest that there are few 'realms of meaning' (Phenix, 1964) or 'forms of knowledge' (Hirst and Peters, 1970). These disciplines, the authors argue, have legitimate claims to inclusion in school curricula. More significantly, the existence of these discrete knowledge disciplines makes integration extremely difficult if not entirely impossible. Extreme advocates of this perspective, such as Bantock (1980, p. 44), argue that unless subject matter organization is strictly adhered to, the curriculum becomes nothing more than 'a magpie' approach, of 'bits and pieces' which are 'unrelated and ephemeral'. The less trenchant perspective, represented by Hirst and Phenix, is that there are subject disciplines such as mathematics, morality and science that have their own internal logic and criteria of truth (Alexander, 1984). Under this rubric it would be possible to integrate subjects such as biology and physics within the same discipline. What these disciplines provide is a 'network of relationships through which experience is understood' in ways that others have found helpful (Kelly, 1977, p. 81). While various subjects overlap, the argument suggests that the internal structures of disciplines render interdisciplinary work impossible.

Multi-disciplinary topics are feasible (even from a rationalist perspective) and could be investigated from economic, social, historical and geographical perspectives without doing violence to the internal logic of individual disciplines. What occurs in these situations is what Peters (1966) refers to as 'cognitive overspill'. For Whitehead (1962, p. 33) the challenge is 'to weave in the learner's mind a harmony of patterns' by promoting links between the 'subordinate cycles' of the different knowledge components of the curriculum. Experience suggests that there is a great deal of cross-fertilization between disciplines on a casual basis. An ever-expanding plethora of new degree and diploma programmes indicates that ways of integrating and restructuring knowledge continue to be found. However, mindful of my postmodern stance, there is merit also in the argument that cross-fertilization is better served when it comes from an in-depth knowledge of particular subjects and disciplines.

In contrast with the rationalist perspective which focuses on the importance of curriculum content, its integrity and unique internal logic, advocates of progressive ideology place greater emphasis on the process of knowledge construction (Kelly 1977, 1986; Blenkin and Kelly, 1981, 1983). It is, they say, the process of meaning-making that matters to the progressive tradition. However, when criticism concerning the inert nature of the received tradition and its potentially stifling effect on development has been considered, a practitioner is still faced with the task of providing what Kelly (1986) terms a 'balanced' curriculum diet. It is tedious in the extreme, therefore, to continue to suggest that teaching is a matter of 'curriculum process' rather than 'curriculum content' (Kelly, 1986, p. 153). While teaching is quite appropriately concerned with individual development, the process is inseparable from its content. It is difficult to envisage teaching or development taking place without engagement with content however concrete or abstract. To this end, Eisner's (1982, 1988) plea for a wider definition of cognition, and thus, also, for what counts as knowledge, is potentially more significant than the either/or perspective of the rationalist/empiricist dichotomy. From a psychological perspective we do experience the world in a holistic fashion but what we experience depends on the conceptual apparatus into which we have been socialized. Eisner's (1979, 1982, 1985) plea is for a broader church that enables learners to construct meaning other than by propositional knowledge.

Knowledge: Socially Constructed

The new sociology of education has, during the past thirty years, sought to undermine the dominance of the received rationalist perspective in relation to knowledge. It has done this by espousing knowledge as being socially constructed, and this reflexive perspective has exposed how rationalism has been used to successfully bolster the privileged positions of socially advantaged groups. These groups maintain positions of privilege by according high status to particular kinds of knowledge (Young, 1971; Keddie, 1971; Bernstein, 1976, 1971; Eggleston, 1977; Goodson and Ball, 1984; Goodson, 1994). The knowledge explosion of recent years has heightened the sense of urgency felt by curriculum reformers that it is futile to continue to emphasize subject matter content which will be redundant before students leave school and/or college. Consequently, they suggest that greater emphasis should be placed on the skills required to process information rather than to retain it. However, even with this emphasis, acquisition of cognitive skills is inextricably linked to the cognitive concepts which are the glue that holds the entire process together. It appears, therefore, that practitioners must be cognizant of both content and its attendant pedagogy.

One possible resolution of this apparent impasse is to accept, for the purpose of cognitive development, the conceptual constructs which are our cultural inheritance, while at the same time recognizing their tentative nature. The primary purpose of education may then be understood as the transformation of this cultural inheritance by the learner, rather than its transmission by the teacher. This arrangement leaves the question of integration in the hands of practitioners and it is reasonable to expect that responses will vary because of issues such as: age of learners;

availability of resources; as well as teachers' values and beliefs. However, it should be noted that the design and implementation of an integrated curriculum presupposes a great deal of sophistication on the part of practitioners. After his experience of attempting to develop an integrated programme for 'a medical school curriculum', Shulman comments that: 'the more we attempted to integrate the curriculum, the more we had to rationalise the curricular and programmatic organisation in which the curriculum was embedded' (1988, p. 35). His considered conclusion is that 'a program that values integration . . . must be more highly organised and coordinated than one in which the disciplines are permitted to hold sway' (p. 35). Planning and delivering an integrated curriculum is a severe test of the subject matter expertise, pedagogical skills and organizational abilities of the most able teachers. Enabling learners to build sophisticated conceptual frameworks which allow for individual integrity and a coherent world-view may be the more fundamental challenge to schooling than the packaging of information.

My experience of schooling indicates that the tensions surrounding the principle of integration are frequently resolved along pragmatic lines, with scant attention to theoretical considerations. Availability of time and resources frequently dictate the extent to which curricula are integrated. Only in the weakest sense could it be said that epistemological, psychological or sociological concerns indicate appropriate classroom action. In the final analysis, the litmus test of integration is not *a priori* justification but the sophistication of its delivery. Barrow's (1984, p. 125) conclusion, that 'it is for particular schools to determine what, on balance, is the degree and type of integration most suited to their resources', seems most appropriate: that it is necessary to look to actual practice to gain further insight. It may be concluded, therefore, that integration of subject matter in the hands of skilled practitioners may be a significant advance on the sterility of the content and delivery of traditional curricula. In the absence of such sophistication, the curriculum may be reduced to an unchallenging mish-mash that lacks rigour, coherence and cognitive challenge. Integration becomes an asset or a liability depending on the subject matter knowledge and pedagogical expertise of practitioners.

Environment-based Learning

The Primary Teacher's Handbooks (Ireland, 1971, p. 20) evoke the horticultural metaphor when they state that: '. . . the child's environment provides the most congenial ground in which the seeds of knowledge may be sown and its organic growth fostered'. The Plowden Report (CACE, 1967, p. 544) echoes this sentiment when it claims that 'the newer methods start with the direct impact of the environment on the child and the child's individual response to it. The results are unpredictable but extremely worthwhile'. More recently, published documents in the Irish context indicate that this principle should be understood as providing 'a badly needed balance to approaches that tended to rely exclusively on textbooks' (Ireland, 1990a, p. 20) while other such documents advocate that 'learning should be based in the environment' (Ireland, 1987, p. 13). The principle's sentiment focuses attention on the importance, distinctiveness, and integrity of childhood experience, with its attendant need for practitioners to respect this by mediating between learners' experiences and those provided by the teaching process. It challenges teachers to identify ways in which the individuality, needs, interests, inclinations and potentialities of learners may be nurtured through a rigorous, though flexible and sensitive, programme provision. An environmentally based curriculum is thought to be desirable because it accommodates the natural curiosity of learners and avoids the inertness of a transmission approach. However, without careful analysis, such a principle might well lead to a very narrow provision thus reducing the degree of challenge to learners in favour of relevance, while limiting rather than broadening their interests and educational horizons.

One of the major influences of psychology on education has been the development and dissemination of tests and testing. Those who emphasized environmental factors over inherited potential in the development of intelligence, argued that environmental influences were of key significance in fostering intellectual growth and this has led to preferential funding for areas of disadvantage (Holland, 1979; Kellaghan, Weir, Ó hUllacháin and Morgan, 1995). Awareness of the impact of environment is not something new in education, but its relative importance continues to fuel debate and acrimony (Hernstein and Murray, 1994). What kind of environment, then, is most conducive to learning?

Learning Environment?

Urban blight, decay and neglect, which contribute to economic poverty, deprivation and ill-health provide contexts that are part of many learner's immediate environment. Dewey (1916, p. 21) recognizes that 'cliques, clubs and Fagin houses', even jails, may have some educative value, but he does not recommend them. Parents of learners (and indeed their teachers) will almost certainly choose more desirable alternatives than the immediate surroundings mentioned above because of their greater educative potential. They recognize that what is immediate in a child's environment has influence in shaping its outlook. Dewey (1916, p. 21) is very explicit about the need for schools to provide 'a simplified environment' which implicitly recognizes the need to structure learning, so that it is tailored to the developmental stage(s) of the learner. However, he is insistent that this curriculum should also strive to 'eliminate . . . unworthy features of the existing environment' thus bringing the learner into 'contact with a broader environment' (p. 20). Noddings (1992, p. 70) elaborates on this point when she says that students should be able to have some influence over 'the material offered in school' to ensure that it 'pass[es] the important test of being connected to students' personal experience — past and future'. However, she is quick to point out that choice, which is uninformed by intelligent advice and dialogue between students and teachers, is likely to lead to 'chaos rather than continuity'. It is readily apparent, therefore, that personal investment in and engagement with curriculum content is an important asset of child-centred rhetoric, with important caveats as to how this principle is transformed into classroom actions. Dewey (1938, p. 44) argues that environment is 'whatever conditions interact with personal needs, desires, purposes and capacities to create the experience which is had'. However, it seems unhelpful to interpret Dewey's (1938, pp. 33–50) criteria of experience (continuity and interaction) as necessitating attention to what is immediately contiguous to the learner, for he was adamant also that schools provide a 'balance' in the curriculum to ensure that 'each individual gets an opportunity to escape from the limitations of the social group in which he was born, and to come into living contact with a broader environment' (Dewey, 1916, p. 20).

The *Report of the Review Body on the Primary Curriculum* (Ireland, 1990a, p. 20) identifies the environment as a 'valuable resource' which can be an 'antidote to the book-bound-approach' of a traditional curriculum. The latter limited the possibilities for connecting with learners' previous experiences, thus leading to the charge of presenting inert ideas (Whitehead, 1962). However, this is not the same as advocating that learners' education should be located in or on the environment. Rather, in many instances the previous experiences of learners or something in the immediate environment will be the point of departure for the curriculum rather than its fulcrum. However, without simplification, careful planning, structuring and sequencing on the part of teachers, significant development will be unlikely to occur and be too dependent on happenstance. Development is likely to happen most advantageously when manipulation of the environment enables learners to connect new stimuli with previous experiences, thus giving continuity to the learning process. It is the extent to which practitioners can manipulate the environment for genuinely educative ends that brings about the appropriate match between learners and curricula. This developmental process serves the dual purpose of broadening learners' horizons while opening up the possibility of reaching unanticipated horizons.

It is possible, therefore, to recognize that the sentiment of environmentally based learning has significance for curriculum and teaching. Yet, this recognition is tempered by the knowledge that the manner of its execution will differ greatly from one context to another. Practitioners' judgment will determine how the principle is transformed into classroom actions. Consequently, the principle is weak and, thus, a necessary but not sufficient criterion to determine curriculum action.

Summary

The principles of child-centredness are ambiguous in their implications for classroom actions and are therefore problematic. However, the seamless tapestry of their sentiment admits no such ambiguity. In an uncritical moment it can be said that child-centred ideology has its heart in the right place. The sentiment arouses different passions in practitioners which are tempered by personal biography, professional experience and local circumstance. Consequently, progressive practices vary according to practitioners' interpretations of these principles as well as the circumstances of their work, both immediate and remote. Analysis of key principles of child-centredness in terms of sentiment, assets and liabilities helps to situate the central question concerning practitioners' interpretations and constructions of this ideology. It reveals also that progressive rhetoric tends to be clearer about what it opposes rather than proposes. A more complete, inclusive and grounded understanding of practitioners' intentions and classroom actions, therefore, can be provided by situating and reconstructing them within both grand narratives.

Research on Child-centred Teaching

As already indicated, previously conducted research into aspects of progressive teaching has a shaping influence on the central question of this study with implications also for the methodology it employs. All the usual sources were systematically searched for literature on child-centred teaching. However, many seemingly relevant journal articles had particular foci such as grouping, whole class activities, or individualization and were deemed to be too narrow for inclusion in a general literature review which had child-centred teaching as its central focus (Tobin and Malone, 1989; Russell, Mills and Reiff-Musgrove, 1990; Spodek, 1989; Barker-Lunn, 1982; Bennett and Jordan, 1975; Boydell, 1975, 1980). Three categories of studies emerged from this extensive search: survey, observational and case study. Four studies were classified as survey, while additional research conducted in the Irish context is also included in this section of the review (Ashton, 1975; Bennett, 1976; Bassey, 1978; DES, 1978).[4] Four studies were analysed under the observational rubric (Galton, Simon and Croll, 1980; Mortimore, Sammons, Stoll, Lewis and Ecob, 1988; Berlak and Berlak, 1975; King, 1978) while three studies are loosely identified as case studies (Gracey, 1974; Sharp and Green, 1975; Alexander, Willcocks and Kinder, 1989).

This review was undertaken for two particular reasons. First, it was anticipated from a substantive point of view that this literature would provide insights into the practice of child-centred teaching which would differ from the rhetorical perspective outlined above. Second, fastidious attention would be paid to the manner in which the research questions of these studies were framed and their respective research methodologies constructed. These methodological issues are addressed within the wider modernist, postmodernist perspective in which this study is situated. The purpose of this second focus is to provide a critique of previously conducted research which has a shaping influence on the research design of the present study. The overarching consideration in grouping these studies was the extent to which they ignored or took seriously context as an integral element of investigation.

Survey Research

While there are differences in approach and methodology in the four studies discussed here, they are similar to the extent that they all sought to identify and to categorize practitioners' teaching styles. It is significant also that all four studies were completed in the mid to late 1970s in Britain. They came in the wake of an economic downturn internationally with an attendant loss of optimism which put the brakes on educational expansionist policies and efficiency and effectiveness gained in currency. Domestically the William Tyndale (Ellis, 1976) affair and prime minister Callaghan's (1976; Whitty, 1985) famous Ruskin College speech calling for more 'relevance' in the school curriculum were all straws in the wind which shaped the thinking and the context of the research being discussed (Hargreaves, 1989). The general economic climate fuelled the educational controversy between proponents of 'back to basics' (as exemplified in the Black Papers) and those who favoured the reforms which were enshrined in the Plowden Report. It is clichéd to assert that the first casualty of war is truth, and ideological wars are probably no exception to this rule. More importantly, in the context of this study, a quintessential modernist cycloptic perspective is maintained by the supporters of traditional and progressive ideologies so that research findings are rarely discussed in the round but are quoted selectively to bolster espoused paradigms. Alexander, Rose and Woodhead express this point forcefully as follows:

> ... the debate about standards and classroom practice is all too often conducted in terms of a simplistic dichotomy between 'traditional' and 'progressive', or 'formal' and 'informal'. The move to a more mature and balanced discussion of the issues is long overdue ... (1992, p. 5)

Ashton (1975, p. 89) describes teachers as 'individualistic' or 'societal'; the former are, he suggests, predisposed towards developing capacity in learners for 'making reasoned judgements' as well as 'autonomy, both intellectually and personally' and self-confidence is highly prized. Societal teachers, on the other hand, emphasize 'a strong 3Rs flavour ...', expect learners to 'conform to externally accepted standards' and believe decisions about curriculum content to be the exclusive preserve of teachers. Similarly, Bennett's (1976, p. 37) controversial study begins from the perspective that there are two 'global terms "progressive" and "traditional"'. As a consequence of this modernist starting point, teachers in the study are categorized as being 'formal' or 'informal'. While cluster analysis is employed to impose further categories, resulting in a total of twelve, Bennett (1976, p. 47) concludes that only 'the extreme types could be adequately described ... the remaining types all contain both informal and formal elements'. He deduces that 'the majority of teachers appear to adopt a mixed or intermediate style for which the progressive–traditional dimension provides inadequate description' (p. 48). Bassey's (1978, p. 9) study seeks to 'describe the major practices of primary school teachers'. There is less emphasis, therefore, on categorization and greater opportunity for complexity to emerge. While there is a propensity towards 'classwork' among junior teachers, infant teachers seem to favour individualization. These polarities conform in broad outline with Ashton's individualistic and societal teachers. However, Bassey recognizes, like Bennett, that there are many teachers who include elements of traditional and progressive ideology in their practice rather than practising at the extremes.

Primary Education in England (DES, 1978, p. 206) appears to institution-alize the extremes and the middle ground with its categorization of teachers into 'didactic', 'exploratory', and 'mixed methods'. Its general findings concur with Bennett's and others' that many teachers give 'high priority' to the 3Rs, while the more able are not challenged sufficiently. It concludes also that 'there is no evid-ence . . . to suggest that a narrower curriculum enables children to do better in the basic skills or leads to the work being more aptly chosen to suit the capabilities of the children' (p. 114). This seems to endorse a more broadly based curriculum. Campbell's summary of the HMI report's implications can be extended to embrace the others. He concludes that primary practitioners 'had not implemented Plowden's policies . . . and . . . [were] reducing what little there had been' (1985, p. 28). The studies reveal that exclusive interpretations of the progressive grand narrative were no longer an adequate means of explaining the complexities of classroom life: a more januform and more complex, rather than cycloptic, perspective on teaching was emerging as a necessity.

In a number of survey studies conducted in the Irish context during the past twenty-five years, teachers overwhelmingly endorse progressive ideology (Sugrue, 1990). However, when data on actual practice are isolated from these studies teachers seem to endorse a child-centred rhetoric while practising a more formal pedagogical style. Egan (1981, p. 8) recognizes this dilemma when he suggests that practitioners are informal in 'approach' while being more formal in their actual 'technique'. He is not merely suggesting, as indicated in the studies mentioned above, that teachers employ mixed methods but that they can apparently live with the tensions created by espousing progressive intentions while their actions resonate with aspects of tra-ditional pedagogy. Egan's perspective attempts to grapple with the realization that the complexity of classroom life does not submit readily to neatly defined categories. However, without recourse to observational studies of actual classroom practice, understanding of this complex confluence of rhetoric, intentions and classroom actions remains vague.

The limitations of survey research in general have been well documented by a number of writers who are critical of a technical–rational approach to the invest-igation of human affairs (Erickson, 1986; Lincoln and Guba, 1985; Eisner and Peshkin, 1990; Eisner, 1991b; Jackson, 1992; Denzin and Lincoln, 1994; LeCompte, Millroy and Preissle, 1992). Similarly, the Bennett (1976) study, which is the most widely known of the four studies discussed above, has become as infamous for 'criticisms of its methodology' (Gray and Satterly, 1976, 1981; Aitken, Bennett and Heshketh, 1981) as for the 'publicity associated with the launch of [the] book' (Campbell, 1985, p. 28). Barrow indicates that without recourse to observational studies

. . . there is absolutely no a *priori* reason to suppose, as is implied by talking about styles and models, that what is important in the teacher's performance is caught in any of the various styles and models that have been produced. (1984, p. 193)

Bassey (1978, p. 18) recognizes also that providing detailed descriptions of teaching styles from self-reporting is a poor substitute for what is 'closest to their actual practice'. Likewise, Bennett acknowledges that formal and informal teaching practices have assets and liabilities; they complement as much as they conflict. He states:

> . . . formal teaching fulfils its aims in the academic area without detriment to the social and emotional development of pupils, whereas informal teaching only partially fulfils its aims in the latter area as well as engendering comparatively poorer outcomes in academic development. (Bennett, 1976, p. 162)

An alternative methodological approach is necessary which recognizes the commonalities and complexities while avoiding modernist paradigms which seek to dichotomize. Bennett recognizes the necessity for such a methodological shift, as well as a rapprochement between the grand narratives, when he says:

> It is surely time to ignore the rhetoric which would have us believe that informal methods are pernicious and permissive, and that the most accurate description of the formal methods is that found in Dicken's *Hard Times*. (1976, p. 163)

Studies will be necessary, he concludes, which enable teachers to 'submit their practices to critical scrutiny' so that 'deeper understanding' of actual practice can 'underlie what all teachers do' (Bennett, 1976, p. 163). The HMI Report (DES, 1978, p. 125) draws a remarkably similar conclusion when it states that 'the only sure way forward' is 'a slow but steady build up from the points of strength of individual teachers'. These conclusions implicity recognize that it is necessary to move beyond the rigidities of grand narratives to a postmodern perspective that seeks to accommodate complexity and diversity while according greater recognition to, and acknowledgment of, practitioners' voices and the contexts of their work.

Observational Research

Observational research methods seek to redress some of the inadequacies of survey studies. The Observational Research and Classroom Learning Evaluation (ORACLE) study sought to provide 'a mass of objective data' that would enable the public to adjudicate on 'the relative effectiveness of different teaching approaches across the main subject areas of primary school teaching' and to address 'the criticisms of the new approaches in primary schools' which had been pilloried in the wake of the Bennett study (Galton *et al.*, 1980, p. 1). From a substantive point of view, the study concludes that 'progressive teaching . . . hardly exists in practice' (p. 156) and 'didacticism still largely prevails' (Simon, 1981, p. 24). In classrooms where there was evidence of 'structure' and high levels of 'interaction', the study claimed that achievement levels were higher. A rise in the significance of 'relationships' was reported also. From the perspective of the present study, there was further evidence of complexity and some coexistence between traditional and progressive pedagogy in the same classrooms. Such classrooms were 'informally organised' while 'didacticism still largely prevailed' and there was a 'major emphasis on the basics' (Simon, 1981, pp. 23–4).

The more recently conducted study, *School Matters* (Mortimore *et al.*, 1988) was a longitudinal study of primary pupils (7–11) which used an elaborate research design including the use of standardized tests, the observation schedules of the ORACLE study, some observation and details of 'school life' to give some context to the data. The study documents the growing importance being attached by teachers to good relationships; language and mathematics in particular tended to be taught as separate rather than integrated subjects, class teaching had declined and many interactions between teachers and pupils were of an individual nature. The study claims that 'the amount of time spent interacting with the class . . . had a significant positive relationship with progress in a wide range of areas'. However, it is important to acknowledge also that interacting with the class 'did not necessarily mean whole class teaching' (p. 228). Some 'project work' was advocated by the teachers, about one project per term, and visits were 'important sources of ideas' for this kind of work. The happiest and most productive classrooms, according to the study, were task-oriented environments that were 'intellectually challenging' (pp. 229–30). They concluded also that 'teaching strategies [are] . . . much more complex than the notion of teaching style implies' (p. 81). Implicitly this conclusion recognizes that arbitrary categorization of teaching fails to recognize the complexity of classroom life and that research methods that respect, acknowledge and capture this complexity are more appropriate for investigating the substance and process of child-centred teaching.

All Things Bright and Beautiful? (King, 1978) is a descriptive sociological study of infant classrooms, which is based on observations primarily with some interview data also. The importance of context is acknowledged as King spends time in the staffroom, playground and attending special events in an attempt to capture the atmosphere and ethos of the three schools studied. These schools were situated in different social contexts described by their respective teachers as 'problem area', 'council houses' and 'professional', thus clearly indicating that their intentions and classroom actions were shaped significantly by context. There was further evidence of emphasis on 3Rs. Even in infant schools, where teachers were firmly in control of content and pedagogy, learners' interests were manipulated to bring them within the teaching framework created by teachers. The 'loosest kind of planning' was being done to enable teachers 'to . . . play it by ear' in their classrooms (p. 72). This study's findings reinforce the emergent perspective from the other studies mentioned above that some aspects of classroom practice appear to resonate with traditional conceptions of teaching, while others connect with progressive ideology. Increasingly, however, these studies suggest that a dichotomous conceptualization of teaching is unhelpful and that the context of teaching and the intentions of teachers have significance for classroom practice. Therefore, observational studies, particularly if they employ predetermined categories, may actually ignore or deliberately exclude from consideration critically important aspects of classroom life. In this regard, Edwards' and Mercers' comments on the methodological limitations of observational studies in general are apposite.

> The kind of data obtained from systematic observation studies does not allow researchers to reconstruct the course of any given lesson; the only information available about the course of events after the lesson has finished is in the form of numerical frequency codings. (1987, p. 25)

Alexander's comments on the ORACLE study and, it may be suggested, observational studies generally, is that they are 'tacitly behaviourist', and

> ... the quasi-objective observation study both imposes on behaviour the observer's interpretations and theoretical frameworks, and fails to explicate the meanings which the observed behaviours have for the 'actors' involved (i.e. the teachers and children). (1984, pp. 49–50)

To overcome these methodological difficulties, Berlak, Berlak, Tushnet Bagentos and Mikel (1976) set out to 'conceptualise the complex relationship between thought and action' (p. 88) by participant observation which, until then, had not been employed in the study of primary classrooms. As might be expected, the complexity of the teaching situation emerges when this methodology is employed. When it comes to teaching the basics teachers do 'not rely very heavily on intrinsic motivation' as the rhetoric of child-centred teaching suggests, but they 'force gently' and 'forbid ... kindly' (p. 93). This is a significant advance on the bullying, haranguing, and cajoling that characterized some traditional classrooms. Subtle differences also emerge in relation to standards where they tend to be set for 'individuals rather than for groups' and where learners, in Vygotskian style, were expected to appropriate for themselves the standards which had been set for them by teachers. In this way, students were encouraged to evaluate themselves rather than being evaluated by the teacher; this allowed for individual difference and learners taking responsibility for their own learning. The subtlety of these insights suggested to Berlak *et al.* that understanding the complexity of teaching would be better served by 'conceptualising schooling ... in terms of a set of persisting dilemmas' where teachers, through their practice, had to find 'de facto resolutions' to competing issues (1976, p. 95). However, the dilemmas encountered by teachers in their classrooms do not happen in a vacuum and the study may be criticized because it defines context rather narrowly. Nevertheless, traditional and progressive conceptions of teaching merge into the thoughts, actions and contexts of teachers; they conclude that 'questions such as whether a teacher is child centred or not are ... better conceptualised in terms of how teachers deal with the conflicting claims implicit in the dilemmas' faced daily in their classrooms (p. 96). Acknowledging complexity and context requires a more januform rather than cycloptic perspective on teaching traditions and enables the researcher to reconstruct these narratives by grounding them in the multiple realities of classroom life and in teachers' biographies.

Case-study Research

'Case study' is being used in the present context in a generic sense, which includes qualitative and quantitative approaches to research or an amalgam of both (Jaeger, 1988). Gracey's (1974) study sought to examine the relationship between organizational structures and achievement goals in a New York elementary school and employed observation and interview as the means of data collection. He began from the perspective that context has implications for teachers' constructions of practice. However, typical of the period, he classifies teachers as being 'individualistic' or 'productive' (p. 3). The latter, he suggests, adopt a 'lockstep' approach and emphasize 'the basics' while students are expected to conform to curriculum guidelines. The former were more likely to espouse self-expression, creativity and spontaneity. Predictably, therefore, he argues that educational bureaucracy and local structures are congruent with the intentions and actions of production teachers but are inimical to those of individualistic teachers. Despite considerable detail about particular practitioners who, according to Gracey, conform to these types, my reading of these thick descriptions suggests that they have much more in common than the conceptualization of his study allows. The oppositional, adversarial framing of the research question prevents more sophisticated understandings of commonalities, complexities and dilemmas.

Sharp and Green's study (1975) has similarities with Gracey's. It sought to increase understanding of 'the child-centred approach to education' in infant classrooms in a working-class context. They describe the study as exploratory rather than verificatory as they were attempting to come to terms with the new methods of 'social phenomenology' which had emerged with the new sociology (Young, 1971; Keddie, 1971). Their data was gathered through a combination of unstructured observations and interviews. From the perspective of the present inquiry, the distinction they make between 'teaching ideology' and 'teaching perspective' is particularly useful and the latter seems homologous with Berlak and Berlak's (1975) concept of 'persistent dilemmas': a 'teaching ideology' is 'a connected set of systematically related beliefs and ideas about what are felt to be the essential features of teaching' (p. 68). This ideology is a complex matrix of personal experience, professional education and general socialization. Consequently, the authors insist that it is quite difficult to determine with precision what this ideology consists of for the individual teacher. Teaching perspectives, on the other hand, lack the 'high level of generality' associated with ideology and consist of 'a set of beliefs and practices which emerge when social actors in an organisation confront specific problems in their situation' (p. 69). They recognize that practitioners derive principles inductively from reflection on their practice (Hunt, 1987, 1992; Schön, 1983, 1987, 1991).

Implicit in the authors' argument is the suggestion that a reflexive capacity has more significance for practitioners' understanding of their experience than ideals or prescriptions derived from an ideology's axioms. This insight concurs with the Berlaks' claim above that practitioners' intentions and actions are transformed through their interaction with local conditions. Sharp and Green (1975) conclude that the teachers employ the language of child-centredness in a 'ritual of commitment' which is 'rhetorical rather than' indicative of 'intricate meanings' (p. 170). This insight resonates with the distinction made by Egan (1981) between approach and technique. In order to provide accounts of child-centred teaching that are grounded in the perspectives and practices of teachers, it is necessary to design a study that pays attention to the ideology, intentions (approach or ritualistic language), actions and contexts of practitioners. However, Sharp and Green do admit to some significant methodological limitations in their study. They accept that their observations were 'unstructured' and they were unclear as to how 'the problem should be formulated' (p. 234) and King (1978, p. 130) points out that their analysis relies too heavily on 'the accounts teachers gave of what they did and why they did it, more so than what they were observed to do'. They arbitrarily introduced a Marxist critique with the result that the study becomes rather 'doctrinaire' thus lacking theoretical sensitivity (Glaser and Strauss, 1967). Greater attention needs to be paid to the interaction of actual classroom routines and their wider context.

In the 'Leeds case', Alexander (1992, p. xiii) discerns that it is necessary to 'move freely between . . . practices as observed or described and the ideas by which they are sustained'. Though the Leeds case study has several elements, it is essentially an evaluation of change and innovation over a number of years rather than a study of progressive teaching. Nevertheless, its basic conceptualization recognizes the inherent complexity of classroom life. The authors state that:

> . . . teaching is as much about ideas as it is about action; that the teacher's thinking is as significant a determinant of the quality of children's learning as are the teacher's movements round the classroom; and that the 'practice' of teaching is properly conceived as a fusion of knowledge and understanding, interpersonal commitment and competence, situational skill and judgement, and on-the-spot capacities for rapid diagnosis and decision-making. (Alexander *et al.*, 1989, p. 17)

Apart from an acknowledgment of the complexity of teaching and learning by the authors of the various publications which emanated from the Leeds case study, the controversy that followed their availability, which in many ways mirrored the arrival of the Bennett study almost two decades earlier, is further evidence of the importance of context: a multi-layered context that extends from classrooms to schools while embracing communities as well as prevailing economic and socio-political climates. The present study differs from Alexander's work because its primary function is to increase understanding rather than make judgments about the quality of primary provision. The postmodern approach to grand narratives espoused in this study recognizes that it is necessary to move beyond the 'cheap expedient' characteristic of traditional schooling and the 'unquestioned educational ideal' which progressive ideology has become in the heads and hands of some policy-makers and practitioners (Alexander, 1992, p. xiii).

One of the functions of an interpretive inquiry is to provide accounts that enable practitioners to move beyond the frequently sloganized terminology of child-centred ideology to a critically reflexive dialogue where the tensions between intentions, actions and the dilemmas they pose for practice are brought into higher relief. It is the absence of such a reflexive dialogue, as well as the routine of practice itself, which enables Sharp and Green (1975) to conclude that 'there is no direct logical relationship between the child centred vocabulary and the teachers' actions in all their intricate complexity' (p. 175). By promoting and sustaining such a reflexive dialogue, interpretive inquiry can increase understanding of the what and the why of classroom actions, as well as practitioners' potential for professional growth and programme development.

Behind the ritual commitment to child-centredness that the researchers identified, there was much ambivalence regarding curriculum content and pedagogy. It was accepted that children need to be numerate and literate and this was a non-negotiable element of the curriculum. However, practitioners felt that it was permissible to push 'bright secure children . . . while the dull ones . . . should be provided with an unthreatening classroom environment' (p. 172). This concurs with a conclusion in the HMI Report (DES, 1978, p. 116) that inner-city children were 'under-estimated by their teachers' and were more likely to be given work that did not extend their capabilities while in many instances the most able were not challenged adequately (Alexander, 1992). In relation to readiness, teachers were torn between allowing learners to 'become ready' or to 'make them ready' (Sharp and Green, 1975, p. 179). While the Leeds case study, and the Sharp and Green study differ significantly in their conceptualization, they agree that the work of practitioners is highly problematic with decision-making, compromise and dilemmas at its core. It is precisely because interpretations and constructions of child-centred ideology (and traditional teaching) are problematic that the present inquiry has been undertaken. By documenting the details of actual practice, the expectation is that understanding of child-centred teaching will be enhanced. Further, the particulars of practice will facilitate the grounding of a postmodern account of progressive teaching which avoids the kinds of polarizations evident in the majority of studies discussed here because of their modernist preoccupation with oppositional and adversarial categorizations and discourses.

Personal Biography and Traditions of Teaching

This chapter has consistently highlighted the importance of context for teachers' constructions of practice. I concur wholeheartedly with Polanyi when he states that:

> I started as a person intellectually fashioned by a particular idiom, acquired
> through my affiliation to a civilisation that prevailed in the places where
> I had grown up, at this particular period of history. (1958, p. 145)

My 'intellectual passions' concerning teaching traditions have been shaped by my 'apprenticeship of observation' (Lortie, 1975) within the Irish educational system:

from my days as a student in a small rural school in the 1950s and early 1960s; through teacher education in the early 1970s; followed by a decade of classroom teaching; a period in the primary schools inspectorate; and my involvement in teacher education and research. My earliest schooling was in classrooms with bare wooden floors where we sat in long wooden benches (without support) sitting in rows facing the 'mistress' or the 'master' (Sugrue, 1996a). The curriculum was dominated by 'the basics' which, in the Irish context, are Irish, English and mathematics. It is compulsory for each pupil to begin the Irish language from the first day in school. Corporal punishment, verbal abuse and sarcasm were commonplace. There were no 'frills'; art and drama were non-existent while in fine weather there were occasional football matches after school. Teaching was heavily dependent on textbooks, there were no library books and much of our efforts involved rote learning. We were compliant, passive and learned to speak only when spoken to and we kept out of trouble if we completed the homework which was assigned regularly.

Child-centred teaching became official policy in Irish primary schools in 1971 and this major shift coincided with the beginning of my teaching career. I recall being enthused by the ideas of the great educators (Rusk, 1979); developmental psychology seemed to hold much promise, while the prospect of group work, creative writing and project work appealed to my youthful enthusiasm in comparison to dictation and the writing of standard essays.

While I regarded the above as important developments, large classes and lack of resources, the tradition of teaching in the setting, the isolation inherent in the prevailing 'culture of individualism' (Hargreaves, 1992, 1994; Lieberman, 1990; Sugrue, 1996c) and the nature of inspection (Sugrue, 1996b) all served to circumscribe my practice in ways that perpetuated the tensions between the rhetoric of child-centredness and the realities of my teaching. Older colleagues suggested that too much of what was valuable from traditional teaching had been sacrificed in a spirit of reforming zeal. In a tacit, unarticulated manner I was conscious of a tension between theoretical and ideological issues arising from postgraduate studies in education, my classroom actions and the social context of my work. As a practitioner and inspector I also became increasingly aware that when primary education was discussed in public fora, voices of practitioners were typically absent or silent: there was no language of practice.

As a teacher educator and researcher there were opportunities to visit schools in England, Scotland, France, Holland, Germany and North America, and it was intriguing to note that despite significant variations in context, staffing and resource provision, the term 'child-centred' was applied in all these situations. Perplexed by this conundrum, my musings entertained the notion that child-centred teaching had many forms which were constructed chameleon-like in a variety of settings. Rather than seek an essentialist (and modernist) uni-dimensional interpretation of child-centred ideology, it seemed more beneficial to document this pluriformity of practice as a means of grounding more inclusive understandings of progressive primary teaching. A qualitative approach to this task had, I thought, the potential to capture aspects of classroom life that were neglected or ignored by more traditional approaches to the conduct of research. Such an approach further recommended itself as it had the potential to develop and contribute to a language of practice, to be more inclusive: a postmodern perspective that would respect complexities and commonalities while not being blind to variations. In this manner, the grand narratives of teaching could be reconstructed albeit from a child-centred perspective. Chapter 2 takes up this theme as it returns to the substantive issue of this inquiry and describes its research design.

Notes

1 The seven principles were: 1) freedom to develop naturally; 2) interest, the motive of all work; 3) the teacher as a guide, not a taskmaster; 4) scientific study of pupil development; 5) greater attention to all that affects the child's development; 6) cooperation between school and home to meet the needs of child life; and 7) the progressive school as a leader in educational movements. For further details see Potter (1967).

2 The Survey Report (Ireland, 1987, p. 12) and the *Report of the Review Body on the Primary Curriculum* (Ireland, 1990a, p. 16) quote the same lines from *The Primary Teacher's Handbooks* as reproduced here, to indicate that the principle of activity and discovery was implicit in the child-centred policy originally advocated in 1971. The Survey Report states that the principle to which this rhetoric gives rise is that 'activity and discovery should be used' (p. 12).

3 Forman and Twomey Fosnot (1982, p. 186) contrast constructivism with 'naïve realism' and argue the latter 'assumes that knowledge is a direct product of making better mental copies of an external world', while 'constructivism assumes that we have no direct accessibility to an external world and therefore have to construct representations that have more to do with the act of knowing than they do with the external object per se'.

4 The Irish studies included in this general review, only some of which were actually published, include *Primary School Curriculum* (INTO, 1976); *Evaluation of the New Curriculum for Primary Schools* (Conference of Convent Primary Schools in Ireland, 1975); *The New Primary Curriculum* (Fontes and Kellaghan, 1977); *Report of the Primary Curriculum Review Body* (Ireland, 1990a); *Report of the Primary Education Review Body* (Ireland, 1990b); the Survey Report (Ireland, 1987) as well as small-scale studies such as Burke and Fontes (1986); and Egan (1981).

Chapter 2

Substance, Setting and Method

Introduction

Three distinct but related tasks are the focus of this chapter. First, the substance of the inquiry is revisited in the light of analysis and argument in Chapter 1. Second, due to the complexity of practice; the ambiguity of child-centred ideology in its implications for classroom actions; and the dialogical relationship between ideology, policy, intentions and actions, the problem is matched with an appropriately complex research design for its investigation. Third, because of the importance of context for shaping progressive practice, a brief contextualization of the problem is provided by identifying the contours of primary education in Ireland.

Substance

Chapter 1 indicated that, despite the powerful and seductive sentiment of child-centred ideology, its implications for teaching are vague, imprecise and problematic. Consequently, practitioners' interpretations of child-centredness vary significantly, and its investigation needs to pay attention to these varied understandings. The literature review indicated that intentions are influenced by factors other than principles, policy and ideology. Consequently, an inquiry that focuses exclusively on ideology and its interpretations by practitioners, provides a partial account only of that ideology's transformation in practice. A majority of these studies assumed an unarticulated, ideal interpretation of child-centred teaching. The researchers proceeded to demonstrate that this holy grail was being converted to reality by a minority of teachers only. Consequently, these studies concluded that either child-centred ideology is inadequate and defective or practitioners need to pull up their socks and be more effective: 'full implementation' is necessary (Ireland, 1990a). However, in the studies where contextual details were documented, a more complex picture of practice (intentions and ideology) emerged. Context not only influenced the form and substance of teaching that practitioners constructed, but it had significance for their beliefs also. Constructing teaching and learning, therefore, is a complex interaction of ideology, practitioners' intentions, actions and their contexts. Failure to deal adequately with any one of these ingredients provides an incomplete picture of it.

Arising from this matrix, practitioners are understood as active transformative agents rather than as passive implementers of preconceived policy. It is assumed that all the elements of the inquiry's problem enjoy a dialectical relationship through the reflexivity of practitioners. This study is not an attempt to determine the extent to which official policy has been implemented. A question such as this, assumes theory and practice (intentions and action) to be dichotomous so that policy is 'prescriptive' and reform 'managerial' (Carr and Kemmis, 1986, p. 219). In contrast with this 'positivistic' (Schön, 1983; Sheldrake, 1990) approach to research, interpretive inquiry:

> . . . aims to transform the consciousness of practitioners and, by so doing, aims to give them grounds upon which to decide how to change themselves . . . it assumes [that] . . . practitioners are free to make up their own minds about how to change their practices in the light of their informed practical deliberations. (Carr and Kemmis, 1986, p. 219)

The research question of this inquiry, therefore, is not seeking to measure degrees of congruence between policy and practice or intention and action. Rather, it seeks to understand how practitioners construct their teaching. The assumption is that by illuminating the particulars of teaching constructions, understanding of child-centredness in general is increased also. It is to apply the Gadamerian hermeneutic rule that 'we must understand the whole in terms of the detail and the detail in terms of the whole' (1975, p. 291). Due to the problematic nature of the inquiry's question, this task is never quite complete. However, it assumes that to 'understand in a *different* way' increases potential for alternative actions (Gadamer, 1975, p. 297; Dunne, 1992; Grundy, 1987). Documenting the multiple realities of classroom practice helps to ground understanding of child-centred teaching in ways that respect the voices of teachers, the problematic nature of child-centredness, and the dialectical relationship between its constitutive elements. Additionally, it recognizes that:

> The restructuring of schools, the composition of national . . . curricula, the development of bench-mark assessment — all these things are of little value if they do not take the teacher into account. Teachers don't merely deliver curriculum. They develop, define it and reinterpret it too. It is what teachers think, what teachers believe and what teachers do at the level of the classroom that ultimately shapes the kind of learning that young people get. (Hargreaves, 1992, p. ix)

Because of this more elaborate conceptualization of child-centred teaching and the manner of its investigation in the present inquiry, it can legitimately claim to have significance for professional growth and programme development also.

Method

Reiterating the inquiry's problem as an investigation of practitioners' interpretations and constructions of child-centred teaching is helpful in setting the scene for constructing its research design. Rendering a more inclusive, grounded account of practice cannot ignore the grand narratives of teaching and the manner in which these are played out within school cultures and classroom routines.

The research design is 'emergent' (Lincoln and Guba, 1985; Hammersley and Atkinson, 1983) and, though its structure and rationale are discussed here, it is entirely consistent with the approach that some methodological details are fore-grounded at appropriate points in the text, rather than in this chapter. The research design provides a firm structure within which the methodology remains 'flexible' (Bogdan and Biklen, 1982, p. 55) so that the 'strategy and even the direction of the research . . . [can] be changed relatively easily' (Hammersley and Atkinson, 1983, p. 24). Nevertheless, it is the substantive issue of the inquiry that drives the study, while the research design chameleon-like serves its investigation as the focus is altered. An emergent design is particularly suited to coping with the unexpected and ephemeral, as well as with the detail of routine. It is an effective means of rebutting the charge that the researcher merely superimposes his 'prejudiced' per-spective on the data, though every study is prejudiced in the Gadamerian sense of the term (1975, p. 270). A design emerges when the 'investigator' engages in '*con-tinuous* data analysis so that every act of investigation takes into account every-thing that has been learned so far' (Lincoln and Guba, 1985, p. 209). This approach enabled me to begin with a 'wide-angle lens' (Spradley, 1980, p. 56) and to isolate gradually (through progressive focusing) a number of salient aspects of the problem as having particular importance for the actors. Such selectivity is necessary as it is impossible to give equal attention at once to all aspects of a complex situation (Hammersley and Atkinson, 1983).

Having established the problematic and multi-faceted nature of child-centredness, the most immediate task of the inquiry is to document practitioners' interpretations of such a policy and ideology, as an entrée for more focused investigations of actual practice. However, details of intentions alone would be a very partial account of classroom routines. Therefore, it is necessary to include accounts of how a rather elusive child-centred ideology is transformed by practitioners through their clas-sroom action. Such documentation needs to take particular account of contextual influences on practitioners' classroom constructions including deeply embedded understandings and routines of traditional teaching. Child-centred teaching, in its ideology and in the detail of its construction, has an ephemerality which eludes more conventional modes of research. A methodological filament is required which captures the very detail that slips through the net of other modes of investigation. Documentation of this detail needs to be conducted in a systematic and rigorous manner so that the investigation is 'credible', 'dependable' and 'confirmable' (Lincoln and Guba, 1985, pp. 289–331).

The research design is 'interpretive' with three distinct phases, and these facil-itate the progressive focusing of the inquiry, sacrificing breadth for depth as the scope of the problem is reduced from one phase to the next (Erickson, 1986). Intepretive inquiry is particularly suited to investigation of the study's substance because of its focus on 'human meaning in social life and in its elucidation and exposition . . .' (Erickson, 1986, p. 119). It is concerned also with 'issues of human choice and meaning', and 'issues of improvement in educational practice' (p. 122). Consequently, interpretive inquiry is 'a matter of substantive focus and intent, rather than of procedure in data collection . . .' (Erickson, 1986, p. 120). This substantive focus is maintained through the three distinct but intimately related phases of the inquiry.

Phase One: Sixteen Interviews

Sixteen practitioners were interviewed and they were encouraged to provide detailed descriptive accounts of their interpretations of child-centredness through the focus of their teaching practices. The interviews, which are the substance of Chapter 3, were conducted primarily in July 1990. Initial contact with potential participants was made during the last week of the school year (the last week in June) after a list of potential interviewees had been generated through consultation with inspectors, colleagues, school principals and practitioners. During consultations indication was given that I wished to interview practitioners who, despite constraints, had made a significant effort to construct child-centred practice. I was deliberately indicating my preference for documenting good practice without articulating in detail what I had in mind. I began a process of 'theoretical sampling' which gave me a 'foothold in the research' and enabled me to simultaneously collect, code, and analyse data and decide 'what data to collect next and where to find them' (Glaser and Strauss, 1967, p. 45). Once initiated, the process is one of 'continual development' whereby ongoing analysis of interview data becomes the key to determining 'where to go next' (Glaser, 1978, p. 37). Seeking good practitioners also carries within it the more pragmatic expectation that such teachers are more likely to participate in subsequent phases of the research.

The most frequently used shorthand by inspectors to decode my request was: 'you want me to name good teachers in my district.' School principals frequently mentioned a practitioner by name and continued: 'she is a good teacher, but I don't know if she is what you are looking for.' For some, child-centred teaching and good teaching seemed synonymous, while others were more open to the possibility that good teaching, however defined, might not include many of the distinguishing features of child-centredness. These exchanges gave implicit recognition to the ambiguities surrounding concepts like good teaching, child-centredness and traditional teaching (Alexander, 1992).

Requesting names of potential participants from a variety of sources facilitated a limited amount of cross-referencing. School principals were not appraised of consultations with inspectors and some practitioners. Consequently, when teachers were identified who had been named by inspectors or colleagues, they became more valuable as potential participants.

When structuring and conducting the interviews, I took seriously Spradley's (1979, p. 78) two 'complementary' dictats; that the process involves '*developing rapport*' and '*eliciting information*'. I trod a middle ground between a very 'exploratory' structure and a 'depth' and 'focused' approach (Lincoln and Guba, 1985, p. 268) while more inclined towards 'non-directive', 'reflexive interviewing' (Hammersley and Atkinson, 1983, p. 113). Each audio-taped interview was scheduled to last for an hour though the vast majority were of seventy to eighty minutes duration. Two very supportive individuals transcribed the audio-taped interviews.[1] Consequently, I was more focused on the interview process and data analysis which became an important means of extending the scope of subsequent interviews through the identification of additional questions. In general, the approach adopted was 'not to decide beforehand the questions . . .' but I did 'enter the interview with a list of issues to be covered' (Hammersley and Atkinson, 1983, p. 113). To do this successfully it is necessary to understand that 'the qualitative interview project is cumulative' so that 'it is what you learn from the total study that counts' (Bogdan and Biklen, 1982, p. 137). The general interview strategy adopted was to use the information that the participant was providing to ensure continuity and structure as well as to enable me to change focus when necessary. Questions were framed to avoid cueing the interviewees into providing particular answers.

The interviews and their data analysis progressed in tandem so that the nature of questions and the range of issues to be covered were under constant review. The number of interviews it would be necessary to complete was part of my ongoing deliberations. Initially a minimum of ten and a maximum of twenty were planned, though these figures were not absolute. When ten interviews had been completed the process was running smoothly and many issues were recurring with interesting variations. At that point I began to re-focus the purposive sampling so as to take more cognizance of the gender, school contexts and experience of participants while retaining a focus on practitioners' interpretations of child-centred ideology. Adding further variety to the data, as well as enriching the pool of potential participants for subsequent phases of the inquiry, were additional considerations. Consequently, teachers were sought from smaller, rural, and single-sex schools. When sixteen interviews were completed, I decided that 'saturation' had been reached, though the possibility remained that additional interviews could be conducted later in the research process if necessary (Lincoln and Guba, 1985). When a broad spectrum of practitioners' interpretations of child-centred ideology had been secured, it was necessary, through ongoing data analysis, to orient this detail towards subsequent phases of the inquiry which were focused on practitioners' actions and contexts, as well as their intentions. The dialectic was extended from interpretations of child-centred ideology to include classroom actions and the context in which they occurred.

A more systematic analysis of the interview data was undertaken as the 400 pages of transcripts were being generated. Data were sorted into a total of forty-nine separate computer files which were printed for further analysis. It became apparent that variation in interpretation of child-centredness was influenced significantly by the school context of the participants, though it was impossible to specify precisely the nature or extent of this influence. Consequently, context had significance for determining the classrooms in which observations were undertaken and detailed fieldnotes completed in the second phase of the research. By selecting a wide variety of contexts it was possible to document variations in teaching constructions and to isolate common themes. When the fieldwork for all three phases of the research was completed, and the serious task of continuing the analysis into the writing stage had been initiated, repeated analysis reduced the large number of files to twenty-four by eliminating some which appeared insignificant and by amalgamating others (Hammersley and Atkinson, 1983; Spradley, 1979, 1980). The final distillation of this data is presented in Chapter 3 as three general themes with particular emphasis on commonalities, complexities and variations. These themes, in addition to their various subheadings, emerged from the ongoing data analysis as being a valuable means of adding structure and coherence to practitioners' intentions in relation to their practice of child-centred teaching. These accounts (in addition to the literature review in Chapter 1) constitute the interpretive backdrop to, as well as the basis for, more focused investigations in subsequent phases of the inquiry.

Phase Two: Six Mini Case Studies

Chapter 3 reveals a panoply of practitioners' intentions in relation to practice. These accounts indicate that context influences both intentions and classroom actions. However, without knowing more about these contexts and the moment-by-moment details of teaching routines, it is impossible to understand the process from practitioners' perspectives. Providing insider accounts is the means through which the why of practice can be explored. It is necessary, therefore, to move beyond descriptive accounts of intentions to the nuts and bolts of classroom actions.

The inquiry's second phase brings together all the important dimensions of the substantive question: ideology, intentions, actions and context. However, investigation was circumscribed by limited time in the field. The purposive sampling of the inquiry was continued with a narrowed focus. The purpose of this second phase was to isolate persistent themes which, despite differing intentions and contexts, were at the heart of the teaching process. These themes emerged from ongoing and sustained analysis of detailed accounts of individual practitioner's classroom actions.

Six mini case studies were conducted in a variety of contexts. The criteria by which participants for the case studies were selected from the interviewees in phase one are discussed at the beginning of Chapter 4. Five consecutive school days were spent in each classroom, and the fieldnotes written up at the end of each day were shared with the practitioners concerned. Through reflective dialogue with the practitioners, stimulated by the content of the fieldnotes, the dynamic of intentions, actions and context are explored for their contributions to each practitioner's teaching constructions. The considerable variation in the location of these practitioners has significance for providing insight into contextual influences on practice. The progressive focusing of the problem through the phases of the research is intended to illuminate the issues involved in a cumulative fashion. While five of these six mini case studies were written up as an integral part of the original inquiry, they are not reproduced here (Sugrue, 1992). Rather, concentration is on the substantive themes which emerged from this second phase and this complex collage of practice is the focus of Chapter 4. The sixth mini case study was incorporated into the major case study which is the final phase of the inquiry.

Reducing the number of participants in the second phase is a trade-off between breadth and depth in the study. There were a number of pragmatic considerations that informed this methodological strategy also. I was keen to document teaching practices at the beginning of the school year when rules, routines and structures are in the process of being constructed and agreed between pupils and their teachers.

Negotiating entry and cultivating good field relations were important dimensions of all three phases of the research. Because the second phase involved being in the classrooms of participating teachers, it was necessary to seek permission from school principals and Boards of Management for each case study, as well as the consent of participants. Cultivation of good relations with participants and their colleagues was particularly important also. This importance stems from the indispensable need for dialogue as an integral element of 'thick description' and the process of revealing various layers of contextual meaning and strengthening interpretations of data (Bogdan and Biklen, 1982; Lincoln and Guba, 1985; Erickson, 1986; Goetz and LeCompte, 1984). Consequently, it was necessary to alternate 'between the insider and the outsider experience . . . simultaneously' (Spradley, 1980, p. 57). Due to the relatively short time planned for fieldwork in each classroom, my intention was to tend towards 'complete observer' rather than 'complete participant' though this did not prevent me from providing assistance when appropriate or when invited to do so by the collaborating teachers (Hammersley and Atkinson, 1983, p. 93).

When fieldwork for the second phase was completed, it was possible, through cumulative, ongoing data analysis, to identify three recurring themes that had particular importance for participants; themes that also transcend the boundaries of each case. Although these themes were emergent, they are presented in Chapter 4 as if they had clearly emerged at the outset of the second phase; in real time it was only as the cases progressed and through subsequent intensive data analysis that these cultural themes became manifest.

The three substantive themes narrowed the inquiry's focus. These themes became the lens through which an in-depth investigation of one individual's classroom practice was documented in a major case study. In this way, the most significant aspects of child-centred teaching for practitioners were allowed to emerge from the study's data through continuous analysis, progressive focusing, and purposive sampling. Interpretive accounts of these themes are the collective lens through which an in-depth investigation of one practitioner's constructions of child-centred teaching are reconstructed. These interpretive accounts become the basis also for a grounded, more inclusive revisioning of progressive teaching.

Phase Three: A Major Case Study

While the three cultural themes, which emerged from progressive focusing of the inquiry's problem during phases one and two, were to provide the substantive lens for the third phase, criteria were required also to select one of the six participants in the second phase who would collaborate in the major case study. These criteria are discussed in detail at the beginning of Chapter 5. Cultural themes apart, field relations were an inevitable consideration due to the nature of the task and the intensity of the research process of observations, reflections and dialogue over an extended period of time.

At the beginning of the third phase, renegotiation of entry with various individuals and bodies had to be repeated. As the cultivation of field relations continued, the combination of teacher–researcher dialogue, in addition to the inquiry's detail, became the catalyst for much more interpretive reflective comments in the fieldnotes, indicating a growing confidence in the evidence of the case as it advanced. It was necessary to pay attention to the specific details of practice to achieve this confidence in the evidence without losing sight of the practitioner's context (Wolcott, 1992). Though the three cultural themes provided the lens through which this practitioner's practice was investigated in detail, it was necessary to remain open to the possibility of surprise (Hammersley and Atkinson, 1983). Consequently, the focus on the various cultural themes was altered continuously in an effort to document the richness, complexity and multi-layered reality of this practitioner's teaching.

Time in the field is important to the trustworthiness of a case (Hammersley and Atkinson, 1983). When time spent in a particular site is limited, such as happened with the mini case studies, interpretations are limited and (of necessity) tentative. It becomes obvious, therefore, that an in-depth case study requires a more sustained period of time in the site, without being able to specify in advance how much time is necessary. This major case provides 'insider accounts' of how a particular practitioner interprets and constructs the various emergent themes of child-centred teaching in her particular context (Hammersley and Atkinson, 1983). These details become the study's means of grounding a more inclusive account of child-centred teaching. The first of three cultural themes, which collectively comprise the major case, is reported in Chapter 6 while the other two are documented separately in subsequent chapters.

Substance, Method and Audience

In case study research of an interpretive nature, to generalize beyond the bounds of a case is problematic. Consequently, it is important to explain how the interpretive accounts of the inquiry are intended to function.

The emergent design of the inquiry (as already indicated) is cumulative in relation to illuminating the central problem so that its final phase does not stand alone. Rather, its chief benefit is that, based on the forensic-like scrutiny of the data generated in the earlier phases, the contours of the in-depth case study are already framed. By providing thick descriptions and insider accounts, it is anticipated that the reader will have sufficient detail to reconstruct imaginatively the practitioner's teaching experience. Instead of being presented with findings, the audience is invited to come to terms with the issues raised. Readers are drawn into the dialogue through their own reflexive capacities. Part of the challenge to the researcher is to provide this rich description in a language which illuminates and challenges readers' under-standings of the issues concerned; to describe practice in a language which makes the reader's own tacit understandings more available for critical scrutiny. When case-study research functions effectively, it becomes a catalyst which enables practitioners to become more explicit about their own practices. Kilbourn (1990a, p. 112) indic-ates that 'one of the ways we learn about practice is by reflecting on realistic accounts of it' so that 'each new case contributes to our repertoire of understandings and skills for dealing with future cases'. There would be no point, he suggests, in documenting the details of the particular case if they were not 'in some sense relevant to future instances . . .' (p. 112).

A case study is 'a bounded system' that is primarily concerned with under-standing its focus 'in its own habitat' (Stake, 1988, p. 260). Nevertheless, it is based on the premise 'that the unique case helps us understand the more typical cases' (p. 261). One means of avoiding this issue of 'generalization' is to suggest that responsibility for determining universalisability rests with the reader. There is general agreement within the interpretive tradition that 'practitioners can learn from a case study even if the circumstances of the case do not match those of their own situation' (Erickson, 1986, p. 153; Stake, 1988). However, the possibility of gaining insight from the particulars of a case is not confined to practitioners since 'highly descriptive accounts of practice allow a reader to put him or herself in the place of those in the account' (Kilbourn, 1990a, p. 113). Such accounts expand the potential audience well beyond practitioners.

The extent to which a reader is able to overcome the contextual boundaries of a particular case study is (in part) dependent on the degree of specificity of detail which is provided in the case. The quality of data which constitute the evidence in any case, are the most effective means of overcoming the limitations of the bounded study. The challenge to the researcher is to provide sufficient contextual detail to enable the reader to reconstruct the substantive issue and, thus, participate in the meaning-making process. It is not, therefore, a question of regarding context as important, yet, wishing to ignore it in the interest of satisfying a need for univer-salization. Rather, rich contextual details enable readers to overcome the boundar-ies of the in-depth case study. Nevertheless, Chapter 9 moves beyond the bounds of the study to reconstruct a grounded understanding of child-centredness that respects practitioners' voices. Providing a more inclusive account necessitates paying atten-tion to traditional and progressive ideologies as they are manifest in the study's context and by nesting the inquiry's problem in this larger canvas 'a deeper set of principles' (Shulman, 1988, p. 33) is sought which celebrate complexity and variation while seeking some 'situated certainty' also amidst the uncertainties of postmodernity (Hargreaves, 1994).

Setting

It has been suggested repeatedly that the contexts of teachers' work are an import-ant shaping influence on their actions. However, it is not their immediate context alone which has such importance because 'the traditions through which particular practices are transmitted and reshaped never exist in isolation from larger social traditions' (Goodson, 1992a, p. 242). A recent OECD report on education in Ireland, supports Goodson's assertion when it states that:

> To understand contemporary Ireland, it is necessary to recognise how much its remote as well as more recent history still affects public values and attitudes and offers a key to understanding its institutions, not least its system of education. (1991, p. 11)

Child-centred teaching (as already indicated) became official policy in Irish primary schools with the publication of *The Primary Teacher's Handbooks* in 1971. Progressive education enjoyed considerable popularity in England and North America in the early part of this century, and, through a genuine spirit of reform, in the decades after the second world war (Zilversmit, 1993; Cunningham, 1988; Darling, 1994). Its rather recent arrival in Ireland, therefore, warrants explanation, and lends substance to my claim at the outset that traditions of schooling in Ireland have their own particular rhythms with consequent potential to illuminate educational debate elsewhere. The setting gains importance from being the 'ground or the background for' interpretations of the inquiry's details (Greene, 1990, p. 175).

It is generally accepted that Irish primary teachers responded very favourably to progressive policy (Sugrue, 1990a). Just a decade after its introduction the Irish government claimed that 'the child-centred approach, instead of being swamped by the more traditional approach of the primary school . . . took on for all classes of the primary school' (van der Eyken, 1982, p. 123). Several researchers have commented subsequently that this new policy was 'radical' and it represented a 'radical departure from the past' (McDonagh, 1969; Coolahan, 1981), as well as being 'a radical shift of ideological position and methodological approach' (Ireland, 1990a, p. 5). Yet, thirty years of literature on planned educational reforms suggests that radical change does not work (Fullan, 1991; Sarason, 1990). It becomes all the more important, therefore, to provide some contextual information on primary education in Ireland including the various conditions which shaped and paved the way for this 'radical shift' of educational policy.

Primary Education in Ireland in the 1990s

There are many features of primary education in Ireland which are a curious amalgam of historical circumstances. For example, though the legal age of school entry is six, a majority of children begin formal schooling on the September following their fourth birthdays. Primary schooling is an eight-year cycle: two years in 'infants' followed by grades one to six. Transfer to second level schooling typically happens on the September following a child's twelfth birthday. Education is compulsory from the age of 6 to 15 and this upper age limit is to be increased to 16 (Ireland, 1995). Schools are obliged to provide a minimum of 183 school days per year for approximately five and a half hours per day. This is shorter than in many countries but the school day tends to be intense as a consequence (Burke, Dobrich and Sugrue, 1991, 1992; OECD, 1995).

There are 3,427 primary schools in the state and about 3,217 are ordinary national schools. There are approximately 500,000 primary pupils who keep about 20,000 primary teachers gainfully employed. Almost 65 per cent of primary teachers are between the ages of 30 and 50 years, in mid-career in a contracting system which, due to its size in the first instance, has very little opportunity for promotion, and is characterized by a general lack of mobility and the absence of a career structure (INTO, 1994a).

Despite a reduction of approximately one third in teacher–pupil ratios in Irish primary schools during the past twenty years to their present level of 25.6, recent comparative figures indicate that Turkey is the only country in Europe with a higher ratio (OECD, 1995). Similarly, in comparative studies on educational expenditure, per capita funding of primary education in Ireland is very low and the fact that significantly more is spent on pupils at second level is regarded by many as regressive. Ninety-one per cent of funding at primary level is devoted to teachers' salaries leaving extremely little for provision of resources.

The management of Irish primary schools is at once highly centralized and decentralized. The state pays teachers' salaries, while teachers are employed by individual schools. There are no district or regional structures, though there are proposals for the creation of regional boards (Ireland, 1995; Coolahan and McGuinness, 1994). A recent report describes the arrangement thus:

> In most cases, National Schools are State-aided parish schools, operating under Diocesan patronage. The ownership of school buildings is generally vested in trustees appointed by the patron [Bishop]. Since 1975, nearly all schools have been managed by a board of management, consisting of 6 to 8 members, depending on school size. (Ireland, 1994, p. 3)

Management structures reflect the system as a whole, which is almost exclusively denominational.

Quality control in the system is primarily the domain of the schools inspectorate which is employed by the state. It aims to provide reports on individual schools every four years. It has responsibility also for the probation of newly qualified teachers. However, recent government publications indicate that school principals, in future, will be expected to increase their responsibilities for induction of new staff and for the quality of teaching and learning in their schools, including the observation and evaluation of teacher's work (Ireland, 1992, 1995; Coolahan, 1994; Sugrue, 1996b).

When child-centredness became official policy, the Department of Education dispensed with provision of detailed syllabi in favour of a menu of options, thus conferring greater autonomy on individual school staffs to 'outline a plan of work for the school' (The Primary Teacher's Handbooks, 1971, p. 21). There has been no revision of *The Primary Teacher's Handbooks* in the past twenty-five years and at the time of writing a series of new curriculum guidelines are awaited from the government's advisory body: the National Council for Curriculum and Assessment (NCCA) which has several subcommittees working on various subject matter areas. This brief account outlines the contemporary situation.

It is generally accepted that Irish society has changed rapidly and radically during the past quarter of a century. As a further element of situating the present inquiry, the confluence of social and economic circumstances which led to a radical shift of educational policy and thinking at the time and some of the system's defining characteristics in the preceding decades need to be described in broad brush strokes. For, as Kearney (1985, p. 37) suggests, correctly in my view, 'to ignore or to disregard our past is . . . to remain in corrosive collusion with it'.

Traditions of Primary Teaching in Ireland

For the first half of this century Irish society, and its educational system which reflected its wider context, were remarkably homogenous. When welcoming the draft 'New Curriculum', the Teachers' Study Group commented that: 'For over forty years the national schools have followed the same programme of instruction which has, to a great extent, shaped their work and atmosphere' (McDonagh, 1969, p. 5). Though circumspect in their criticism, the group ventures that for 'some teachers . . . the old programme has for a generation damaged the relationship between teacher and pupil and run counter to the grain of the child's mind' (p. 5). These comments are remarkably similar to those of Holmes (1911, p. 110) who, when criticizing the payments by results era in England, suggests that elementary schooling was 'an ingenious instrument for arresting the mental growth of the child and deadening all higher faculties'.

One of the most significant shaping influences on primary teaching in Ireland this century has been the importance attached to revival of the Irish language. While progressive education was enjoying some popularity internationally during the early decades of this century, the primary curriculum in Ireland was being restricted significantly. Shortly after independence (1922) it became compulsory for all pupils to learn the language from the beginning of schooling. The 3Rs of the primary curriculum have been (and remain) Irish, English and mathematics, while religious instruction is compulsory also, though parents reserve the right to withdraw their children from it. Although the profile of entrants to primary teaching has altered in recent years, McCarthy (1968) provides a valuable description of the traditional entrant to the profession:

> These young men and women were drawn from the most academically able in the country, but, certainly in the case of the men, from a remarkably limited social group. It appears to me that they came primarily from small farmers and small shopkeepers in the south and west, and in many cases had themselves left home as early as thirteen or fourteen years of age, attending first the preparatory colleges (which now fortunately have been

disestablished) and also the diocesan colleges, all residential in character. From there they went to a residential training college which was conducted on remarkably authoritarian lines. (quoted by Brown, 1985, p. 249)

MacMahon, in his autobiographical text *The Master* (1992), paints an interesting picutre as to the prevailing social context which spawned the kinds of teachers identified above. He says:

> It was enjoined upon us by the state to undertake the revival of Irish as a spoken language, a task that, by and large, we manfully faced; and it was also enjoined upon us by the Catholic Church, which to put it as its mildest, was powerful at the time, to transfer from one generation to the next their corpus of catholic belief . . . (1992, p. 89)

Primary teacher education, which remains denominational in nature, was a further influence in the selection and formation of intending primary teachers. Control and domination were part of a wider anti-intellectualism within the culture, which in its classic formulation decreed that to question is to be disloyal. For many, the result is a form of intellectual laziness, which, at best, regards ideas or theoretical considerations as bothersome (Lee, 1989). With particular reference to Irish schooling in the sixties, Fitzgerald (1991, p. 66) describes this anti-intellectualism as an attitude that 'finds expression in the flagrant pressure towards conformism in the schools, the discouragement of original thought or effort, the cult of the second-rate . . .'. In a recent interview McGahern (a former primary teacher who was sacked after his second novel, *The Dark* (1965), was banned under draconian censorship legislation) provides an important insight as to how this anti-intellectualism functioned in relation to student teachers. He says:

> When I was in training college, and that's not all that long ago, 1953–1955, four or five boys founded a little debating society, and they were nicknamed Oideachas Eireann, which is awfully sarcastic: it translates 'The Higher Institute of Irish Learning.' They were absolutely hounded in the place. These were people of nineteen and twenty, and they were to go out and teach and would be leaders of most rural communities. This fellow would prowl up and down the study hall, and if you were reading Eliot or some book that wasn't on the course, you could actually get biffed at the back of your ears. (quoted by Carlson, 1990, p. 66)

This widespread anti-intellectualism has a particularly Foucauldian ring to it where docile minds and 'docile bodies' appear to be the object of the system, with particular implications for curriculum and teaching (Foucault, 1979; Jones, 1990; Ball, 1990).

In the late 1950s and early 1960s, changes, which had been occurring in Europe and North America since the end of the second world war, began to happen in an Irish context at an accelerated pace. For example, the Primary Certificate

Examination was abolished in 1967, while universal secondary education and a school transport system were introduced. Despite these rapid changes, it was into a predominantly conservative, anti-intellectual context that child-centred teaching was introduced. Child-centredness presupposes knowledge to be relativist, a social construct, acknowledging the existence of multiple, often competing, realities. It is reasonable to surmise that the relativist epistemology of child-centredness would sit uneasily, if not ambiguously and a trifle precariously, within the socio-cultural tradition just described. An ambiguous ideology which has not been adequately articulated runs the risk of being reduced to doctrinaire shibboleths: a 'consensus on cliches' (Williams, 1995, p. 83). By paying attention to context, therefore, the present inquiry attempts to increase understanding of how a child-centred ideology has been interpreted by practitioners, given the prevailing cultural climate in the setting, as well as documenting how these interpretations have been constructed in and through classroom actions.

From a postmodern perspective, it is important to recognize that a paradigm shift was intended by policy architects in 1971. Such a shift or revolution occurs when 'an older paradigm is replaced in whole or in part by an incompatible new one' (Kuhn, 1970, p. 92). However, when a paradigm is 'first proposed, it has seldom solved more than a few of the problems that confront it . . .' and even where it has made inroads, these 'solutions are still far from perfect' (Kuhn, 1970, p. 156). Accepting a new paradigm is, therefore, primarily an act of faith: an indication that the community which adopts it has lost faith in its antecedent. Yet the new system is largely unproven. Apart from significant ambiguities surrounding the actual ideology of child-centredness, the many unique features of this inquiry's setting fan the flames of this uncertainty. In the past decade there have been calls for an 'overview of actual practice in classrooms' in the setting because there are 'relatively large areas still unresearched' (Ireland, 1985, p. 40). Without recourse to 'actual classrooms' it is difficult to move beyond rhetoric, on the one hand, and claim and counter-claim on the other. For example, the OECD report (1991, p. 67) on Irish education argues that 'the emphasis is still largely on a didactic approach' and this, the report suggests, is due to pressure from 'selective secondary schools' and 'a result of a long pedagogical tradition', which I have attempted to sketch above. Side by side with the above claim, a counter-claim by the Irish National Teachers' Organisation suggests that the paradigm revolution is complete, when it says that:

> The current broad-based, child-centred, integrated curriculum provides a firm foundation for pupils entering the competitive worlds of second and third level education. The Irish educational system has achieved international recognition as one of the best in the world . . . (1991, p. 3)

It is not my intention to arbitrate between these apparently irreconcilable perspectives. Rather, efforts are made to get beyond judgmental questions regarding degrees of implementation, which deal in unarticulated ideals, and to increase understanding of what actually happens in classrooms. By documenting particular instances of actual practice, insight will be gained also into the general problem of child-centred teaching. Perhaps, as Kearney (1985, p. 9) suggests in his introduction to *The Irish Mind*: 'in contradistinction to the orthodox dualistic logic of *either/or*, the Irish mind may be seen to favour a more dialectical logic of *both/ and . . .*'. In support of his thesis he cites Joyce's capacity to describe Dublin as 'lugly', 'simultaneously communicating his ambiguous perception of his native city as both lovely and ugly' (p. 10). This inquiry is an attempt to identify, describe, interpret and reconstruct the 'lugly' features of exemplary practitioners' teaching in child-centred contexts while being mindful of persistent threads in the socio-cultural setting and, through this pluriformity of practice, revision a more inclusive account of child-centred teaching. Such revisioning seeks to recognize the januform nature of practice as a means of moving beyond the cycloptic promotion, defence and predatory instincts of earlier approaches to the grand narratives of teaching.

Note

1   My thanks to Siobhán Nolan and Joyce Fitzsimons Markey who completed this tedious task cheerfully and efficiently.

Chapter 3

Practitioners' Teaching Intentions

Introduction

This chapter presents empirical data on practitioners' interpretations of child-centred policy. The purpose of this data analysis is to identify commonalities, complexities and variations in teachers' reconstructions of official policy in a setting where traditional teaching has been securely embedded within the dominant 'cultures of teaching' (Hargreaves, 1994, 1992; Lieberman, 1990). In keeping with the postmodern perspective adopted throughout this text, representation of their intentions acknowledges the influences of competing traditions of teaching.

The more than four hundred pages of transcript, which resulted from sixteen semi-structured, open-ended interviews, were subjected to repeated data analysis resulting in the emergence of three cultural themes. Poised between their actions and a policy of child-centredness in the setting, these practitioners' intentions become an important means of gaining insight into the dialectic between ideology, intentions, actions and context while enabling me to construct a collage of how such a policy is transformed. I did not wish to superimpose on the interview data what, in the setting, are identified as the fundamental principles of child-centredness as this would have been inimical to the emergent design of the study, though they did inform the nature of the questions asked. Consequently, the three themes, and their sub-headings, have emerged primarily from analysis and interpretation of the material. Within the research design of the study, documenting practitioners' intentions is an important first step in a process of more focused investigation of child-centred practice, as well as a partial means of grounding a reconstructed vision of child-centredness.

The first theme, *Practitioners' Images of Child-centred Teaching*, is the most general of the three. It focuses on practitioners' broad metaphoric statements about teaching. The second theme, *Practitioners' Planning Intentions*, deals with teachers' attitudes towards planning and organizing the content and process of teaching. The third theme, *Practitioners' Pedagogical Intentions*, discusses the interviewees' purposes in relation to the pedagogical strategies which they employ as part of their classroom routines.

Theme One: Practitioners' Images of Child-centred Teaching

The sixteen interviewees, whose interpretations of child-centred policy are reported in this chapter, were all qualified as primary teachers, though they pursued five alternative means towards that end (see Appendix, p. 228). Interviewees were invited to provide an image or metaphor which encapsulated the teaching process for them (Hunt, 1987; Elbaz, 1983; Clandinin, 1986; Connelly and Clandinin, 1988; Lakoff and Johnson, 1980). Aoife, who has been teaching 'infants' (4–5-year-olds) for more than thirty years, described how the disadvantaged context in which she teaches has shaped her image.

> . . . I think in the situation where I am, . . . part of it is only teaching, you have to be a social worker, you know, really, I do, . . . you're not only dealing with children in our situation, you have a lot of family, parents, mothers particularly to deal with . . . (transcript 1, p. 12).

Though Jane has been teaching for five years only, she is already in her third school. The previous two were in areas of social and economic disadvantage. She extends the caring and nurturing, mentioned by Aoife, to include additional responsibilities arising from her more recent relocation to rustic surroundings, thus demonstrating the importance of context for shaping images.

> . . . sometimes I think teaching involves so many different jobs — like one day last year we even had to go out and rescue a sheep that was caught in a fence outside the classroom window you know [laugh], and I'm saying, . . . you've to be a nurse, and a mother, a social worker and even a sheep farmer. (transcript 10, p. 2)

Jane added further complexity to this image by suggesting that it included the idea of 'someone who is there for the children', to fulfil an essentially moral role and who, regardless of the nature of the demands made by learners, would be 'ready to see what the good thing to do is in that situation' (transcript 10, p. 2). Jane's espoused perspective resonates with Nodding's (1992) plea for caring and moral development to be given a more central role in teaching.

Variation on these images is provided by Orla, who has been teaching for nearly twenty years. In addition to her teaching responsibilities, she is principal of a small rural school. Her comments indicate that her experience and context have altered her perspective and, in the process, her allegiance has shifted from teaching as transmission to a position more readily identifiable with child-centred teaching.

> I suppose that would have changed for me a bit over the years, I would have thought in the beginning I had to have all the knowledge and that the success of what happened in the classroom depended on how well I could get that across. Now, the change I would have seen in my own attitude would be sort of looking at education from the point of view of drawing out what's already there. (transcript 15, pp. 1–2)

Frank has been teaching for more than ten years. As a pupil he attended a small rural school. His comments connect with a growing volume of research literature which suggests that personal biography, life history, and 'apprentice-ship of observation' (Lortie, 1975) play a significant part in forming practitioners' images of teaching (Clandinin, 1986; Connelly and Clandinin, 1988; Goodson, 1992a, 1992b; Ball and Goodson, 1985; Goodson and Walker, 1991; Sugrue, 1996). Recognition of this dimension in teachers' work increases its complexity signific-antly. Frank was quite explicit about the influence of his apprenticeship of obser-vation on his image of teaching.

> ... when I was in primary school itself, I really looked up to and admired my own, what we call a school master, still call a school master, and even 'till this day I will still call him master. I refer to him as being master, instead of Mister. I admired that man and I respected that man you know and to a certain extent I've nearly modelled myself on him. (transcript 6, p. 4)

Variation on the influence of apprenticeship of observation is provided by Kate who has been teaching for less than five years (in Ireland and in North America). While still a very young child, holiday visits to her aunts' and great-aunts' class-rooms have influenced her both in terms of being 'very strict' as well as putting an emphasis on learning 'things off by heart' (transcript 11, p. 2). These comments, and those which follow, suggest that Kate's image of teaching embraces aspects of traditional and progressive ideologies and she presents as being comfortable with this pluriformity.

> Well, my children don't sit in rows [laugh], that's a visible difference. There's a lot of grouping, whilst I can't remember grouping in their class-rooms. Maybe I wasn't there for long enough and I was very young. But, there are a lot of groups in my class especially in English and maths. I suppose I let them do, I give them a lot of encouragement you know, I make them get up and they're responsible for their own group reading ... [They're given] far more responsibility and there's a reward system of stickers and that sort of thing [laugh] sweets, or whatever. (transcript 11, pp. 2–3)

Ian recognized that there are many metaphors that could give particular repres-entation to teaching and his favourite image was that of magician. As he articulates how this image functions, the complexity of practice is revealed. Though teacher directed, the experience he describes may be intensely engaging for learners. Con-sequently, it could be simultaneously understood as homologous with or inimical towards interpretations of child-centredness and teaching as transmission. Implicitly he is arguing for an image of teaching that embraces aspects of both traditions.

> I remember myself as a magician. Now when you think of magician you think of maybe sleight of hand, tricks or that, that's not what I mean. The magician is the one who makes magic and casts spells and potions. And

that's what I regard myself as doing. For example, to give children a very intense experience of something . . . For example . . . there are teachers, 'progressive,' 'experimental,' whatever the words are, who actually elicit their teaching from the children. They might be teaching something and most of the lesson comes just from the children. Now I'm the opposite. When I'm teaching — silence I want. But then I try to use the silence to create a very intense image, . . . the story mode,[1] to introduce something with a story, something very graphic, something very compelling. The point is to try and engage them with a sense of suspense, children love suspense. (transcript 9, p. 25)

Not all the participants were familiar with describing their practice in terms of images and metaphors. Consequently, some did not respond to the question directly, electing instead to describe other intentions in relation to their practice. In the various and overlapping images and metaphors presented above, the common thread is that they implicity subscribe to a particular set of values. I invited the practitioners to surface the values they considered to be of greatest significance.

Values and Teaching

Respect for individual difference is an important touchstone of child-centred ideology (Darling, 1994). In the Irish context, by contrast, our capacity for 'self-denigration' has been documented by many (Clare, 1991). Poverty privileges collective endeavour more than it indulges idiosyncrasy and, it is suggested, our literature reflects this emphasis.

. . . almost nowhere between 1920 and 1960 is this [Irish] society and its relationship with the individual destiny seriously examined or dramatised, explored or exploited in works of fiction. Instead, there are those brief moments of defeat, novels about the lives and loneliness of priests, the decay of the Big House [see Genet, 1991], a stagnant world full of pathos and set scenes. (Tóibín, 1991, p. 51)

In contrast with this rather bleak socio-cultural inheritance from the perspective of the individual, or perhaps because of it, one of the more heartening aspects of the interviews is the extent to which 'confidence', 'self-image' and 'happiness' of learners are mentioned repeatedly by the participants as being of fundamental importance. However, this should be tempered by an awareness of 'the Irish ability to say one thing and do another' (Clare, 1991, p. 16).

Kate and Helen teach in very different social circumstances, yet the basic values they espouse are very similar. The former indicates that 'to respect others . . .' (transcript 11, p. 27) is fundamental and the latter expands on this basic tenet:

Just respect for one another, just the whole thing of fair play, of being honest you know, of not being afraid to tell the truth. I always say, what's the worst that can happen if you tell the truth . . . (transcript 8, p. 20)

David provides variation on this theme while indicating that his priorities are a complex mix of personality, personal values and contextual influences which, in his case, is one of social disadvantage.

> Number one, the motivation to do things, to motivate them, motivate them to work, that's very very big with me personally, I would regard myself as, maybe not a hard worker, but I'm a busy person myself and I suppose you do try to transmit your own values . . . (transcript 4, p. 11)

Further variation is provided by Mark who also teaches in socially deprived circumstances. He indicates that he favours Watt's (1989) altruistic individualism over more egocentric behaviour. It is also worth noting that the values implicit in these intentions provide a strong social orientation to teaching (Alexander *et al.*, 1992).

> I want them to know how to co-operate with each other, I want them to be able to . . . [have] some sort of balance in themselves, that they can work with others and work with me and get on with each other . . . (transcript 13, p. 11)

Implicit in these comments is an emphasis on the social development of learners which is more inclusive than the austerity associated with archetypal notions of the master and the mistress (Sugrue, 1996a). Valuing individuals through cultivation of classroom relationships constitutes further complexity and variation in the interviewees' images of teaching.

Teacher–Pupil Relationships

Laura expected her class to 'go away with' a feeling that she is 'fair with them'; that she is 'their friend more or less'. However, she qualifies friendship when she says: 'I don't go overboard on the friendly bit, I don't get too involved with them' (transcript 12, p. 8). Helen added further ingredients to the process of cultivating relationships.

> Its fun, they've fun, a sense of humour, something we enjoy, a very energetic, a lot of doing, active stuff like that. I don't want the children in my class to fear me, they'd respect me, and they know, they understand the rules, they know exactly what the borderline is. Like I am firm with them but fair, and I think there's a happy atmosphere in the class. The sense of humour, I enjoy them . . . the repartee with them. And they're not afraid to be wrong, they're not afraid to comment on something, they're not afraid to ask questions . . . (transcript 8, p. 6)

These extracts suggest that practitioners are in sympathy with commonly held interpretations of child-centredness: there is a significant distancing from austerity, fear and oppression, yet there remains a need for limits and rules.

Barry is a seasoned campaigner in a socially disadvantaged area. He readily acknowledged the importance of personal investment in classroom relationships and implicitly reveals something of his own apprenticeship of observation as he juxtaposes the competing traditions of teaching while clearly indicating his own preference.

> I think if you don't let a certain amount of yourself be known to them, then . . . I would find it very hard to teach otherwise you know. To go in and just throw up the information to them, that's the real old style you know. The amount of interaction between children and teachers today is so much greater than when I was going to school . . . (transcript 2, p. 22)

Barry also recognized that since use of corporal punishment in schools was prohibited (in the early 1980s), he has found it necessary to devote more time to relationships in the interest of creating a positive classroom climate. This, he claims, has positive benefits for his teaching and for teachers in general.

> You have to devise ways and means, you've got to have better relationships with them, because I mean before that you could just 'sling two' and that was the end of it, but I can tell you, you've to work a lot harder, and you've to spend a lot more time talking to them as individuals now . . . I've certainly spent far more time since [the abolition of corporal punishment], and I think it's made better teachers out of a lot of people, that they had to draw on some other side of themselves to discipline, [and] if you can achieve [it], it's far nicer discipline than the stick, but there again, I often wished to God I had it back, you know, because, I mean . . . [there are] certain individuals who can't ever get . . . [their act together regardless of how many times they have rules explained to them]. (transcript 2, pp. 22–3)

It is apparent that Barry's preferred practice was not brought about without significant effort on his part. His comments implicitly recognize that without alterations to local structures and support for the individual practitioner, there is a great temptation to revert to the old order. Changing practice is a gradual and often painful process (Fullan, 1991, 1993).

Both Paula and Frank adopted a contractual approach to classroom relationships, which is underpinned by respect and reciprocality. However important these relationships may be on a day-to-day basis, practitioners who teach in disadvantaged areas virtually all indicated that involvement in extra-curricular activities made a significant contribution. The stories they told to substantiate their argument corroborated each other: involvement with learners outside classrooms enables teachers to discover aspects of learners' personalities which otherwise would remain hidden. Their comments implicitly suggest that what counts as 'basic to education' could be extended profitably to include much that is currently deemed to be extra-curricular (Eisner, 1996). There was general agreement that good relationships strengthened their contractual nature. Consequently, it is more difficult for learners to break rules repeatedly, thus running the risk of damaging rapport with teachers.

Jane had a number of children in her third class (8–9-year-olds) who were attending the local psychiatric clinic. One of these boys was particularly disruptive, and he had recently broken an arm by hitching a ride (scuttin') by hanging on to the rear of a lorry. Jane and a colleague determined to bring some of these children, including the one-armed bandit, to a local park on Saturday mornings.

> When we got to the adventure centre in the park — that fella was up on everything you know. Arm or no arm he was hanging out of every branch and everything. He was kind of disruptive there too at the beginning but a kid lent him a bucket and spade, a 3-year-old. Now this fella was nine, and he sat in the sand pit for an hour and a half and made sandcastles without a move out of him. He didn't bother anyone else he was just totally enthralled. When he came to the park first, there was this kind of a bridge made out of logs that the kids would go across and he had positioned himself in the middle of that and he said that he was a 'Troll' and any child that tried to get past he knocked them [laugh]. We had to literally take him down, broken arm or not, and say you really cannot knock other kids off this bridge you know. But just before we left the park he said, 'Oh I never locked my Troll's cave under that thing', and he ran back and with an imaginary key he turned the lock. That just gave me a real insight into him, that he was very imaginative and creative in that sense, that I'd never seen in school. I mean, really with him, all I had seen to a large extent was disruption and I'd seen he was intelligent but . . . he never applied himself to work and he never allowed anyone near him to work either you know. So I tried then, this was June, to work on his imagination a bit and like it had great results. (transcript 10, pp. 28–30)

The insight gained through this 'critical incident' (Woods and Jeffrey, 1996; Woods, 1993a, 1993b) enabled Jane 'to handle [the situation] a bit better . . . not being dogmatic' (transcript 10, p. 28). Barry provided variation on this out-of-class contact when he used lunch-time football as a means of building up a working relationship with a sixth class of pretty tough boys. Relinquishing his break was a good investment, he thought. Laura, who taught in disadvantaged circumstances also, recognized the value of out-of-class contact.

> I think you can have a different relationship with them in the extra-curricular. You can also develop the relationship that you have already in the class, though not necessarily [with] your own children but it helps in relations throughout the school. For example, if you're 'on the yard' and you've children from every year — they know you, you know them — it filters through . . . (transcript 12, pp. 21–2)

All of these comments suggest that in various ways, both inside and outside of classrooms, teachers value relationships with learners and this resonates with popular interpretations of child-centred ideology.

Interviewees were less comfortable with the manner in which relationships had developed more recently and policies enunciated which were more inclusive of parents. Mark describes how relationships with parents had altered during the past twenty years. When he began teaching, he remarked, 'I did not know any parent', but today 'I know all the mothers and . . . quite a few of the fathers'. Neither, he suggests, are learners as 'controlled as they were . . . not as regimented' (transcript 13, p. 27). Some interviewees expressed the view that parents were 'far more critical and are more aware of what's going on . . . and [they] find it hard to accept that their son or whatever is not brilliant' (transcript 7, p. 22). In a similar middle-class situation to the one just quoted, Noel was aware of the paradigm shift that had occurred: 'I am very conscious of the fact that . . . gone are the days when a teacher was the oracle . . .' (transcript 4, p. 10).

These comments seem to suggest that an important dimension of interviewees' images of teaching embrace the notion of full and harmonious development: one of the tenets of child-centredness.

Teaching the 'Whole Child'

An important dimension of policy shift with the adoption of child-centredness was to extend traditional curricula to give a more balanced education that included social, personal, emotional as well as cognitive development. When these elements of teachers' images of teaching were discussed contextual influences became more apparent. Kate taught first grade learners (6–7-year-olds) in middle-class circumstances. She commented: 'I want the children to learn but to be happy too' (transcript 11, p. 17). Noel's context was similar, though he taught at the senior end of school where preparing learners for entrance examinations for the secondary school system was a priority. Consequently, he acknowledged that there was tension in his work between individual learner's needs and the demands of the system:

> How I can fulfil that aspiration [full and harmonious development]; it's very difficult obviously because every child is an individual, they all have individual talents, but again, I've spoken so favourably about teaching in an advantaged area that, I suppose, with such an emphasis on entrance exams, a child say that might have talents in art or whatever, those talents probably wouldn't be as highlighted as they could be because of exam pressure . . . (transcript 14, p. 10)

Orla taught middle standards (third and fourth classes) in a rural setting. She indicated 'that a good experience of school is very important if they are going to learn.' Consequently, she insisted that 'unless a child is basically happy she's not even in a frame of mind for learning' (transcript 15, p. 17). When Jane taught in disadvantaged contexts, she did not 'get much satisfaction' from teaching the 3Rs, 'because a lot of the energy went into the other things', not least of which was 'keeping the peace'.

Although I did not realize it at the time, what Jane revealed next was to fore-shadow an issue of particular importance for the inquiry. Her comments have addi-tional significance because they reveal the importance of reflection for gaining insight into one's practice (Schön, 1983, 1987, 1991; Grimmett and Erickson, 1988; Russell and Munby, 1992; Eraut, 1995).

> It was only . . . that summer I just sat down and I really tried to work out what had happened during that year and how things had gone and [I asked myself] did we actually achieve anything in that class? And, it really began to strike me yes we did achieve something but it wasn't actually in academic terms. I mean, there was some achievement there but not a lot, not what I would have hoped for but, that there were other areas . . . (transcript 10, p. 26)

By way of illustration, Jane told a story of how living in the disadvantaged com-munity in which she was teaching, provided important out-of-school contact with a difficult learner which helped her to get through to him. This learner came by her house and sowed seeds in her garden, and Jane's newly acquired understand-ing increased her awareness that social development through relationships was an integral element of her classroom routines. Her extra-curricular activities were increasing the learners' 'continuity of experience' (Dewey, 1938, pp. 33–50).

> By the end of the year a lot of children would call round or drop in now and then and we'd meet them in the shops and I found living there a great help. So, that kind of flowed into school and I suppose some of school flowed into life outside of school and it has made me really, really aware of trying to do something different to just the academic side of school. That I would try to keep going through the academics in class, you know. (transcript 10, pp. 15–16)

These comments suggest that there is a tension between the social and cognitive needs of learners which varies significantly depending on the context of teachers' work. Laura, who taught in similarly deprived circumstances, indicates that social development is a significant element of her agenda.

> It's not a thing I don't think of at all [full and harmonious development] but for certain children my main aim would be social; to socialize them. I find that it's very difficult to teach them the 3Rs shall we say . . . (tran-script 12, p. 19)

Helen does not identify readily with the theoretical language of full and har-monious development. Her final comment indicates that the rhetorical language of theory did not come to mind when asked to articulate her understanding of the prin-ciple. Implicitly her comments resonate with the perspective articulated by Berlak and Berlak (1975); that practitioners' intentions are fashioned more by tensions and dilemmas than by ideology. When this occurs, ideology may alienate and isolate practitioners rather than become a source of vision and sustenance. Helen's context increases the complexity of relationships by revealing their internal tension between: familiarity and distance; caring and challenging (Hargreaves and Tucker, 1991; Noddings, 1992).

> I want them to be as happy as possible. If you get very emotionally involved with all their problems you won't be effective as a teacher either. So there's a very thin line there between being so worried and concerned about them that you say, ah well, just don't make any demands of them. So you have to be very careful. But that full and harmonious thing I never actually, I would never think of what I'm doing as that . . . (transcript 8, pp. 15–16)

Many of the other interviewees also indicated a need for curricular balance, which Chapter 1 suggested was characteristic of child-centredness. However, none of the interviewees linked this need so eloquently as Paula with concern for self-confidence and cultivation of additional interests in learners. When responding to a question as to how her practice related to the full and harmonious development of learners, she too indicates that the rhetoric of child-centred ideology is not a language which comes to mind automatically when she reflects on her practice.

> The first thing I want to do is, I think the full development of a person by building their confidence. And I don't feel that I'm a 'knocker'; every effort really the child makes I feel that it is their effort and I would praise utterly. I don't believe in knocking so I think that the full and harmonious development of the child, while . . . it's not in my head the whole time, I think everything I do really is very much influenced by it because I want to develop them as full people really, build their confidence give them as many skills, open their minds as much as possible to the world. I think that if I just teach the curriculum rigidly I don't think I'd do that. (transcript 16, p. 13)

Many of the above extracts indicate that context, personal biography and professional experience, play a critical role in shaping the intentions of practitioners. They share images, values and intentions that are extremely complex yet highly individual. Some of their intentions appear to be consistent with commonly held interpretations of child-centredness, while others seem to include aspects of teaching as transmission: a januniformity as well as a pluriformity of intentions.

Theme Two: Practitioners' Planning Intentions

Introduction

Traditional schooling (in the Irish context) was strictly controlled by a combination of detailed syllabi, rigorous inspection and state examinations in a narrow range of subject areas. Progressive policy sought to supplant this narrow rigidity with a more broadly based curriculum to be determined at school level, thus conferring greater autonomy on teachers to exercise professional judgment and to plan and structure teaching locally in order to match learners' needs and interests with appropriately selected and organized learning opportunities. Teachers were encouraged to develop plans collaboratively at school level though traditional rules continue to demand individual long-term, short-term preparation and monthly progress records of learners. Greater emphasis was placed on whole school planning, which has been pursued more vigorously since the early 1980s as the influence of effective schools literature and international trends towards devolution of decision-making to local levels have increased (Smyth, 1993; Campbell, 1985; Skilbeck, 1984; Hargreaves, 1989; Rudduck, 1991; Nias, Southworth and Campbell, 1992; Little and McLaughlin, 1993). Under a series of sub-headings, this theme seeks to document practitioners' intentions in relation to approaches to planning advocated by child-centred policies.

Planning Teaching and Learning

Frank (sixth grade) indicates that, in his school, a pragmatic approach was adopted to putting schemes of work (content) together for different class groupings. He readily acknowledges that he was unclear as to what precisely was meant by a school plan. What he and his colleagues cobbled together created tensions between collaborative planning and the 'legendary autonomy' of Irish practitioners (OECD, 1991). His comments suggest that their interpretation of the process owes much to traditional rules which specify individual teacher's planning responsibilities rather than collective duties more commonly associated with child-centredness. Furthermore, the extract supports the view that teaching was content driven. Frank's comments suggest also that he is more comfortable with the old-fashioned language of rules than with more recent advocacy of collaborative planning.

> Well there is a 'plean scoile' [school plan] yes, there's a set of schemes say for third, fourth, fifth, and sixth [classes]. What we did at the start was we decided that 3rd class [teachers] would make out their scheme of work in maths, English and Irish. There is a kind of a plean scoile there. I wouldn't call it a plean scoile but it is a certain scheme of work that goes right through the school. (transcript 6, pp. 34–5)

His comments suggest that the manner in which schemes, rather than plans, were developed indicates horizontal rather than vertical planning in the school, thus promoting a kind of balkanization, with priority being accorded to 'basic' subjects (Hargreaves, 1992, 1994).

In the large urban school where Kate (first grade) began teaching, her account of the staff's collective planning bears a striking resemblance to Frank's experience of the process. They had a plan for each subject area of the curriculum but, despite this, she adopted a more pragmatic approach when it came to furnishing a scheme of her own.

> I got a first class scheme from a teacher who'd been teaching first class the year previous to me [laugh]. Well I had to get one some place and it had been given to the school. (transcript 11, pp. 10–11)

Emer provides further variation on this general theme when she states that completing the school plan was 'a chore that had to be done' so that the completed document could sit 'in the [principal's] office'. She thought that it was an unequal burden as 'some poor sods got landed with some subjects' and this was most likely in the case of individual teachers who were particularly talented in a specific subject area. The expertise is primarily in the subject matter as opposed to expertise in planning or pedagogy. Despite the approach, she feels that a school plan is 'handy to have', even 'valuable' for certain aspects of subjects. However, she identifies tensions similar to those commented on above by Frank when she says: 'I don't think it's right to limit teachers to what's in the plan.' In her experience, however, plans did not limit individual teachers because they had 'gone [on] doing what they were going to do anyway' regardless of the school plan (transcript 5, p. 11). Her comments suggest a tradition of teachers operating in isolation rather than a more collegial, collaborative approach. This 'culture of individualism' (Hargreaves, 1992, pp. 220–2) she described as follows:

> For example, somebody's good at music and they get a second class, well they're not going to stop at the end of whatever is on the programme for second class. I think there's so many talented people . . . it's valuable to go and do your own thing . . . (transcript 5, pp. 11–12)

For Noel planning is 'individual to himself' (transcript 14, p. 6) and the only commonality with his colleagues is a shared set of textbooks, while Mark comments that planning is 'all very much up to ourselves' (transcript 13, p. 6).

In sharp contrast with this perspective, Orla, in her position as school principal, was committed to the process of school planning as opposed to the production of a 'tome' as an end in itself. Orla and her four colleagues attempted to use the process as a means of 'keeping the curriculum under review' (Leithwood, 1987). Her comments suggest that when a plan is kept under review it remains more flexible, thus remaining responsive to the change process, as well as increasing awareness of the need for continuity. Such an approach also appears to be consistent with what is popularly thought to be child-centred.

> Oh very definitely [planning is cooperative] and that's something we have tried to do over the last few years, especially since the idea of 'plean scoile' came in, we have tried to stay with that, and not just give it lip service. We were trying to do it subject by subject and area by area and things that weren't specific subjects. Music is one area that comes to mind but we decided to work on a scheme and sort of see if it satisfied what we saw as our aim in teaching music. Now we're trying to keep with that and to review it . . . We're very much trying to take it from where the other person left off. (transcript 15, p. 3)

Gena had been involved in the drafting of a school plan and she found it useful when approaching her own preparation, particularly in the absence of textbooks.

> Very useful, particularly with the junior level when you don't have text-
> books as such, and all this pre-reading and pre-maths and that, the plean
> scoile is invaluable . . . (transcript 7, p. 4)

These short extracts indicate that there was significant divergence of practitioners' intentions in relation to curriculum planning. They also illustrate tensions between the tradition of teacher autonomy and isolation, and a more collegial approach.

It is reasonable to assume that the variations documented above have significance for the nature and quality of classroom experiences. The evidence provides some indication also that greatest attention is paid to planning in the absence of appropriate textbooks. Consequently, the extent to which practitioners rely on textbooks to plan their curricula, will provide some insight into the tension between teaching which is primarily interpreted as prescribed as opposed to a teaching approach which attempts to match the needs, interests and abilities of individual learners with appropriately structured learning experiences.

Planning: The Use of Textbooks

Unlike systems of schooling elsewhere, such as Britain and Canada, learners in Irish schools are obliged to purchase their own textbooks with some financial assistance for disadvantaged learners. In schools situated in poor economic and social circumstances, such as David's, he and his colleagues '. . . are under some kind of a sub-conscious . . . order to limit the number of books we ask the children to buy' (transcript 4, p. 2). Barry teaches in similar social circumstances and, having stated that textbooks 'have absolutely no importance what-so-ever', he readily acknowledges that he is supporting this stance with 'a well-worn argument' which states 'that they're not really suitable for . . . the children we teach' (transcript 2, p. 10). To illustrate his point he indicates that though his sixth class did have a mathematics textbook, they used it as little as a half-dozen times during the year. Similarly, he suggests an Irish reader would 'have a bearing' on what he describes as 'my own programme' (transcript 2, p. 10). Within his own programme he questions the relevance of textbook content though he is aware that he may be advocating 'relevance' at the expense of 'intellectual rigour or challenge' thus placing his working-class students at a disadvantage (Hargreaves, 1989).

David (third grade) is 'sceptical of the use of textbooks' but he did 'use them as a sort of a prop'. He elaborates on this by saying that in 'history I would use a textbook . . . as a kind-of-a theme for keeping the course going together' (transcript 4, p. 4).

Laura (fourth grade) thinks that once textbooks had been acquired by learners 'we have a lot of parental pressure . . . to try our best to get through those [textbooks] as much as possible' (transcript 12, p. 3). Because of the economic circumstances of the pupils in Laura's school, the principal and staff had begun to accumulate school textbooks for rental by pupils in an effort to reduce the financial burden on poor parents. Over a period of time this had the unanticipated consequence of lending variety and diversity to the curriculum through a greater supply of materials than would be the case if pupils purchased a set of books annually. However, as Laura indicated, there were times also — such as when World Cup (soccer) fever was at an all-time national high in June (1990) — when it was possible to harness such enthusiasm for educational purposes, rather than attempt to stick rigidly to a textbook or a planned programme.

> You're not constrained by textbooks which does help in a way, particularly in environmental studies. Like I did a huge thing on the World Cup . . . I just found the easiest thing to do, they could read coordinates on a map in third class and they knew where all these countries were totally because they were just really into it, they loved doing the flags . . . (transcript 12, pp. 18–19)

Other variations on the extent to which textbooks influence the nature of learning experiences were provided by Emer (fifth grade). She suggests that they are valuable for providing structure as well as for suggesting goals, and there is clear indication that content drives the teaching process.

> It [a textbook] does give a structure and it shows you where you're going and . . . if you've planned [that] you want to get to the end of a certain block or that you'd like them to know this much in a certain amount of time, well, then you drive yourself and you drive them to get that done . . . (transcript 5, pp. 3–4)

In contrast with Emer's suggestion above that practitioners should be allowed to do their own thing, Orla declares a firm commitment to cooperative planning, though she likes the security provided by a text: 'Planning is one of my own weakest areas. I find it hard to plan especially long term and . . . I feel dependent on textbooks.' Yet, there is nothing slavish about this: 'I use them very much as my basis and I want to have something that I could fall back on . . . I'll try and adapt them to suit myself' (transcript 14, p. 2). Noel provides some variation on this general theme when he suggested that it would be foolhardy to abandon textbooks given 'the amount of expertise that goes into the writing' of them. They can, he says, be used 'as the foundation you can build around . . . textbooks are good and they serve a purpose' (transcript 14, p. 5).

Without recourse to actual practice it is difficult to determine the extent to which textbooks are used with flexibility and imagination. These comments certainly do not communicate a sense that these practitioners' teaching is *laissez faire*: an accusation sometimes levelled at progressive teaching by its detractors. Many features of their comments also suggest much that is homologous with what passes for traditional teaching.

Planning: Themes and Integration

Some interviewees declared that their planning reflected such principles as environment-based learning and integration thus resonating in intent, at least, with axioms of child-centred teaching. Jane made use of textbooks in tandem with 'a lot of environmental things and . . . objects'. She liked to plan this work thematically but previous socialization of learners ensured that they thought in terms of discrete subjects.

> I tend to plan around the topic and bring in the different subjects into that, even though we might actually do it in subject terms in school 'cause they would say, 'Teacher, when are we doing history this week?' or whatever. At the same time, I would tend to work on two themes for a month. (transcript 10, p. 3)

Paula provides further variation on this when she declares that her work is not based on textbooks, she plans thematically in a very integrated coherent manner: 'Yea, anything I do is totally integrated. Everything I do is integrated really as much as I possibly can without having a false kind of an integration . . .' (transcript 16, p. 14). Paula has no hesitation in saying that her lack of dependence on textbooks and her interest in pursuing a programme thematically, requires enormous commitment and attention to detail when planning due to a distinct lack of resource provision (Sugrue, 1990). However, she understands this meticulous planning to be quite homologous with common interpretations of child-centred ideology.

> I don't use my planning though as . . . having a kind of imprisoning effect on the children. Anything that comes up from the children or enters the subject spontaneously, I then develop that. If I could develop it within the bounds of the classroom I would, or if I couldn't, I would bring it with me and I would try to develop it for the following day or whatever. So I don't allow that [to] restrict me or make my teaching rigid in any way . . . (transcript 15, p. 4)

Paula's comments support a more inclusive interpretation of child-centred teaching where structure, flexibility, definite content and learners' interests can be brought into productive tension through the imaginative and creative efforts of the teacher.

Jane planned thematically to enable students to make connections, thus facilitating a Vygotskian style structuring of learning experiences.

> Planning thematically is something I try to do specifically. I'm not sure that children always make the connections in the way that we [adults] would make or that we would expect them to make automatically. . . . I would say their interest flows out of subject areas all right. But sometimes connections that I would expect them to make, I'd find they don't actually make [them] and I would have to point out the links between them. I think

> that is why I tend to use a theme . . . It makes the links more specific, in a sense, than leaving it up to themselves to try and find out. (transcript 10, p. 23)

For similar reasons, Helen tries 'as much as possible to integrate' because subject matter 'makes an awful lot more sense than doing scraps, dividing the day up into little scrappy bits' (transcript 8, p. 16).

Orla is torn by the tensions created between competing traditions where a content-driven perspective competes with notions of patch studies which are more time consuming and exploratory, but potentially more engaging and meaningful for learners.

> I look for the following-through of themes [by] trying to put things together in planning, but I find what happens to me is, say on a subject like History, I feel there's a great need to look at local history when they're in third and fourth and then I feel, dear God, that's all I've done this year, and I find there's something in me which says you should have covered much more [content]; maybe a fear of not trusting my own in-built mechanism that says it's ok, you've done that and . . . if they have that, they have a lot . . . (transcript 15, p. 17)

Orla's perception of these tensions may support the claim made by much implementation literature that, in the absence of local support structures which facilitate change, it is extremely difficult for an innovation to be consolidated and 'institutionalized' (Fullan, 1982, 1991; Rudduck, 1991). Despite Orla's conviction regarding the virtues of integration, the security of a prescribed curriculum and its implicit assumptions about a gold bar standard to be attained by all do not cease to have their attractions. Her predicament also supports the suggestion that looking at practice as a series of dilemmas is potentially illuminating (Berlak and Berlak, 1975). As Nias (1989, p. 195) indicates, 'the varying philosophical roots of primary teaching contribute to its stresses'.

In contrast with these devotees of thematic planning and integration, for Barry, 'integration would happen rather than be planned' (transcript 2, p. 21). His comments suggest opportunism rather than lending flexibility to a coherent plan:

> If I'm teaching maths or whatever I could switch to geography just as fast and just because we're supposed to be doing maths I could maybe, 20 minutes later, finish up with history or anything . . . That would be my idea of integration rather than planning it before hand . . . (transcript 2, p. 21)

Frank had been teaching senior standards also for more than a decade and he suggests that 'there has been a certain amount of integration in [his] teaching' but this 'has been very casual . . . and it certainly wasn't planned'. His comments indicate, more so than Barry's, that integration is a form of 'improvisation': significantly dependent on thinking on his feet, or 'reflection-in-action' (Schön, 1983), calypso teaching!

I've often found when I might have been doing maths and I might have picked the subject of time, and we ended up doing geography; we ended up doing time zones or something like that. Whether you call that integration or not. I often find that if we're doing history, I might try and get them an old song . . . an old ballad or something like that . . . (transcript 6, pp. 35–7)

Practitioners' perceptions of integration in relation to younger learners differ significantly. In the context of the first grade that Chris was teaching, he uses 'integration when it arises' and he does not 'try to integrate things'. Neither does he 'write it down' because 'experience of the children' is limited so that there is, he thinks, a 'high level of integration — things overlap a lot anyway' (transcript 3, pp. 17–18). Similarly, Kate views integration as 'great', though her comment that 'it just happens and it's just a little bit of effort' seems to indicate the inherent tension between planning and spontaneity and the extent to which subject teaching is embedded in school cultures and reinforced by the purchasing of texts for each, thus reducing the necessity for planing a programme rather than following a text (transcript 11, p. 24).

Other interviewees were less enamoured by the principle of integration. David comments: 'I don't do it very much to be honest with you . . . I do agree with it but it doesn't happen in my class' (transcript 4, p. 18). Noel does not 'regard [integration] as being particularly important' and in any event he would have great difficulty planning such an approach preferring, as he says, 'my content [to be] largely based on textbooks' (transcript 14, p. 12).

Teachers of older pupils were more likely to think in terms of subjects. This perspective is consistent with Whitehead's (1962) view that the curriculum for older pupils should be characterized by greater degrees of subject differentiation. Gena had taught across the primary age range and her experience corroborated the perspective that the junior end was 'under a lot of integration' and 'certainly far more than at the senior end . . .' (transcript 7, p. 16). These comments suggest a strong affinity with individual subjects rather than popular notions of subject integration usually associated with child-centred policy.

The above extracts indicate a wide spectrum of practitioners' intentions in relation to planning an integrated curriculum. However, apart from focusing on divergence of intention, these extracts also indicate that without recourse to actual practice it is impossible to comprehend how these intentions are transformed into learning experiences. Clearly these declared intentions derive sustenance from both traditions of teaching.

Planning: Using Time

Traditional schooling is associated with rigid timetabling and clockwork precision in transition from one subject area to the next: a place for everything and everything in its place, confined in this instance to carefully prescribed doses of the 3Rs, usually taken orally! Progressive ideology, by comparison, favours 'blocks' of time to allow for prolonged engagement with topics, fieldtrips, various activities and more practical exploratory work, all of which require more time than conventional teaching-as-telling.

The Irish primary school day, a little in excess of five hours, is commonly divided into three time periods of approximately ninety minutes each. My own experience of school as learner and practitioner was that the day typically began with Irish language teaching, while religious instruction was usually conducted during the half-hour immediately before or after the main break. This basic structure forms the backdrop against which individual teachers plan, organize and allocate time for teaching and learning.

Chris (first grade) indicated that he experiences tension between the need for attention to basics and the other areas of the curriculum. His comments suggest also that his timetable is designed so that *he* can do as much work as possible, thus espousing a content/teacher-driven approach.

> I try and keep a balance if possible, but there is that fear, that tendency to try and give the most to the 3Rs because there's such importance placed on it. The timetable is crucial though; . . . I think that's why things run so effectively and why I can get through a lot of work, it's because I have a good timetable and I stick really rigidly to it . . . (transcript 3, p. 7)

Mark provides additional evidence of giving prime time to what he describes as the 'heavier subjects' whereby he begins each morning with Irish conversation and 'after that I would do maths and that would be always, every morning practically . . . history, geography in the afternoon generally, art in the afternoon . . .' (transcript 13, p. 2).

Gena (fifth grade) provides an interesting variation on the theme of the basics (3Rs) plus the rest by concentrating the former in the early part of the week. Her comments implicitly suggest that the formal curriculum is structured within the timetable while the informal curriculum, which includes aspects of aesthetic development, receive attention when the real work has been completed. The informal also carried the implication of being fun while the other work was serious.

> So sticking to the timetable say Monday, Tuesday, Wednesday and Thursday, we really get the work done, and on Friday then I would always do songs and poems and creative writing and I know I suppose I should do them every day and vary it a bit but on Friday I'm inclined to leave the timetable and we do a table quiz which would be based on homework for the week . . . (transcript 7, p. 4)

Further comments reveal that, when necessary, she does not 'stick rigidly to a timetable' because, on occasion, 'some lesson I'm doing is just going nowhere [so] I abandon it . . .' (transcript 7, p. 4).

Aoife, a veteran infant teacher, indicates that the process of transforming a timetable into action is invariably complex, giving rise to particular tensions in a socially disadvantaged context.

> You just have to play it day by day. Now people don't understand that. If something is beginning to happen, go along with it, to hell with a time-table sometimes. Now you have to have a timetable in infants, because — I've often found if you 'go from' the timetable, and you go back some place [else], they'll say, 'Teacher, but we didn't do such a thing, you know' . . . they become dependent on your timetable, on the discipline of the timetable — its amazing. Because they haven't that discipline at home — they haven't it any place else and you know, people say, 'Oh, discipline — they [learners] appreciate it'. (transcript 1, pp. 9–10)

The evidence presented here suggests that there is a concentration, during prime time, on the 3Rs, and this is frequently understood as running counter to common interpretations of child-centred teaching. It is apparent also that some practitioners favour a definite structure that a timetable provides while this structure may be set aside when emergent situations appear to warrant such action. Consequently, there are conflicting messages about structure and flexibility, though a more inclusive account of practitioners' planning intentions might venture that in the absence of structure there is nothing about which to be flexible!

In contrast with this degree of structuring, Ian declared with a certain disdain that: 'I don't have any timetable.' Not only does he not have a timetable — 'I don't need a timetable. Now does that mean things suffer? The answer is yes, of course' (transcript 9). Ian's dissenting voice apart, timetabling seems to be well rooted in the intentions of the interviewees, indicating particularly strong continuity with tradi-tion in the priority accorded to 'the basics' (Alexander, 1984; Bennett, 1976; Galton and Simon, 1980; Galton, Simon and Croll, 1980).

Planning: Recording Pupils' Progress

Policy documents in the setting indicate the desirability of teachers keeping 'detailed records of [pupils'] all-round progress' (Ireland, 1971, p. 22). More recent research suggests that 35 per cent of schools have written policies in this regard, though many more may have *de facto* policies which are not recorded (INTO, 1990). The *Report of the Review Body on the Primary Curriculum* (Ireland, 1990a, p. 81) sug-gests that 'Assessment should provide a basis for decisions about pupils' further learning needs . . . [be] comprehensive enough to allow the full range of abilities across all the subjects of the curriculum . . . [and] . . . allow for effective commun-ication of relevant information to parents, teachers and others.' By contrast, tradi-tional teaching was externally assessed by robust inspection and state examinations. Research indicates that, in the absence of adequate record-keeping, matching tasks with learners' abilities is extremely difficult (Mortimore *et al.*, 1988; DES, 1978; Alexander, 1992).

Frank taught senior classes in a middle-class area where doing well in entrance examinations was considered important by parents. He gave tests regularly 'to find out . . . if they know what I've been teaching them' (transcript 6, p. 9). This regular testing was confined to the 3Rs. In mathematics he conducted regular testing of 'the old tables' because 'they may have got the concept but they might be very careless at computation' (transcript 6, pp. 13–14). Due to a confluence of parental expectations and the pressures of preparing students for entrance examinations, Noel elaborates on the consequent dilemma.

> The procedures that we follow in school, the entrance exam being the important thing, obviously the more practise you give children at that type of a formula [the exam], the better they are able to cope with it, so therefore the children in my class are tested very regularly in the old style, traditional exam format. (transcript 14, p. 11)

Additionally, Noel had weekly tests in tables and spellings but he did not keep a record of these as it was 'time consuming' and, anyway, 'it becomes very obvious after a while who the children are who are having difficulties'. When this occurred, he would 'keep a close eye' on those who were 'falling behind'. In such cases, Noel indicated that he contacted these learners' parents. His comments suggest an obvious tension between his efforts to cater for individual's needs, while simultaneously feeling that he had little room for manoeuvre because of the demands imposed by 'the system' (Giroux and Simon, 1989; Purpel, 1989; Aronowitz and Giroux, 1985). He admitted that the prospect of students 'falling behind' was 'very unpleasant' and it was 'unfortunate' that some are 'traumatized' by this. However, the strictures and 'standards' imposed by entrance examinations were non-negotiable. Such circumstances appear to have much in common with popular understandings of traditional schooling. 'Reassurance, as far as possible' does not appear to be an adequate response to individual needs (transcript 14, p. 12).

There was universal agreement among the interviewees that their teaching included daily and weekly, oral and written examination and tests of spellings and tables, which provide strong continuity with traditional schooling. Some practitioners kept records while others had special copies or notebooks which the learners were expected to show to parents and have them signed. The practice of having them signed was intended to ensure that parents were aware of learners' performance. The system Laura developed included a diagnostic function, but she did not always have time to make full use of the information these tests provided.

> I keep records in Irish and English reading. And in maths on . . . the skills and the topic. I tick off what they've achieved [conceptually] and the computation laws. And then I usually give them a test at the end of a topic and I try to structure the questions so that there's a question on each particular thing and then I just tick if they got a right or a wrong. And then try to go back and take the ones who didn't grasp such and such a topic and help them, and I don't always manage to do it but I'd like to do it. (transcript 12, p. 12)

Gena discovered that the threat of a test was an effective motivator of reluctant learners, particularly when it came to doing homework. However, one of the consequences of placing an emphasis on written work and written tests was, she discovered, that when she assigned reading it was frequently ignored, because it was not regarded by many learners as real work.

Laura had a selection of 'stamps' which she used regularly in the learners' copies to provide encouragement. Her experience was that 'they love them', and learners commented regularly on the number of stamps they had in their copies. Helen displayed something of the ambivalence in the Irish psyche towards praising children, frequently described as 'spoiling' (Fitzgerald, M., 1991, p. 50), when she suggested that 'I'd never put down [on a report] a child is excellent except for attendance' (transcript 8, p. 22). These declared intentions seem highly resonant with understandings of traditional schooling. The general impression conveyed by all the interviewees was that testing and record-keeping was confined to the 3Rs, particularly English and mathematics. Emer commented disparagingly on the manner in which other subject areas were treated in relation to documenting learners' progress, though she did not indicate the precise nature of her own practice in this regard.

No, they're [music and PE] not taught well enough to keep a record of them. People don't know, say for example, music . . . that you can examine their rhythm and . . . their sight singing . . . (transcript 5, pp. 20–1)

A number of standardized tests, which have been developed in the Irish setting during the past fifteen years, have encouraged testing in English and mathematics and to a lesser extent in Irish. In addition to these test scores, practitioners have developed a more informal system. The majority of interviewees used a standardized test for English and mathematics, both of which tended to be administered at the beginning and end of the school year. These reported intentions are remarkably similar to findings in England which indicate that 'the vast majority of those who used tests (87 per cent) employed them either once or twice a year' and 'very few teachers kept records of any kind in curriculum areas other than language and mathematics' (Mortimore *et al.*, 1988, p. 76; Alexander *et al.*, 1989). If anything, availability of published tests has tended to reinforce existing patterns of recording progress in basic subjects. This concentration on the 3Rs seems more pronounced in areas of social privilege. Though some practitioners did indicate that their testing was diagnostic, this was not an aspect of their practice on which they dwelt at any length. These declared intentions indicate significant variation in practitioners' interpretations of child-centred policy.

The contextual variations which were manifest in the interviewees' intentions in relation to testing and record-keeping, tended to be reinforced by their attitudes towards structuring and assigning homework. In a tentative manner, context was a more identifiable influence on practice (though not necessarily more important) than beliefs and biography.

Homework

In the present context it is legitimate to consider teachers' intentions in relation to homework as a significant dimension of their approach to planning teaching and learning.

Frank and Noel assigned homework each night, including weekends. They expected that pupils would spend approximately ninety minutes per evening completing a combination of written and oral work, almost invariably including spellings, tables and sums, as well as written assignments in the 3Rs. Frank altered the pattern of homework at the weekend to include essays. Both teachers assigned items such as poetry, to be learned by heart. Noel indicated that once entrance examinations were completed he no longer assigned homework at weekends. When asked about the amount of time he expected learners to spend completing assigned work, he replied:

> I'd expect them to spend roughly an hour, no more than an hour and a half; if you have to spend longer than an hour and a half you just get your parents to write a note, and if you've any problems . . . you just tell me what the problems are and I'll try and deal with them. (transcript 14, p. 20)

Here, again, Noel's circumstances seem to dictate that not falling behind and attaining the desired standard are of paramount importance which appear to run counter to commonly held beliefs about child-centred teaching.

Paula took a highly structured approach to assigning homework. She distributed pre-prepared sheets, discussed them in class and, as a consequence of her own efforts, she expected them 'to do their homework properly . . . they would spend an hour to an hour and a half' completing the tasks (transcript 16, p. 10).

Kate expected her socially comfortable first class to do 'half an hour' of homework. It typically consisted of spellings, tables, sums and putting the English spellings into sentences (there might also be additional spellings from the English reader for the more able), and having listed all these elements she indicated: 'half an hour I'd say is minimum' (transcript 11, p. 19). Allowing for a normal distribution of ability in these classrooms, it is reasonable to assume that a significant number of learners spent considerably longer doing homework than anticipated by their teachers. It is not immediately apparent how these declared practices can be readily accommodated within child-centred ideology.

In less favourable social circumstances, intentions were tempered by awareness of home circumstances. Barry included homework as a regular feature of his teaching by simultaneously turning 'a blind eye to certain fellas who actually won't do their homework — because they have far more problems than actually doing homework' (transcript 2, p. 8). Involvement with drugs or fathering children were of much greater concern for him in relation to some learners than completing homework. Context had a bearing also on Aoife's perceptions of the work she could assign to her infants' class. She commented: 'You have to think about the child all the time, or what the child has to cope with at home' (transcript 1, p. 23). Barry's and particularly Aoife's perceptions resonate with a comment in King's (1978) study which suggests that those who teach in socially disadvantaged areas tend to look to learners' social background as the all-encompassing explanation for poor achievement, to the exclusion of curriculum and pedagogy. David provides some variation on this theme when he says that 'We would give a little bit of homework that would be adequate, taking into account . . . where they are'. Consequently, for the third class which he taught, he expected them to do homework for 'no longer than twenty minutes, half an hour at the very most' (transcript 4, p. 15). In the disadvantaged context in which Mark taught a sixth class, his expectation was that they spend 'about an hour', but he emphasized that this 'would be the maximum' (transcript 13, p. 14). Helen commented that 'the only written work they ever get is maths' because 'she doesn't agree with it' and in any case 'there's no one to help them' (transcript 8, p. 7). Neither did she ever assign homework at the weekends.

The emergent pattern expects one group of learners to do homework for longer time-periods and for five or more nights each week, while another group has less demands made on it for four nights per week. The complex variation in intentions indicates a concentration on the 3Rs. Teaching routines are influenced in significant ways by the context of these practitioners. All but one of the practitioners, regardless of context, were in favour of assigning homework. By comparison, research in England suggests that 25 per cent of schools have policies on homework, 17 per cent of schools frowned on the idea and the remainder allowed individual teachers to decide some of whom assigned it when requested by the students! (Mortimore *et al.*, 1988). The interviewees hinted at tensions between more traditional attitudes to teaching and significant aspects of child-centred ideology. However, as suggested previously, details of actual practice would be necessary to illuminate these tensions further. The interviewees' planning intentions are generally januform: keeping an eye to traditional and progressive teaching simultaneously.

Theme Three: Practitioners' Pedagogical Intentions

Introduction

The term 'pedagogical' is being used in a very general sense in the present context to include the entire interactive process in schools and classrooms. While the OECD report (1991, p. 59) on Irish education recognizes the 'vision and thoroughness' of policy statements, it concludes that 'the emphasis is still largely on a didactic approach' particularly 'in the later primary years' and 'in a relatively narrow range of subject matter'. Neither, the report suggests, 'has a satisfactory curriculum balance been struck' in the 'primary' school (p. 59). The inclusion of these comments is not intended as a pre-judgment of the theme that is about to be explored. Rather, the focus is on how practitioners transform policy into pedagogical intentions with particular emphasis on complexities, commonalities and variations. Nevertheless, the sentiment and assets of child-centred ideology, create certain pedagogical expectations which include group work, individualization, activity, discovery, project work, integration and informality without being able to anticipate the precise form these might take. Documenting practitioners' pedagogical intentions contributes towards a more comprehensive composite picture of practitioners' perspectives, and provides additional insights into the problematic nature of child-centred ideology, while situating and grounding these intentions within the wider context of competing traditions of teaching.

The first aspect of the theme to be explored is the extent to which practitioners see their practices as part of a team effort. Hargreaves (1992, p. 227) indicates that from an international perspective 'the culture of collaboration is a rarity' because 'most teachers still teach alone, behind closed doors, in the insulated and isolated environment of their own classroom'.

Pedagogy and Collegiality

The interviewees agreed that 'the secret to running a good school', as Barry expressed it, 'is leadership' (transcript 2, p. 27). Paula added the caveat that it needs to be 'leadership as a member of a team' and not 'leadership from up there' (transcript 16, p. 21). When participants were asked about the extent to which they were part of a team or isolates in their classrooms, a more complex pattern emerged.

Emer had worked in three schools during the previous five years and this experience enabled her to make perceptive observations regarding the prevalence of collegiality among practitioners.

> I think a lot depends on the principal and on the kind of teachers in the school. And I think it also depends on the history, 'cause as a teacher coming into a school you don't know what's been going on before; I've been very lucky in one particular school, the staff were just together. (transcript 5, p. 8)

Kate's first appointment fired her enthusiasm to establish 'a very high standard' and she found the level of cooperation from colleagues to be 'brilliant . . . so professional' during her probationary year. While staff were 'very helpful' she thought that this was 'because the principal is like that too' (transcript 14, pp. 13–14). However, there is no indication that this cooperation violates the traditional autonomy of the class teacher: a form of cooperation that stops short of being collaborative.

Helen and Gena argued that cooperation is dependent on teachers who have responsibility for the same age group and the extent to which, as individuals, they get on together and this may be construed as a form of balkanization (Hargreaves, 1994, 1992). The degree of cooperation varies from one year to the next. Helen expresses this succinctly: '. . . it depends really, but on the whole . . . you would feel quite isolated.' Nevertheless, she identified what may be termed a chain of command which 'sets the whole atmosphere for the school . . . if you have strong leadership you will have a very happy staff . . . happy teachers and happy children . . .' (transcript 8, pp. 12–13). This perspective resonates with the general findings of the effective schools literature which suggests that 'visibility' and 'instructional leadership' are key issues (Purkey and Smith, 1983, 1985; Fullan, 1985; Mortimore *et al.*, 1988). Yet, such strong leadership can be domineering, undemocratic, unethical, and consistent with traditional patriarchal, hierarchical modes epitomized by the 'headmaster' (Southworth, 1995; Grace, 1995).

Frank indicated that there was a complex tension between the legendary autonomy of the class teacher and a more collegial climate. What emerges in his context is a more cooperative spirit which does not encroach on the sanctity of the classroom citadel. His comments compliment Nias' (1989, p. 205) conclusion that 'in essence' teaching is 'a private activity' and Huberman's (1993) concept of teacher as an 'independent artisan'. He says, 'Once I'm inside my own classroom . . . there's nothing I can do about it. But we do work as a team in the school.' By way of illustration, he elaborates, 'We often swop round as well; I've often found that . . . I like doing the PE . . . I'm not mad about music, so I often find maybe a teacher will do my music for me and I do her PE' (transcript 6, pp. 32–3).

Traditional recruitment into primary teaching (in Ireland) insisted that female entrants be able to sing, while this compulsion did not extend to male applicants. Consequently, many schools were dependent on female staff to 'do the music'. This practice may also have helped to perpetuate the myth that music was feminine and not sufficiently macho for boys to take seriously. The 'master', by way of reciprocation, would typically take the boys for football (Gaelic). There is a sense, therefore, in which the cooperation between Frank and his female colleague is perpetuating an established tradition; is illustrative of specialization rather than collaboration; and is perhaps modelling and reinforcing gender stereotypes in the process.

In contrast with this cooperative climate, Mark declares that the prevailing climate in his school is one of isolation: 'I'm not part of a team no, it's fairly much autonomous [within] my own four walls' (transcript 13, p. 7). David's comment in relation to the 'school plan' that '. . . without telling anybody, I can just calmly abandon it and do my own thing in my own class . . .' suggests a form of 'legendary autonomy' (OECD, 1991) that borders on the anarchic (transcript 4, p. 6). Paula felt likewise that her work was 'very much in isolation', but she spoke also with obvious nostalgia for a school she had worked in previously in which 'everybody seemed to have . . . a kind of passion' and commitment to the collegial enterprise (transcript 16, p. 21).

Paula's nostalgic comments apart, the general pattern is one which places emphasis on teachers working in isolation and the degree of cooperation varies from school to school and from year to year. Within the tradition of primary schooling in Ireland, 'good' teaching was prefaced on the strong personality of the individual teacher, in tandem with central control of syllabi, and standards policed by an influential inspectorate (Sugrue, 1996b). Such an emphasis was on individual salvation rather than collective action. In contrast with this isolationism, Nias' (1989, pp. 206–7) research suggests that teachers who 'took a school-wide view' had a much 'broader canvas than the classroom upon which to paint their desires and aspirations', thus, extending their professionalism.

The interviewees' comments suggest that a significant change of emphasis from isolated performer to team player is not part of their experience, though this may be a function (in part) of selecting 'good' practitioners as participants in the inquiry. However, if this is the case then it provides further evidence that perceptions of 'good' teaching continue to be influenced by traditional criteria, thus reducing the impact of child-centred principles. Without a collegial approach, the challenge of providing a more balanced curriculum is a severe test of the knowledge and skills of isolated practitioners as solo performers (Alexander, 1992).

Pedagogical Knowledge and Skill

There was general agreement among virtually all the interviewees that specialist teachers in music, art and physical education would be a valuable addition to the system. The accepted wisdom in the setting is that everyone can teach the 3Rs well and, depending on talents (rather than expertise), other aspects of the curriculum are taught with varying degrees of enthusiasm and competence. There are a number of issues interacting within this received wisdom that are worth exploring. There is the weight of tradition itself which accords such tremendous significance to numeracy and literacy; therefore, all teachers are expected to deliver these subjects competently. Not to be able to teach the 3Rs competently, to even entertain the idea of possible incompetence, would be tantamount to inviting dismissal (Sugrue, 1996a). However, being able to admit to feeling inadequate in other subject matter areas suggests that they are less significant within the primary school tradition. Consequently, acknowledging feelings of inadequacy in these disciplines is less culpable as well as less indictable. It is interesting to note that in a survey of 901 primary teachers conducted for the Leverhulme Primary Project, Bennett (1991, p. 2) and his colleagues established that 'teachers regarded themselves as being most competent in English and mathematics, and least competent in music, science and technology'. However, one of the hallmarks of progressive policy has been greater emphasis on individual development through aesthetic awareness and the expressive arts as well as the basics.

Barry suggests that 'you'd want to be a magician' to do everything that is expected of you and, to illustrate the impossible nature of the task, he continues, 'I'm hopeless at art, literally, I can't draw anything, and I would find it literally impossible to see a progression from one stage of a child's development at art to where I am going' (transcript 2, p. 15). Chris, though a very recent graduate, has not 'really done that much art' because all he knows is a 'few of the basic things' (transcript 3, p. 26). Noel's comments indicate how traditional emphasis on the basics are reinvented when he says, 'I teach best those curriculum areas that were taught best in the training college' and this 'has had a detrimental, knock-on effect which I struggle to overcome . . .' (transcript 14, p. 14).

Laura provides an interesting insight into her own internal tensions as she tries to reconcile the benefits of specialist teaching with the rhetoric of 'whole child'. She implicitly acknowledges the advantages of subject matter expertise when she says, 'Definitely I would do the subjects best that I'm most competent in' but she also feels 'obliged' to attend to all aspects of content. On the subject of specialist teachers, she says; 'Your job is to develop a child fully and if you have to bring in all these specialist people you're not really doing it. On the other hand if you haven't got the ability to do it, the extra person, the skilled person would be good.' She confided also that she had 'let go' PE over the years 'through the worry of insurance' (transcript 12, pp. 20–1). Others also indicated that there was a growing awareness of a more litigation-conscious public, which acted as a disincentive against taking risks with innovative ideas. Inadequate resources and lack of support for teachers also acted as significant disincentives.

David has little hesitation in identifying mathematics as his 'best subject' and he indicates that his 'interpretation' of policy is heavily influenced by his own knowledge and skill.

I have to make an effort with art and music because I'm not very good myself at them. I think you have to be; I do them however badly. PE, no problem; now I don't do the [prescribed] programme PE but . . . we do PE once a week, but it's down to games maybe, its my own interpretation of PE. But as regards opening the book [to] see what's on PE or whatever, I don't do PE in those terms . . . (transcript 4, pp. 18–19)

Jane added some variation to this general theme when she confided that she was only too well aware of the limits placed on her programme content by her own lack of confidence while in these circumstances the 'kids miss out'. She longed for greater collegiality and sharing of expertise where 'somebody else would come in . . . and just work with the kids for a while' so that she 'could learn from them' (transcript 10, pp. 11–12).

The general impression from the interviewees was that taking responsibility for one's own professional development was dependent on the level of confidence and competence one had to begin with. The comments are significant also in their implications for the construction of a balanced and broadly based pedagogy, and thus also, for interpretations of child-centredness. The following extract reinforces the perception that there was a knowledge and a skill component to professional practice. Emer's comments suggest also that expertise and lack of dependency on texts are correlates while professional development requires structured and sustained support.

I think if you bother your head you'd be real enthusiastic about anything . . . it's very easy when your knowledge is limited to say I'll just stick to the text but you get nothing out of it yourself and you know you're teaching badly . . . I'm pounding it in, they're bored, I'm bored, I wish I knew more about this . . . Things like PE, I think if you look up enough books

> you'll find out how to go about it . . . like I don't think I could do a hand-
> stand at this stage . . . but I'd still be willing to have a go . . . (transcript 5,
> p. 18)

'Having a go', implies taking a risk and in a system which has not built up
'the necessary infrastructure for system-wide curriculum development . . .' (OECD,
1991, p. 59), not everybody is 'ready to be vulnerable' (Nias, 1989, p. 187). In an
authoritarian tradition, without collegiality, the tendency has been to pretend that
all is well. This conspiracy of silence tends to foster disempowerment and quiet
despair rather than rouse people to collective action. The ready endorsement by the
interviewees of the need for specialists resonates with the findings of other studies
which suggest that knowledge is divided into 'the basics' and 'the other' subject
matter areas (Galton *et al.*, 1980; DES, 1978; Alexander, 1984). The comments
above suggest that isolationism is a prominent feature of school ethos, though
collegiality is typically understood to be one of the hallmarks of child-centredness
and of effective schools. Mark's comments may be regarded as a motif of the interviewees' perspectives.

> I'm very good teaching maths. I actually like teaching maths and . . . I'd
> say that would be my strongest subject. I have a sort of flair for English
> and I like English too . . . But you see I would also consider them most
> important . . . I wouldn't consider the others as important . . . (transcript
> 13, p. 18)

His comments mirror the hegemonic stranglehold that tradition has over the curriculum, the most disturbing feature of which is its tendency to 'reinforce and
rationalise the existing culture of teaching, not transform it' (Hargreaves, 1989,
p. 59). Reaffirming the tradition may be a convenient means also of hiding one's
lack of competence and confidence in constructing a more balanced and broadly
based pedagogy.

Environment-based Pedagogy

A constructivist epistemology together with students' active engagement with the
learning environment are twin axioms of child-centred ideology. Gena indicated
that at the junior end of the school environmentally based teaching was relatively
simple because of learners' limited experience. Her comments support the view that
an integrated, undifferentiated, thematic approach is more appropriate for young
learners, while greater subject differentiation gains importance as learners mature
(Whitehead, 1962).

> At the junior level, in so far as it's possible everything [is based] on his
> [learner's] environment. We do the language of the home and of the school
> and we take them out for walks and we go outside and do nature things

completely geared towards the school and their home . . . (transcript 7, p. 22)

Laura and Helen were highly committed to improving the linguistic compet- ence of their disadvantaged learners, particularly through structured oral language programmes. Unlike Gena, their intentions were compensatory in nature: to nurture the language potential of the learners precisely because it was not part of their environment (INTO, 1994b). Helen was acutely aware of the tension between her desire to meet learners' real needs while acknowledging the potential of prescribed programmes to deliver equality of opportunity to learners, while also fulfilling the Deweyan desire to broaden their horizons.

You're aware that a lot of them come from an environment where they would not be encouraged to read, to talk, to ask questions. So, therefore, your whole approach to teaching would be to encourage them to talk, to ask questions, to use more elaborate language, to want to use it . . . I know we probably are in conflict [with the background of the learners] but I strongly feel you can't ghettoize the whole area [in which] I'm teaching . . . If we're doing a local study project that's fine, but you work out from their area, out to the outside world. (transcript 8, p. 21)

David provides some variation on Helen's point of view when he says that with colleagues, they 'look at the environment as more or less an interference, a problem in what we're trying to do . . .' (transcript 4, p. 26).

In all of these extracts, there is a persistent tendency to see the teaching of content as important, with varying degrees of accommodation to learners' needs. Even in Mark's working-class situation pressures ensure that content is not aban- doned in the interest of greater emphasis on process; his understanding of popular versions of child-centred ideology are tempered by contextual influences:

I know that it should be [based on the environment], that it's much more interesting for the children and better for them if they're at school for themselves and that it's the experience of learning, that it's not just con- tent, but in the end if you don't do this content stuff — at the end of the year you don't know if you've done anything. You'd be afraid that you'd have done nothing. (transcript 13, pp. 13–14)

As might be anticipated, parental pressure to deliver content rather than engage learners was more pervasive in middle-class contexts and Noel's comments reflect this.

I bring the kids on a lot of walks, history walks, you know. [I] bring them to see different things; its easy to organize buses, finance, parents, cars so from that point of view I try to fulfil that . . . but I think it's a very difficult area because . . . there's a curriculum there I feel that it has to be taught so, therefore, I'm not looking around outside for other things to do. The curriculum is pretty full. My content would be based on the curriculum as prescribed. (transcript 14, p. 13)

Jane provides some variation on this general theme.

You're supposed to be broadening the child's understanding of the world. I would tend to start with what they know and try to work out of that. But I wouldn't be hard and fast about that either because I think kids have a great fascination about the unknown. (transcript 10, p. 22)

She elaborates further with some sophistication as she describes how learners' imaginations, through structured learning situations, can provide a Vygotskian bridge between their experiences and far away places. She describes a recent lesson on Marco Polo.

Doing something like [Marco Polo] they are comparing it with their own experience all the time. One kid told me that Marco Polo brought back 700 television sets from China [laugh]. And I just asked her how? Trains and buses weren't invented then? She said on camels . . . How stupid could you be — of course he used camels. But I felt what was going on there was she tried to compare with the valuable things that he had brought back — television and videos would have been the thing to bring back from China . . . At least she was thinking and she was trying to fit it into her idea of reality. (transcript 10, p. 22)

The general impression created by the interviewees is that content is essential, and context as well as biography determine to a significant degree the amount of pedagogical flexibility exercised by practitioners as they construct their practice. However, some of their comments resonate with descriptions of traditional teaching while there is awareness also of the need to engage learners meaningfully while teaching content.

Pedagogical Rules

A rule of practice is '. . . a brief, clearly formulated statement of what to do or how to do it in a particular situation frequently encountered in practice' (Elbaz, 1983, p. 132). Interviewees were unfamiliar with describing their routines in such language. Consequently, they tended to respond with details concerning rules which they constructed that were intended to govern learners' behaviour. Nevertheless, their responses provide insights into classroom climate as well as indications of the extent to which teaching–learning processes are teacher centred or reflect more democratic classroom dynamics.

Paula expresses her fundamental expectation thus: 'Respect yourself and . . .

respect others and I feel that if I can instil this into them that everything else . . . falls into place' (transcript 16, p. 7). This sentiment is similar to those teachers in Nias' (1989, p. 188) study who saw themselves as 'willing to exercise authority' to enable them to 'do the rest of the job'. Noel, conscious of his context, suggests that he works 'in a hassle-free environment' but he begins the year by putting 'three or four things' on the blackboard. For him: 'Respect is a two-way thing that . . . I just don't want respect from them but I also will respect their point of view . . .' (transcript 14, p. 8). Barry was keen to promote 'a sense of friendship among the kids' and there was a strong contextual influence on his claim to have 'more interest in that side of it', suggesting that social development has status within his teaching (transcript 2, p. 19). Frank identifies his 'sacred rule' which is: '[When] I speak in class, you listen.' Such a rule has the *ex cathedra* force of a 'command-ment' reflecting the dominant socio-cultural paradigm in the setting. Generating rules is his domain exclusively.

> They take down a little list of rules from me at the start of the year. And if they break that rule, it's nearly like a little commandment to a certain extent, they know themselves that was rule no. 6. (transcript 6, p. 30)

He expresses sentiments which are shared by Barry that, although senior pupils are conversant with the rules, they will, nevertheless, 'try you out' at the beginning of the school year. When this occurs, Frank likes to 'nip it in the bud' (transcript 6, p. 31). As secularism and pluralism gain greater purchase in Irish society these pedagogical commandments are being challenged more and more by students and increasingly by their parents also. 'Having a laff' (Willis, 1977, p. 29) is a burgeon-ing phenomenon in many primary schools (and more particularly in second-level schools) where students tacitly and explicitly become more conscious of classroom routines and 'school rituals . . . [as] gatekeeping devices which regulate the social and economic reward system of the dominant culture' (McLaren, 1986, p. 26). In these circumstances, teachers engage in containment and retrenchment or seek to construct and negotiate new, more appropriate, rules and routines.

Although interviewees discussed rules with learners at the beginning of the year, none indicated that the learners had a say in the formulation of these rules. Laura suggests that 'You have it sort of pushed into their minds what you want and you usually get [that] from them . . .' (transcript 12, p. 11). This implies that learners themselves very quickly internalize the rules that operate in classrooms and schools, and the vast majority learn to live within them. David was even more emphatic about the determination of rules when he said, 'I have never got children to determine a rule, I've got them to understand them, to implement them and to organize them . . .' (transcript 4, p. 16). While interviewees indicated in their earlier comments above that they invested considerable time and energy in estab-lishing rapport and relationships with learners, their rules suggest that they were very much in authority within these relationships: a situation which seems more homologous with versions of traditional teaching than with popular images of child-centredness.

Chris had just completed his second year of teaching with a group of first class pupils. Yet his rules suggest a great deal of continuity with traditional schooling as he requires them to 'work quietly' because 'activity needs silence'. He condemns the twin evils of 'clicking your fingers' to the accompanying strains of 'Teacher! Teacher!', because they create 'a noise factor' which he does not tolerate; these rituals are strongly evocative of class teaching also. The language of the dominant socio-cultural paradigm, which Frank invoked above, appears as a significant element of Chris' consciousness also. The cultural value which informs the following rule suggests that silence surrounding a rule has the cultural potency of a taboo (McLaren, 1986). Chris explains how he approaches his rule in relation to copying.

> Copying, of course, but that's the rule I would be . . . quite vehement about in the sense that I wouldn't even mention that. It's a kind of a mortal sin . . . you know, the way you have your mortal sins in Ireland that are not mentioned even. (transcript 3, pp. 15–16)

Kate had been teaching first class also, and one can imagine the 39 middle-class 6-year-olds, all attempting to please teacher by keeping her rules. These rules are remarkably similar to those articulated by Frank.

> No talking while the teacher is talking; number two — listen or you're expected to if you can *all of the time* [my emphasis]. And never take their eyes off the teacher if they're talking to the teacher [laugh], and if they're told to watch the blackboard, watch the blackboard [laugh]. (transcript 11, p. 16)

Collectively, these rules suggest that interviewees are very much in authority in their classrooms. Closer scrutiny of other aspects of their pedagogies: class teaching, group teaching, discovery learning and project work, as well as their interpretations of the term child-centred teaching, are the grounds on which a more adequate account of how that authority is practised. Details of this pedagogical pastiche reflect the extent to which the authority they appropriate serves to dominate and dictate learning or to promote participation, cooperation and meaning-making.

Class Teaching

Through a combination of effective schools research (Mortimore *et al.*, 1988), time on task, studies on primary schooling, (Alexander, 1992; Alexander *et al.*, 1989), and promotion of cognitive structuring, (Tharp and Gallimore, 1993; Oser, Dick and Patry, 1992), class teaching, in recent years, has been enjoying something of a renaissance internationally.

Frank characterizes his teaching as follows: 'I've no groups . . . but I will give individual attention.' For the 'very good' learners he deploys 'extra material' but one of his primary aims is to 'bring each and every one of them to the same level' and to do this he employs 'a lot of class teaching and a lot of blackboard and chalk' (transcript 6, pp. 12–13). Frank implicitly invokes the gold bar standard of the entrance examination which is the benchmark against which all students in his class are ultimately measured. While there is no escaping this constraint in his context, such an approach seems to deny individual difference where — regardless of ability, interest, motivation and cultural capital — standards are identical for all. Mark varies this pedagogical pattern by providing individual attention primarily at arms length.

> There wouldn't be an awful lot of individual teaching. I suppose it would be . . . heavily class teaching; group work on occasions, individual work when sort of absolutely necessary but I would try to do it on the board. To explain something . . . I would . . . generally go for the chalk and explain it on the board rather than go down to an individual child, but eventually I would go to a child and explain. (transcript 13, p. 4)

Emer categorized her practice as 'mostly class teaching' but she would like to be able to get herself 'organized enough' to plan more group teaching. She continues: 'I'd love to try this group effort to see does it work and if it does fine and if it doesn't . . .' (transcript 5, p. 25). Her comments suggest an essentialist perspective where 'the best way' could be identified and all other pedagogical approaches abandoned. Noel's comments provide further illustrative evidence of the preferences among many interviewees for class teaching. He rejects group work for fear of 'labelling' learners.

> I feel very uncomfortable with it. Again, teaching in an advantaged area, the children have a certain degree of proficiency . . . the amount of remedial problems that we would have in the school I would say would be quite small. There's great back up from parents so I feel that using groups . . . militates against the confidence of some of the children. I think confidence is essential so therefore I . . . minimize grouping . . . I feel very uncomfortable with the idea. (transcript 14, p. 3)

Paula employs 'a lot of class teaching' while retaining some flexibility to accommodate the extremes of the ability range.

> I think a lot has been talked about remedial and weak children and they are getting more opportunities than they did get, but there is very little talk about the top three or four so that I try to zone in on them as well, and to stretch them more. (transcript 16, p. 6)

David waxed eloquently about the virtues of various organizational strategies, but his own particular pedagogical intentions proved more elusive. However, when asked directly about his classroom routines, he certainly seemed to place himself centre stage: 'In my class . . . I would see myself as being important, that's my own attitude; I don't let it run way from me if you know what I mean?' It is important for David to be 'in control' and while he might inherit groups (from other teachers), particularly in English reading, he says: '. . . my aim would be that groups would reduce themselves' (transcript 4, p. 20). These comments on the prevalence of class teaching indicate significant continuity with traditional schooling rather than identification with popular interpretations of child-centred ideology. However, other interviewees indicated that groups and grouping play a more significant part in their pedagogical routines.

Group Teaching

Jane devotes the first hour of everyday to mathematics. The class is organized into five ability groups (formed on the basis of performance on standardized tests). Four groups are engaged with different aspects of the same topic, while a fifth group does art. These activities are rotated each morning. Kate frequently introduces a new topic in mathematics as a class lesson with subsequent group work. She 'goes over the same lesson again the following day' for the less able because 'they are at different stages' but she does not 'group for the sake of grouping' (transcript 11, p. 17). Both practitioners indicated that there were times when groups worked on different topics, but it was more common to organize different activities which dealt with the same concepts. Even where group teaching was practised, it appears as a modification of whole class teaching rather than a radical departure from it: a reconstruction of the gold bar standard with some accommodation to cooperative learning and, to a lesser extent, individual difference.

Laura provides further variation on grouping. Her class is permanently organized in social groups and these are rearranged in ability groups for English and mathematics. For younger pupils she considers social grouping 'essential' because 'younger children are lost in a big classroom'. However, with middle and senior standards (which was where she gained her experience), their primary purpose is control and discipline. Competition between the groups is kept on a knife-edge through the allocation of marks for behaviour and school work, while manipulation of this tension serves the twin aims of control and as a motivational spur to learners. Without recourse to actual practice, it is impossible to know the extent to which such practices motivate or oppress learners and their consequences for their self-esteem, confidence, efficacy and personal integrity.

> Usually, I find it's great because if you have a misbehaver in the group there is terrible peer pressure on the particular child to conform. And it's far more effective than me giving out to that child if their own peers . . . feel let down by them. And I usually make a big thing then if they have let the group down; then they'd come back and do something good and get good marks for the group — we'd make a big thing of it and . . . it has worked very well for me. (transcript 12, p. 5)

There are shades of the Vygotskian 'zo-ped' to these mixed ability groups and the comments above generally concur with findings elsewhere that there is an increase in group work and greater thought given to grouping options (Alexander *et al.*, 1989). Despite Laura's apparent endorsement of grouping, she indicated that with an opportunity to team-teach the following year, she was reluctant to include ability grouping. This rejection was based on the belief that 'if you split them up you're always going to lose the few . . . they just won't bother'. She thought that if they were with their peers 'they will try and achieve a certain amount' (transcript 12, p. 12). However, such strategies constantly face the dilemma of requiring group cohesion, as well as needing to 'match' the needs of individual group members.

Helen indicated that, in her particular social circumstances, she attempted a complex blend which included class teaching, mixed ability and ability group work because of the emphasis she placed on oral work in the 3Rs and her general practice of teaching thematically.

> I like the mixed abilities . . . because the weaker children are often more hesitant about talking and often more inhibited. So, I always conduct my language lessons as a class and then maybe spin off group activities. (transcript 8, p. 7)

Orla's context was complicated by having responsibility for two classes (third and fourth). Consequently, she expressed concern about the amount of written work she assigned: 'I tend to use writing as a kind of necessity . . .' It also increases the amount of 'correction work' which is very 'time consuming'. She feels that correcting is 'not that valuable' when completed in the absence of the learners: a comment which concurs with recent research (Alexander *et al.*, 1989; Alexander, 1992). Part of her dilemma in relation to writing is that even when one class is doing 'creative' work, she feels obliged 'to be present to them' rather than having to teach the other class (transcript 15, p. 5). One of the hidden elements of this and other comments is the extent to which pedagogical routines cultivate dependence or challenge learners to be more independent.

Despite these details, it is difficult to imagine, with any precision, how these complex pedagogical arrangements actually function in practice, or the impact which they have on learners. It is clear that practitioners hold a pluriformity of interpretations of child-centred policy which are influenced to varying degrees by their immediate context, and the traditional affinity in Ireland with class teaching. Without details of actual practice, the picture remains incomplete.

Project Work, Discovery Learning

Project work and its potential for promoting interdisciplinary, independent and cooperative learning has been firmly established as a tenet of child-centredness (Zilversmit, 1993).

Hesitancy on the part of interviewees suggests that they were uncomfortable when describing their pedagogical routines in these terms. Perhaps it was these terms more than any others which triggered the ideology file in teachers' minds. They did not readily describe their teaching strategies in theoretical terms, though neither did they have a language of practice that came immediately to mind. After more than thirty years with infants, Aoife indicated that discovery was frequently a collaborative enterprise between teacher and learner, more Vygotskian than Plowdenesque: 'The self-discovery thing, I find, you have to be at their elbow — you have to discover for them . . . they're discovering it, but you have to point out the discovery in a lot of cases' (transcript 1, p. 8). Jane was uncertain that her interpretation of discovery corresponded with textbook definitions, and her elaboration reveals the tensions she experienced when grounding the concept.

> Sometimes I look at myself and say I'm not really allowing them to dis-cover, I'm sort of telling them — in this exercise you will find such a thing, you know. So, I'm not quite sure whether that's really discovery method. But, I would try to have a project going all the time on something. They work in groups for that but they are choice groups, they decide themselves on what aspect of a thing they would like, or whatever, and then they can work on that themselves. (transcript 10, pp. 7–8)

Jane equated discovery learning with project work, where learners, both individu-ally and in groups, take responsibility for, and initiative with, a piece of independ-ent work. Helen's comments further strengthen the link between discovery learning and project work, while she too voiced reservations about the rhetoric. There is a suggestion also that it is possible to indulge learners a little more in subject areas which are perceived as lacking the conceptual rigour of mathematics, perhaps re-inforcing the basics and the other syndrome. Helen's comments reveal a further dilemma posed by the ambiguity of ideology when attempting its transformation into classroom actions.

> When you see child-centred, you think — the discovery method. Children learn by discovery, you don't want this stage until they're all ready and in theory that's what I'd love to do. In certain areas like maths it just doesn't work. In a lot of cases, you do what you're meant to do — the concrete material, experiences and all that kind of stuff — and there's some [learners] who'll never [grasp what you're about] . . . when you get to your number [work] and you just know when you're doing it that this [is] rote learning and that is what you do. In other areas . . . it's much easier to implement the child-centred curriculum and to let children progress at their own level. (transcript 8, pp. 28–9)

For Emer, doing project work is an opportunity to do 'something worthwhile'. As an example, she cites projects which dealt with European countries that had been selected by her sixth class during the year. She became uncertain about the merits of the entire exercise when she asked about 'the facts', such as currency and capitals, and found the learners' responses less than adequate (transcript 5, p. 6). This was an obvious recurrence of the ongoing tension between content and process in classroom interactions. As Emer continued to reflect on the issue, she claimed that it is teachers' knowledge and expertise that determine the quality of teaching and learning regardless of prescription, while their interpretations of child-centredness remain highly individual.

> I think it depends on the teacher; if you're the kind of person that can teach one subject in a particular way well then . . . if you can strive for your child-centredness in one particular way, in one subject and that's the way you do it and you do it well, fine maybe the next teacher will do it in another. (transcript 5, pp. 6–7)

The views expressed above run the full gamut of traditional and progressive thinking from teaching-as-telling to more open-ended projects. However, structure and guidance are favoured over more *laissez-faire* interpretations of discovery: a perspective endorsed by recent distinctions between 'free' and 'directed' discovery (Ireland, 1990a).

A further variation on these pedagogical practices was provided by Paula. She had been assigning traditional English and Irish essays to her fifth class each week but she found that, apart from spending a significant portion of her weekend correcting them, the feedback to the learners was pretty useless. On reflection, she decided that there must be a better way. With mixed ability groups she began to do project work as a substitute and the extract below takes up the story. Her comments indicate the importance of reflection also as a key to new understandings which frequently presage change in actual practice.

> I said (to myself) there's something wrong here . . . A lot of the work I do creatively now is actually project work and I find that they're getting much more out of it. Even in Irish now, we'll say rather than giving an essay on an t-Earrach [Spring], they do project work on an t-Earrach; they do art on it, then they can write their sentences about it, or they can write a paragraph about it. I would break an t-Earrach up into an aimsir [weather], dúlra [fauna], ainmhithe [animals] and they would do their art and they'd make a little booklet and they're getting way more out of it . . . or I'll take an Irish poem, and we'd illustrate it, and we'd write our own ideas on it, and we maybe put our verse of the poem under what we had done, rather than this essay copy. (transcript 16, p. 15)

Paula's comments indicate that she was pleased with the greater scope that this approach allowed. Nevertheless, this more flexible arrangement was structured within a teacher-directed framework which sought to engage students more meaningfully. Taken collectively, therefore, there is considerable variation in the degree to which learners are 'scaffolded' within the pedagogical rubric of project work, discovery learning or creative activity with a strong element of class teaching — in-keeping with long established traditions of schooling — rather than what commonly passes as child-centred. Their comments are in tune with Alexander's (1989, p. 241) assertion that primary teaching is characterized by 'private doubts, dilemmas and compromises' and this contrasts 'starkly with the doctrinal certainties delivered in public'.

The number of projects these practitioners initiated during the school year varied. Some had a project ongoing throughout the year, while others employed this pedagogical strategy more intermittently. Their practices were broadly in line with the data from *School Matters* which indicates that 'the average number of projects completed over the year was three' (Mortimore *et al.*, 1988, p. 89). Those who did not link child-centredness directly with discovery learning and project work, were asked how they interpreted the term.

Child-centred Teaching

In the Irish context, the term 'child-centred teaching' is rarely used by practitioners, teacher educators, inspectors or researchers. The preferred term is 'child-centred curriculum' and I take this to be a kind of metaphor, a linguistic rallying cry for a merging of two traditions: an attempt to bring about a metamorphosis between a content-driven curriculum and a raft of progressive strategies for engaging learners. Such exhortations may amount to little more than a thin veneer of the latter overlaid on the former leading to *surface* reforms or it may bring about genuine enrichment where core axioms are revisited, reconstructed, enhanced and enriched through *deep* change (Fullan, 1993).

Emer understood child-centredness thus: 'when you know you're getting through to a particular child' (transcript 5, p. 7), while Gena's interpretation was: 'to work individually with the child and that he could develop at his own pace and that you'd know exactly what he was doing . . .'. However, she did not think that working with individuals was realistic (Alexander, 1992). Her comments revealed that there were many contextual constraints that inhibited actualization of her intentions.

> With thirty-six in a class there just isn't time for that [individual attention], and I would be far less aware of the [need for it at] senior [level] than . . . [at] the junior . . . because once a child is able to read and write . . . it's quite difficult after that then because when the child is into extra reading and you've got children with special interest areas . . . [transcript 7, p. 24)

Although her comments suggest that learners' needs and interests became more diverse as they mature, her practice was to persist with class teaching.

Ian was dismissive of terminology such as child-centred curriculum and methodology; he did not 'think in those terms' at all. He invoked the growth metaphor to acknowledge that 'every child was different' while he was much clearer about what he was against rather than what he actually espoused. He was ambivalent about the need for structure and support for learners: 'The trouble is the curriculum is a scaffolding. The scaffolding is not meant to bury the building. But I think the children are buried in scaffolding and they can hardly breathe' (transcript 9, p. 33). Without observation of actual practice, articulation of practitioners' intentions serves to indicate that there are several variations on key aspects of practice, and this pluriformity is influenced significantly by context and beliefs.

Mark corroborated this point of view when, at the end of his interview, he declared: 'It's really what's happening everyday is what it is about . . .' (transcript 13, p. 31). His comments encapsulate his struggle to articulate tacit understandings of practice as something which is routine, and repetitious, while uncertain and spontaneous, thus putting it beyond easy reach of critical scrutiny.

> I don't analyse it [practice] a lot . . . [what I've been saying] doesn't get the picture in a way . . . it's really what's happening everyday is what it is about you know. There is a little certain hum-drum about it but there's also [variation] . . . it's actually the . . . doing of that day is what it is about. Now that's a sort of a cop-out in a way. It's only the next day that you realize what . . . you did that day. Its not really good to plan . . . you just come in in the morning [and] at the end of the day you know what you've done . . . (transcript 13)

Yet, his employment of a very popular North American metaphor indicates that adequate understanding of practice must look beyond intentions to 'praxis' which includes an intuitive sense of how the teaching process functions (Dunne, 1992; Grundy, 1987; Carr and Kemmis, 1986).

> It's only at the end of the day, you only realize whether you're happy or sad, or whether it was good or bad . . . everyday is a bit different you see; it's . . . only in the actual happening of the day . . . that's where the rubber meets the road. (transcript 13, p. 31)

His comments suggest that it is the variation (within the routine) which tends to stand out thus, making the more permanent and impermeable elements of teaching practice less accessible to scrutiny and, therefore, less amenable to change. Consequently, it becomes necessary to identify key features of where 'the rubber meets the road', and to document them in detail to come to a more complete understanding of practitioners' constructions of child-centred teaching. Documenting these details is a means also of grounding a more inclusive revisioning of child-centredness.

Conclusions

The purposive survey of practitioners' images of teaching, their planning intentions and espoused pedagogical strategies revealed commonalities, complexities and significant variations. In many instances they appeared to adopt a januform stance towards traditional and progressive teaching. These competing horizons created tensions, dilemmas and contradictions for the interviewees which were influenced significantly by biography (including apprenticeship of observation) and professional context without being able to evaluate these influences with accuracy. However, their januform stance towards the grand narratives of teaching was far from uniform. Some seemed transfixed by particular elements of traditional teaching while others appeared to have been transformed by aspects of progressive ideology. The intentions of the vast majority had been touched, tinged, shaped and singed by both.

Without evidence on the dynamics of actual practice, however, as revealed in the moment-by-moment exchanges between learners and teachers, understanding of practice remains general and incomplete. Neither was it possible to identify those intentions that were key. Without recourse to actual practice, it is not feasible to differentiate between the plethora of intentions documented above, and their relative importance for practice. Consequently, despite the comprehensive details of this chapter, investigation of the inquiry's problem remains partial.

It is necessary, therefore, to turn to a variety of classroom settings to begin to identify key elements of child-centred practice as a means of lending depth to the study as well as narrowing its focus. Isolating pervasive elements of practice is necessary for increasing understanding of its complexity and integral to the process of reconstructing a vision of child-centredness that is grounded in the multiple realities of practitioners' classrooms as well as their intentions, ideology/policy and the contexts of their work.

Note

1   This notion of the 'story mode' resonates with the work of Kieran Egan (1979) on the various stages of educational development which, he suggests, include: mythic, romantic, philosophic and ironic.

Chapter 4

Practitioners' Teaching Constructions

Introduction

This chapter reports on the second phase of the inquiry which, through the conduct of six mini case studies, seeks to document the teaching constructions of practitioners to identify common cultural themes of practice for closer scrutiny in the final phase. It begins with some comment on substance and method, followed by discussion of criteria for selecting participants, analysis and presentation of data, and the identification of cultural themes. The case studies are not reported. Rather, the three emergent cultural themes from this second phase are identified and described. Extracts from five cases are provided to illustrate their pervasiveness, complexity and variation. The sixth case is incorporated into the major case study and illustrations of the cultural themes as they became manifest in that case are reported in Chapter 5 as a means of refocusing the substantive question of the inquiry.

Substance and Method

It was not practicable, within the limits of the study, to observe the teaching routines of all sixteen interviewees. The completion of six mini case studies was a reasonable compromise between the need for breadth and a more focused investigation than was the case in phase one. By purposefully selecting practitioners who taught in very different contexts, phase two sought to respect complexity and contextual variation, as well as biographical and professional differences, while simultaneously isolating the most significant tensions and dilemmas which permeated practice.

From a methodological perspective, the progressive focusing of the substantive issue through the three phases of the research implicitly demonstrates the limitations of more narrowly conceived research questions and indicates the distinctive nature of the present inquiry. It also enables the specific details of individual practitioner's practice to illuminate the general problem of child-centred teaching. However, because of the relatively short period of time, five days, spent in each classroom, the three cultural themes are not sufficiently detailed to provide an exhaustive analysis, as well as adequate contextualization, of the most enduring issues of child-centredness. The three themes function as an effective means of narrowing the inquiry's substantive focus. Having isolated these themes, it was necessary to investigate them in greater depth through the detailed accounts of the teaching constructions of one practitioner in a major case study. In this manner, the particulars of a practitioner's teaching, viewed through the cultural lens provided by the second phase, become a vehicle for reconstructing a vision of child-centred teaching that is grounded in the multiple realities of practitioners' classroom actions while nested within the more general backdrop of teaching traditions and previously conducted research on progressivism.

Selecting Participants: Criteria

Factors that influenced selection were practitioners' gender and length of service, location of schools (urban, rural), context (social background of learners), type of school (single sex or co-educational), size of school, as well as the grade levels that participants were teaching. To a lesser extent, the professional training of the participants was a consideration. All of the factors listed can be described as contextual in the sense that they relate either to the biographical and professional experience of the teachers or the immediate school environments in which they worked.

A judicious mix of these factors provides a rationale for the selection of participants for phase two of this inquiry (see Appendix, p. 228). Three of the mini case studies were conducted in rural schools and three in urban contexts while the particulars of each case varied within those two general categories. Only one of the participants had less than ten years' teaching experience and two of them were closer to twenty. This spread of experience enabled me to include practitioners who were graduates, diplomates, and the holder of a postgraduate diploma. Learners' social background was generally more heterogenous in rural schools. Despite this heterogeneity, values and attitudes vary significantly because of local traditions and sources of employment. Consequently, the three rural schools chosen were spread geographically across the country. One of them also provided the opportunity to document practice where a practitioner taught two grade levels, which is a reality in a majority of Irish primary schools. Social background is more homogenous in large urban centres. Therefore, it was important that middle-class and working-class contexts be included. Four of the six participants are female.

The grade levels that the practitioners taught were an important consideration. Of less significance was the gender of learners and the proportion of co-educational and single-sex schools. Because of a general perception that kindergarten classrooms are more child-centred than senior grades, I was more enthusiastic about focusing on teachers of first to sixth classes. I began from the perspective that the official curriculum is divided into four two-year units and my intention was to include practitioners from all but the youngest sector: infants (4–6-year-olds). Consequently, grades two, three and five are represented in the case studies. Three of the case studies were in co-educational schools while the other three were in girls' schools. Due to the many considerations that determined eventual selection, it was not possible to include a boys' school.

Decisions of selection were influenced also by ethical considerations. Permission was sought from practitioners, their principals and Boards of Management. I had intended having greater variety in terms of the grade levels that individuals taught but negotiations failed to yield the preferred combination, for ethical and other reasons.

Five consecutive days were spent in each of the six classrooms. Each participant's interview transcript was re-read immediately prior to entering the field so that, in so far as possible, their practice was documented through the lens of their own declared intentions against the larger canvas of literature and research on child-centred teaching. Short notes were taken in the field, with extensive fieldnotes being written (computerized) each evening. These typically consisted of 8–10 A4 pages of typed (single spaced) fieldnotes, copies of which were shared with the collaborating teacher each day. These fieldnotes became an important catalyst for dialogue between researcher and researched. They were also the data from which the mini case studies were crafted (Sugrue, 1992). Each participant read a draft of his or her case study subsequently. Practitioner's comments on earlier drafts were taken into consideration when redrafting cases.

Analysis and Presentation of Data

Case studies have their own integrity and 'intrinsic' importance (Stake and Mabry, 1993). Nevertheless, the impact of the cases in phase two is intended to be cumulative: respecting individual voice while increasing understanding of practitioners' fundamental concerns when constructing teaching in a child-centred setting. In the interest of brevity and clarity, as well as avoiding the tedium of repetition and 'the trap of recounting' (Hammersley and Atkinson, 1983, p. 213), the emergent cultural themes only are presented as they became manifest in the details of each case. While it is possible to argue that each case 'tells a story' (Hammersley and Atkinson, 1983; Clandinin and Connelly, 1992), in the context of this study their function is the instrumental one of isolating common themes for more in-depth investigation.

Continuous data analysis, during and after the fieldwork for phase two, surfaced three cultural themes with particular importance for practitioners despite significant biographical, professional and contextual differences. The three cultural themes are an instrumental means of shaping and structuring the details from each case while continuing to honour complexity and variation.

Cultural Themes: Communication, Structure and Balance

The theme of *communication* includes the informal dialogue between learners and practitioners that cultivates rapport and sustains relationships. These informal exchanges form the basis for more formal communication routines that are cognitively directed towards learning and mastery of content. Together, personal and pedagogical communication routines form a complex set of rules and routines that have a significant impact on the dynamics of the teaching–learning process.

The theme of *structure* refers to the manner in which practitioners construct learning tasks. Whether practitioners chose to organize and sequence learning as discrete subject matter areas, with limited integration, or in a totally thematic fashion, they seek to challenge, as well as to connect with, learners' previous experience and to organize learning in particular ways.

The theme of *balance* was influenced significantly by contextual constraints, but practitioners sought, in various ways, to bring the cognitive and social needs of learners into productive tension. This equilibrium was brought about by finding space for individuals within the perceived constraints of prescribed curricula and practitioner's expertise in, and inclination towards, mixing the basics and the aesthetic/expressive subject matter areas.

Orla, Jane, Ian, Paula and Noel are five of the six participants in the second phase whose classroom routines are documented in this chapter under the rubric of communication, structure and balance. These themes are not intended as an assessment of participant's work. Their focus is persistent teaching routines, their similarities, variations and differences, and their importance for the teaching–learning process. In an attempt to capture these rules and routines of practice as they were in the process of being constructed, the fieldwork was conducted during the first six weeks of the school year.

Theme One: Communication

Communication first suggested itself as a means of avoiding more conventional terms such as class or group teaching which immediately tend to categorize practitioners as either traditional or progressive, formal or informal. The term communication is intended to be inclusive as the former frequently fail to capture and do justice to the complexity of classroom life. Similarly, the terms methodology and pedagogy are typically identified with formal routines of teaching, thus excluding the informal, yet critically important, interactions that are integral to classroom processes.

As already suggested, there are two distinct but intimately related aspects to the communication theme. There is the more informal manner in which practitioners establish rapport; nurture and sustain relationships with learners; and cultivate a positive classroom climate. These informal interactions, by means of various rules and routines, become more formal and through which the meaning-making process of teaching and learning is conducted. The informal and the formal have a colonizing influence on each other and pervade the entire classroom process; they need to be understood individually, in tandem and in relation to the other two themes.

Orla

Orla had many opportunities as school principal to familiarize herself with learners' names and she had previously taught one of the two class groupings in her classroom. Nevertheless, an important element of the first week of the school year was to establish rapport with learners while negotiating the boundaries of acceptable behaviour and socializing them into her classroom routines. An important ritual at the beginning of the school year is to ensure that learners have the requisite school textbooks. This issue was pursued with less intensity as each day of the first week in school passed by. Pupils' enthusiasm for tackling the task of ensuring that they possessed the required textbooks, in some instances, outstripped their organizational abilities, thus necessitating teacher intervention. The following incident indicates Orla's sensitivity to individual needs, and to establishing rapport, regarded by many as important dimensions of child-centred teaching.

As the religious education texts were about to be checked, a pitiable wail was heard from Jackie, 'My Irish book is gone!' Orla was immediately to the rescue and standing in front of Jackie she recovered the offending text from underneath some other books on Jackie's table. With a gentle pat on the cheek with the back of her hand, Orla reassured her with the mildest of admonitions, 'You're all confused', so that Jackie quickly recovered her equilibrium. A face that was close to tears moments earlier, beamed back a smile of gratitude to a teacher who was already retreating to the top of the classroom. (fieldnote 3/9/'90)

The manner in which Orla fused informal and formal communication routines was apparent through class discussions in social and environmental studies as well as religious education. She exploited these situations to continue to establish rapport with individual pupils.

Informal discussions followed about how a variety of trees could be recognized at different times of the year. Some of the children, particularly the third class girls, displayed a great willingness to engage in story-telling about particular exploits of theirs in local woods etc. One of the advantages of this informal revision work was that a neighbour's house could provide an example of Ash, Oak, Beech, Lime or Fuchsia so that learners could identify these trees through association with a house. Those in charge of the nature table were chastised for not having more exhibits on display and mild threats of sacking were hinted at if matters did not improve. Throughout these exchanges, Orla was careful to acknowledge individual contributions, to give praise where appropriate and in general to strengthen the rapport which was being built with individuals throughout the week. To one individual she said, 'You have such a beautiful garden', and there was the more general positive comment to all, concerning the quality of their writing when she said, 'I notice how well written your work is; if you are going to keep this up for the year it will be great'. Orla herself was conscious that she was being a little over indulgent with the story-telling of the girls when she said, 'We got distracted from where we were going', but the tone of voice indicated that the verbal detours which she had been orchestrating were well worth the time investment. Consequently, she did not have time to hear the children read out what they had written in their copies. She was sensitive to the fact that few had read while many had their hands aloft, to volunteer their stories. Orla responded, 'I will enjoy reading them myself.' (fieldnote 6/9/'90)

Practitioners will readily identify with the importance attaching to agreeing rules of behaviour during the early days of the school year as these have significant implications for the quality of communication in classrooms generally. When Orla inquired about the whereabouts of the learners' dictionaries, their cacophonous response provided an appropriate opportunity to reinforce a rule which would govern more formal communication routines.

. . . 'if we all talk together no one will hear.' It was not the actual incident which was important so much as the situation provided an opportunity for Orla to indicate to the learners the kind of behaviour which was expected and that which would not be tolerated. (fieldnote 3/9/'90)

In a two class situation, more formal routines of transition from one subject area to another have particular significance if time-wasting is to be avoided. Streamlining these transitions was an important dimension of Olra's more formal pedagogical patterns.

As the noise level rose Orla asked, 'Is this going to be the level of noise every time you have to go to your bags for something?' With her fingers resting lightly on her temples she began again, 'Oh my goodness, are we going to stand up every time something is required from our bags?' 'I am going to have a headache for the year' did not seem to be uttered with the same sense of purpose as the two earlier rhetorical expressions. The task of putting the copies in the bags was completed to the sound of further encouragement towards quieter execution of such classroom chores: 'Is there going to be this much noise every time you are asked to get something from your bags?' (fieldnote 3/9/'90)

Another element of pedagogy that Orla lost no time in establishing was a drill and practice routine for the examination of 'number facts', commonly referred to as 'tables'. This routine was complicated by the presence of two classes, not to mention differing levels of ability. Nevertheless, Orla set the agenda by putting a tables wheel on the board while indicating that she would ease them into the process by asking everyone a question initially. Deliberately asking everyone a question made the process highly predictable but, afterwards, she indicated that she would 'hop around'. Also, they would be required to provide a complete number sentence such as $6 + 4 = 10$. On the very first days of the school year, this elaborate initiation into the routine was as concerned with setting standards and expectations as with establishing pedagogical routines. However, there were tensions evident between individual needs and class teaching.

Later, with the random, more rapid questioning she merely pointed to a number on the outside of the circle and the learner shouted out 'just the total'. Orla was conscious of the slow pace at which the initial aspect of this exercise proceeded and commented, having completed the questioning of everyone in both classes, 'I found that a little slow.' (fieldnote 6/9/'90)

This routine appears to have much in common with traditional 'mental arithmetic'. A significant difference appears to be that Orla's practice was conducted in a positive climate whereas many adults will attest to the sarcasm and corporal punishment that accompanied previous incarnations of the routine. In her classroom, formal and informal communication routines appeared to be fused in a positive purposeful manner.

By the end of the first week of the school year, the ritual of examining tables had been substantially fine-tuned. In the following extract, the number wheel had already been written on the board and initial examination of the whole class had been completed.

Orla had mildly rebuked the girls the previous morning for being a little sluggish in their responses. She now acknowledged an improvement: 'Oh! . . . you are very quick at that this morning, I'll give a quick run round.' With a ruler in her hand, she pointed to the numbers of the wheel at random. No number sentences today by way of response just a single word. She began with everyone in the room responding and this was followed by the classes responding as groups, culminating in questioning directed at individuals. (fieldnote 7/9/'90)

These formal routines attached to spellings and tables could be said to be quite traditional fare but both were conducted in a very positive, constructive fashion. There was a tendency towards informality in pursuit of social goals, with more formality associated with cognitive goals.

Jane

Jane's informal communication routines were most apparent in the spontaneous conversation and humour during the first twenty minutes of the school day which she used for correcting homework. Those who arrived early chatted informally among themselves, fetched grass for the class guinea pig, or shared some of the events of the previous evening with Jane. There were many such interactions each morning while art work was being displayed, spellings and tables revised, and favourite TV programmes discussed: all of which suggested that relationships and good communication were prominent features of Jane's practice. The presence of a guinea pig and the general air of informality resonate with Cuban's (1993, p. 157) comments that these were 'artifacts of open [or progressive] classrooms'. The following 'gossip column' exchange was illustrative of the good humoured banter that occurred.

> One girl had a story of her Granny's return from a holiday with a collar
> on her neck as a result of falling down a stairs in a hotel. Another reported
> that her brother had been allocated a place in the engineering faculty of a
> Regional Technical College as a consequence of 'ransom selection'. The
> girl who introduced this topic seemed to be reflecting an adult conversa-
> tion in her household when she said, 'I hope he sticks it now,' to which
> the teacher replied, 'Oh, wait until he gets a girlfriend down there.' (fieldnote
> 20/9/'90)

Further evidence of Jane's commitment to relationships and the time and energy
she invested in establishing them with individual learners was noted in the following extract.

> Three girls whom Jane had taught the previous year, dropped in on their
> way home just to see how she was getting on. Loyalty to old friends
> seemed to be important personal and social aspects of behaviour which
> do not get celebrated generally in a crowded, prescribed curriculum. Jane
> seemed to make time for these little exchanges on a continuous basis.
> (fieldnote 20/9/'90)

Interactions such as these punctuated the school day and this was facilitated by the
fact that Jane had taught the class two years previously so that relationships were
being renewed rather than established *ab initio*. The following extract reinforces
a point made by one of Nias' (1989, p. 186) informants that 'to teach one must
establish a relationship with pupils'. The exchange also suggests that when teacher–
pupil relationships are secure, delineation between street corner and student states
(McLaren, 1993) is not so neatly differentiated.

> Jane began correcting the English questions which had been assigned for
> homework the previous day . . . One of the words that had to be put into
> a sentence was 're-arrange'. She requested sentences from a number of
> the girls, and one volunteered, with a tone of mischief in her voice, 'I will
> re-arrange your face for you'. This is a commonly used street threat
> especially among pre-teenage and adolescent boys. 'I thought that would
> come out sooner or later,' responded Jane, good-humouredly. (fieldnote
> 20/9/'90)

The quality of these informal exchanges spilled over into more formal pedagogical
routines so that the atmosphere remained informal though purposeful. It may be
claimed, therefore, that it is possible to cultivate an informal classroom climate,
beloved of child-centredness advocates, while retaining a didactic edge to pedagogical routines.

A significant dimension of the formal communication structures that Jane employed was her emphasis on group work. Four groups had been formed for English
reading and five groups were being formed for mathematics, though she did not

intend these to be final: 'I will look at the groups . . . see how you are getting on' at the end of October, thus displaying further sensitivity to learners' social and cognitive needs (fieldnote 17/9/'90). A further element of child-centred rhetoric was readily detectable in these communication routines when she invited these groups to select captains and vice-captains as part of the process of giving learners some (limited) responsibility for the organization of their own learning. It is a tribute to the quality of classroom relationships that this selection process was completed without the slightest hint of acrimony.

> The groups then got down to their assigned work. Jane circulated among the groups, initially explaining the task in general and then providing individual tuition in addition to correcting copies. The groups tended to function as a team and when one person had a problem it was discussed with a neighbour. There was also an element of competition within the groups and because they were grouped according to ability they generally kept together. (fieldnote 17/9/'90)

Some general rules of behaviour needed elaboration as part of the process of initiating the learners into the routine, which suggest that Jane continued to control the process and substance of teaching and learning thus retaining elements of traditional teaching that bore many of the hallmarks of child-centredness also.

> It was now 10.00 am and time to move 'quickly and quietly into your maths groups'. While the class were moving around the room, Jane was busy writing the work assigned to each group on the blackboard. Essentially it was the same work that had been assigned the previous day but it was now being allocated to different groups. In other words, the work was being rotated from one group to another. When Jane had written the assignments on the board, she spoke a little sternly, 'You are big enough to have settled down'. Almost immediately she spoke directly to a girl who was out of her place, '. . . if you are looking for a pencil . . . get one from your own group'. Finally she said, 'I don't expect a great racket . . . especially from the art group' which was still in the process of covering the tables with newspapers, mixing paint, distributing jars of water and paint brushes. This group work continued until break time at 10.55 am and each group functioned in a spirit of cooperation. There was a good deal of chat and discussion within each group. (fieldnote 18/9/'90)

The general tenor of the climate within the groups was more cooperative, good-humoured and altruistic, than competitive and egocentric (Watt, 1988). However, the manner in which these groups functioned depended to a significant degree on the subject matter which was its focus. In the next two extracts, group members will be seen to function in isolation where the group effectively has no role (Bassey, 1978; King, 1978; Galton, Simon, and Croll, 1980; Galton, and Simon, 1980), and where there is genuine cooperation and shared learning.

> Ellen asked Emer, 'How do you do it?' There followed a very brief exchange during which the latter told Ellen how to do the sum, i.e., the answer is—. I was curious as to what the question was and how much Ellen had benefited from the explanation that Emer had provided. I went first to Emer and asked the nature of the question. The question was: How many terms in a particular sequence? To which the answer was five. I approached Ellen and asked her what a term was, to which she replied, 'The only term I know is a school term'. We both agreed that this was one way in which the word term is used and went on to discuss possible alternatives in the mathematical context. (fieldnote 21/9/'90)

Jane was fortunate in having secured the support of the school principal to take responsibility for two of her mathematics groups and the remedial teacher had begun to take responsibility for two of the English groups. Without this support, Jane suggested that despite the groupings she would be unable to meet individual needs. Her anxieties support Cuban's (1993) contention that local constraints force teachers to compromise between traditional and progressive approaches to schooling.

> Millie, who was writing a story about her dog, sought assistance with the spelling of the word labrador. While various alternatives were being suggested, Laura was intent on poking fun at Millie for the benefit of the group. However, Millie was not intimidated by this behaviour. She figured out the correct spelling from the various incorrect attempts that had been provided and carried on with her writing. One of the other girls read aloud several sentences that she had written and identified a problem that she had with her story. She correctly indicated that she had begun most of these sentences with 'I woke, I sat, I came,' and so on. I approached her and asked her if she had a problem. She had no intention of identifying what it was. We discussed some alternative approaches and I left her to proceed in whatever manner she chose. A little while later, I noticed that she had begun the writing all over again. Generally I was struck by the social dimension to learning which seemed to pervade the group. Without raising a pen, one learner would spell a word for another which in turn might be passed on to someone else. In this way the group supported itself and, while ultimately each individual was responsible for her own story, the hidden agenda seemed to be that learning is fun and that we learn a great deal from interacting with our peers. (fieldnote 20/9/'90)

When Jane reverted to class teaching, within the limitations of that routine, she continued to be conscious of individual needs thus adding complexity to this traditional approach. When teaching Irish (a second language to all her students), lessons typically began with the correction of homework followed by the use of a grammar/workbook type text. Jane used the text as a stimulus for oral language development, reading and grammar. When questioning alone was insufficient to elicit responses from the learners, she usually drew something on the board or did a mime. In one such lesson, the class was preparing for a picnic. As the next extract indicates, additional elements were added to the pedagogical steps already outlined above.

> As a development of this exercise, individuals were invited to be Mamaí [mother], while others were encouraged to ask her for a variety of items to include in the picnic basket. The class was then divided into pairs and each pair was expected to practise this questioning among themselves. The noise level rose significantly during this activity. Those closest to me were doing what was expected of them and while there was obvious enjoyment, they did seem to be reasonably on task as well. (fieldnote 19/9/'90)

The approach assumes that these smaller groups provide more active involvement for the individual learner than class teaching. Implicit in the extract also is the realization that seeking 'the best' method of teaching something in particular is narrow and self-defeating as it ignores too many contextual details. It is more reasonable to suggest that the complexity of the teaching process needs to be matched by an equally complex arsenal of pedagogical skills.

Ian

Ian utilized the informal time-period at the beginning of the school day to foster good relationships and to cultivate a positive classroom climate also. In the extract that follows, Greg was attempting to negotiate his way to the classroom door having been blindfolded by the teacher:

> This activity created a great deal of excitement which was superseded by the arrival of one of the boys with a young puppy on a lead. The boy's father waited patiently at the classroom door while many of the class got acquainted with it and the teacher also made himself known to this frisky little creature. After some discussion on the possibility of keeping the dog in school for the day, Ian decided to send it home with the boy's Dad. This initiative, a pupil informed me, was intended to enable them to introduce their pets to the other members of the class. (fieldnote 25/9/'90)

Further evidence of this informal atmosphere and good-natured banter between teacher and learners was apparent on my return to the classroom after lunch.

> Ian was already seated at the top of the classroom with what seemed like hedge clippings in his hands, like a posy. A bunch of excited children around him appeared to dispossess him and rushed to the classroom next door to present the bouquet to the female teacher as a gift from Ian, all in good fun. (fieldnote 25/9/'90)

When these relationships were fractured, Ian was keen to restore their equilibrium. In these episodes, the informal and formal became suffused. Brian had been in conflict with the teacher earlier because he did not have the appropriate home-work notebook. Yet Ian was keen to demonstrate that their earlier discord should not mar their relationship. The teacher was encouraging the class to emulate the wolves in their class reader, which they had just begun to read.

> Brian . . . was now being encouraged to howl even louder. The phrase, 'I can't hear this wolf here,' was accompanied by a friendly pat on the head. This seemed to be Ian's way of communicating to Brian that his (teacher's) bark was worse than his bite! (fieldnote 24/9/'90)

On the final day of fieldwork, Ian organized a class party to mark the end of an introductory, getting-to-know-you phase with this class. He expressed tacit understanding of the role of relationships and continuity when he allowed all those in fancy dress to visit the teacher they had had the year before. He reassured them that 'she would be delighted to see them' (fieldnote 28/9/'90). Ian, in common with Orla and Jane, devoted time, energy and ingenuity to the cultivation and mainten-ance of good relations.

In Ian's classroom generally, formal communication routines tended to be dominated by class teaching, though within this framework he attempted to meet individual needs. The new English reader had finally arrived at the beginning of the week. After it had been distributed to all learners, they were keen to begin.

> All were then asked to focus on the first chapter. 'Read the first sentence to yourself . . . the writing is very small but the words are simple so if you take your time you are well able for it.' After a few moments Ian began to read from the very beginning. A picture of the Wisconsin landscape was rapidly being painted for the listeners. He paused occasionally to explain a word such as a trundle bed or he invited the pupils repeatedly as a class or as individuals or small groups to howl like the timber wolf of North America. The class relished this participation. (fieldnote 24/9/'90)

During the next few days there was further reading and discussion of the first chapter. The seven pupils, who attended the remedial teacher regularly for tuition in English, were experiencing difficulty with the size of the print and the level of difficulty of the text (fieldnote 25/9/'90). Ian responded to these details in the fieldnotes in the following terms. Our conversation revealed his intentions and the difficulty sometimes encountered when transforming them into classroom actions.

> Ian explained . . . that he would 'not be asking' individuals to read aloud in class 'in front of the others' so that those who attended the remedial teacher need not worry. He preferred to include them in the listening and the oral discussions that would accompany and develop the language and story of the text. This approach does not exclude the possibility of having them read texts that are more in tune with their current reading ability. (fieldnote 26/9/'90)

In a more general sense, there seemed to be a tension between teaching the class as a whole and meeting the needs of individual learners. His intention of not asking individuals to read seemed designed to enable the less able to participate without fear of having their social selves undermined: it was a trade-off between their social and cognitive development. However, it becomes apparent also that, though class teaching has the advantage of including all learners, it may be beyond its capability to challenge everyone at once. Consequently, class teaching is commonly believed to be anathema to what passes as child-centred teaching.

Ian was committed to providing a broad experiential range to learners that included music and art. It takes courage to equip forty learners with recorders and to begin teaching them the rudiments of sight reading, fingering and playing. The class had begun its first tune earlier in the week and as part of their homework they had been asked to copy its first four bars into their exercise books. Ian had indicated during his interview that he favoured 'remote' preparation for teaching over 'proximate' planning and as a consequence routines were influenced significantly by students' responses. This approach places an additional constraint on the amount of flexibility that can be infused into class teaching. In the following extract, Ian became irritated because some students had not completed the assigned homework. Yet, despite the dilemmas, he continued striving to accommodate individuals' needs:

> . . . Ian, exasperated, declared, 'I've had enough . . . the only way I know that you know the notes is that you write them . . . everybody's going to do it NOW'. This brought muffled groans from those who had already completed the exercise. Ian thought better of this blanket approach almost immediately, and he revised his initial reaction. 'If you have it done, read the next tune,' he told them. Very quickly, Lisa approached Ian to declare that she had read the second tune and he encouraged her to 'finger it' without making any noise. He went on to tell her that it was not her fault that the lesson was 'held up'. (fieldnote 26/9/'90)

Similar tensions were manifest in Ian's approach to decomposition of number exercises, which he had assigned from the class textbook. The child-centred axiom of deploying concrete materials to synchronize the match between learner and learning experience, as well as to enhance conceptual development, are implicit concerns in the following extract, in addition to the ongoing tension between class teaching and the limits to its flexibility when accommodating individual needs.

> As Ian moved about the class providing individual attention where required, he noticed that Dick and Andy were having difficulty de-constructing twelve units into a ten and two units. He decided some general explanation was required and he asked everyone to 'look up here'. Many continued to do their work as Ian proceeded to provide some examples on the board. An individual learner approached me and he expressed difficulty with the concept of decomposition. We collected enough erasers, sharpeners, and pencils to provide ourselves with twelve units. We subdivided these into a ten and

two units and suddenly he remarked, 'Oh yes'. Some further explanation was required, and Ian suggested again, 'Whether you are finished or not ... look up here,' and he began to provide further examples of this decomposition approach to tens and units. (fieldnote 27/9/'90)

Similar tensions were manifest in other subject matter areas. Ian's case suggests that there are real limitations to the flexibility which good informal rapport and relationships can provide to offset the rigidities of formal class teaching.

Paula

Paula prepared extensively (approximately one and a half hours each night) for her teaching, and she expected her students to work very hard also. Consequently, the nature of their relationships tended to be contractual so that she appealed to their better nature.

When Ron, who had been spoken to on a number of occasions during the lesson, gave a good response to a question, Paula reinforced his behaviour with, 'Good man ... I knew you wouldn't let me down'. (fieldnote 1/10/'90)

One of the commonplaces of Paula's teaching was a rather hectic pace. She continuously strove to complete all the work she had planned for any particular day. Though this degree of intensity might appear to contradict popular assumptions about child-centredness, there was time to respond to individual needs, even if there were more subtle messages on occasion:

Despite this apparently hectic schedule, Paula found time to admire what Jack was wearing when she said, 'Jack you're in real style today'. My suspicion was the comments had something to do with the fact that the style to which she referred was the school uniform which he had not worn the previous day. (fieldnote 2/10/'90)

Paula attempted to reinforce the contractual element of relationships by accentuating the positive responses of errant learners, particularly individuals such as Tim who had been less than cooperative the previous day. In the following extract she had attempted to head off a possible recurrence by a more elaborate than usual praise routine:

Tim was thanked profusely for a contribution he made and Paula attempted to reinforce this good behaviour by pointing out the value of 'listening' and that it paid to make that 'extra effort to pay attention'. Yet again, this was drawing attention to the contractual nature of the relationships that Paula attempted to cultivate as a means of minimizing the time spent dealing with classroom management. (fieldnote 3/10/'90)

The classroom climate that Paula cultivated was highly positive though it was task oriented and teacher directed also. Her formal communication routines involved a high commitment to class teaching while, within this framework, respect for individual difference and directed discovery (axioms of child-centredness) were much in evidence. The context of the following episode was that Paula had introduced the basic terms of the metric system of weight the previous day. There had been a general discussion of the conceptual difficulties experienced by many adults when substituting European terms for the Imperial terms with which they were so familiar; this, too, was a conscious effort on her part to connect subject matter with the everyday experiences of learners, something which would be applauded by advocates of progressive teaching.

> Abe informed the teacher that he had weighed the cat at home and discovered it was 3 gms. Paula, somewhat sceptical as to the accuracy of this, asked what an eraser might weigh, and lifting up an empty crisp bag, she disclosed that the contents weighed 26 gms. Having presented this contrary information, she encouraged Abe to repeat the weighing that evening as a means of checking the accuracy of his initial report. (fieldnote 2/10/'90)

As part of her commitment to individual's integrity, Paula was protective of each learner's personal space, particularly in reserving the right to be wrong for all learners, though she had a strong commitment to class teaching, a paragon of traditional teaching. The degree of artistry and detailed planning that Paula brought to her practice enabled her to lend a great deal of flexibility to her formal communication routines, creating a synergic mix of both teaching traditions. The immediate context of the next extract was that she had given the class a quick test in mathematics. They were in the process of correcting some of the more difficult sums on the board, when the reported incident occurred.

> As the number of sums left to be corrected was diminishing, Paula inquired, 'Who didn't do one for me yet . . .' and Ron found himself at the board some moments later attempting to subtract 81 from 53 as a result of his own suggestion that this was the way to do the sum. Many of the class realized the futility of this approach before Ron himself, and some (of them) began to laugh and snigger at his dilemma. Paula became a little irritated by this behaviour and insisted, 'Respect now please'. She encouraged John not to interfere with Ron so that the mistake could 'be spotted for himself'. (fieldnote 3/10/'90)

The relationships Paula fostered were genuinely caring, thus mirroring Noddings' (1992, p. 36) assertion that 'students will do things for people they like and trust', while warning that this situation is open to exploitation and manipulation by practitioners. Paula's interaction with John indicates the complexity of his dilemma as well as the extent to which informal and formal routines contributed significantly to the quality of learning and classroom climate. John had plenty of ability apparently, while he appeared to have more enthusiasm for being the smart-Alec in the class than applying himself more systematically to the task on hand. He had spent much of the previous day in 'quarantine' for minor misbehaviour which was disruptive and infuriating in equal measure. However, Paula was more than willing to forget this. Consequently, she readily acknowledges his positive contribution as part of her strategy of accentuating the positive to create a supportive communication network.

> Many of the learners presented to the class the advertisements they had created. John received the biggest round of applause for his lively and dramatic presentation. Clearly this kid was ideally suited to a curriculum that enabled him to get involved, and provided an outlet for all this energy he displays when unsolicited. Paula, despite her earlier frustration with this individual, exclaimed, 'I'm fit to choke you for talking . . . It's worth it for that'. Some minutes later, after others had also got an opportunity to present their creations, John was rewarded with another opportunity to do his thing. (fieldnote 3/10/'90)

It is possible to argue that it was precisely because Paula planned her daily work in detail that she could devote more attention to caring, thus suggesting that planning, far from being inimical to aspects of child-centred practice, is essential for its construction.

Noel

Noel had a good sense of humour, which is usually an asset in a classroom setting. His spontaneous comments and interjections frequently resulted in equally witty retorts from learners. When these worked well and did not disrupt the fragile classroom ecology of thirty-seven competitive learners, they contributed significantly to the cultivation of rapport and relationships. Immediately preceding the next extract, the class had been discussing Romans' skill at road building as an important aspect of consolidating their empire.

> In attempting to explain what was meant by empire Noel commented that Ireland was once part of an empire. 'Does anyone know what it was?' he asked. 'Don't remind me,' replied Garry as he raised his hand to answer the question. Noel had anticipated the emergence of such a response and he attempted to draw out Garry on the subject. Once it had been established that we had been part of the British Empire, Garry said, 'I hate the English', When Noel asked what this hate was based on, he said that they had no right to come over here and rule us. Noel turned to the rest of the class and asked them if they agreed with this perspective and not one hand was raised in support of their colleague. Instead, some of them murmured the name Jack Charlton. Perhaps this honest miner's son had done more

to change the perception of our historical past at the popular level than all the historians and scholars combined.[1] (fieldnote 11/10/'90)

There were other occasions when Noel found it necessary to establish the boundaries of acceptable interjection and to reiterate the appropriate rule.

> One of the boys over did the smart comments as one of the others was speaking. Noel immediately reminded the transgressor of a classroom rule whereby everyone was expected to have 'the courage to say something' and no one was to be ridiculed for his/her outspokenness. 'I have made about 10 mistakes already myself today,' he went on, so that 'none of us can afford to be too smart.' (fieldnote 8/10/'90)

On another occasion, Noel indicated to the learners, as a consequence of their inattentiveness, that the kind of positive classroom atmosphere they wished him to cultivate could be achieved only if they respected the rules. 'It is impossible to have a good atmosphere in the classroom', Noel began, 'if only two or three hands are going up in response to questions' (fieldnote 9/10/'90). When the rules were not breached, then the classroom atmosphere was enhanced. Mutual regard for the rules facilitated the use of good-natured banter such as when Noel commented, 'That is the disadvantage of having very good students in the class . . . they spot all the mistakes that the teacher makes' (fieldnote 8/10/'90). Sometimes when unanticipated opportunities emerged for the learners they found them too tempting to resist.

> Ken now found his name on the board as a result of a rather loud sneeze which had the desired effect of causing a laugh. Noel acknowledged the importance of a 'good atmosphere' in class but there were limits beyond which pupils should not go. In any case, Ken had been 'warned already'. (fieldnote 9/10/'90)

One of the learners informed me that after the first warning the offender's name was put on the board and, following a third warning, a punishment exercise was given. Noel increased the coercive element of the rule later in the week by excluding those whose names were on the board from the possibility of being assigned classroom duties. While there was a place for wit and humour around the periphery of the school day, Noel's commitment to class teaching, class size, and a generally competitive environment made it difficult to sustain productive tension between formal and informal communication routines.

Noel was attempting to stimulate discussion on fossil fuels and he had brought along some turf for the class to examine, thus giving hands-on experience to the learners in the spirit of child-centred ideology. It was necessary to break the peat to provide each nest of tables with a sample.

> One of the groups in particular grabbed at the piece he had dropped on to the centre of the tables and this annoyed the teacher. Consequently, some

more names were added to the list already on the board and a repetition of the phrase, 'I am fed up with this class'. Noel went on to say that he had been reluctant, due to the presence of a visitor in the room during the week, to be harping on behaviour but that he had seen 'a side of the class' which he did not know existed, and this was 'a great disappointment'. Their behaviour was 'juvenile', he said, and it would not be possible to have 'fun and craic'[2] if there was not mutual 'respect'. He thought that perhaps he was expecting 'too much from the class' and he did not wish to keep on 'fighting to keep the lid on things'. When behaviour of this nature occurs he feels obliged to 'show my displeasure'. (fieldnote 11/10/'90)

Context had a significant shaping influence on Noel's formal communication routines as his exclusively middle-class parents had very high academic expectations for their offspring. Through discussion of the fieldnotes Noel revealed that because he had to complete the prescribed programme, an axiom of traditional teaching, there were real limits to the degree of flexibility he could infuse into formal encounters.

As part of our discussion, I commented that he had a very structured, step-by-step approach to mathematics. Noel's intention was that through a combination of these steps and individual practice, the vast majority would eventually reach mastery. Noel went on to explain that given the amount of work to be completed in the fifth class curriculum, it would not be possible to take too much time at this point to provide additional explanation and elaboration as it would slow the entire class down to an unacceptable degree. (fieldnote 12/10/'90)

As an integral element of formal routines Noel tried to keep a lively pace and to maximize learners' time on task. Our conversation revealed his underlying reasons, which were informed by the context of his practice.

He informed me that another reason for keeping the pressure on, and allowing only a limited amount of time to complete these exercises, was in preparation for entrance examinations when they got 20 questions to complete in an hour. (fieldnote 11/10/'90).

It is apparent from the above extracts that practitioners attach importance and devote significant attention to the cultivation of good relationships and the quality of these relations has importance for the more formal communication patterns in each classroom. Informal routines appear to be more in tune with progressive thinking while more formal routines seem more homologous with traditional practice: a januformity of practice that embraced both traditions to varying degrees. However, when the other two themes are presented a more complex and comprehensive picture emerges.

Theme Two: Structure

Structuring and sequencing learning experiences was an issue of importance for the practitioners who participated in phase two of the inquiry. The complex amalgam of discrete subject matter, topic work, and more integrated thematic planning provided variations on the complex concern of structuring learning to maximize the benefits for learners according to the various intentions of the practitioners and the constraints which operated in their respective contexts. The following extracts indicate that the degree of flexibility in the teaching–learning structures constructed by practitioners, and the extent to which they accommodate individual needs, were meliorated or exacerbated by the sophistication of their communication routines. The impact of structure can only be adequately understood when it is brought to life through formal and informal communication routines. It is necessary, therefore, for the reader to understand that the contribution of the three themes is cumulative and they overlap in significant ways, thus underscoring the essential unity of practice.

Orla

Orla's teaching included detailed instructions to learners about drawing margins in their copies as a prominent structural routine. Additional advice was given to work down the page of the mathematics copies rather than across. Though this degree of specification and circumspection of pupils' work may be anathema to commonly held understandings of child-centred ideology, it enabled the learners to concentrate their energies on the cognitive dimension of the mathematical exercises, and it also streamlined the correction/feedback process which had particular significance in a two class situation.

> No sooner had the third class begun their written work than Orla, with red biro in hand, requested some of the fourth class girls to come to her table so that she could begin to correct their work which was still in the process of being completed. She seemed to do this without even pausing for breath, and again, for the second time that morning, I had the impression of the machine moving up a gear. Further evidence of increased momentum was apparent when I noticed Orla was flying through these corrections as she had prepared a page with the answers. Fleeting glances from copy to page is all that were required, and these were interspersed with swift strokes of the red pen making that familiar correct stroke alongside each sum to the obvious approval of the recipients. Those unfortunate enough to have erred in these initial stages were told, 'Don't rub out anything it will only mess your copy'. The clear implication was that sums, if incorrect, were to be re-done in the next available space. Orla pointed out that if the sum were corrected in situ, it would be marked incorrect by her red biro. Better to make a new beginning than to attempt to re-plough the same patch. (fieldnote 5/9/'90)

Though this degree of rule specification facilitated the correction process, it also circumscribed the autonomy/responsibility of the learners (Holmes, 1911). However, as a consequence, it may be suggested that a significant amount of decision-making, responsibility and ownership, apart from any concern for individual preference, was vested in the practitioner and not in the learner. As Ian had declared in the previous chapter, scaffolding has the potential to facilitate as well as to suffocate, but it is only by sustained observation that its impact on the learning process can be adequately documented. The important point which emerged was that structuring of the learning was deemed essential, though the degree of structure required within the rubric of child-centred ideology is a matter of interpretation.

An important dimension of structure was an emphasis on individual seat work (rather than group work) which was reinforced by a rule that students could not copy each other's work. Both classes were revising a lists of words at the beginning of the spelling text, while Orla was providing a word building exercise on the blackboard. The practice of systematically teaching spellings was seen in the previous chapter to be pervasive, and Orla's use of a textbook for that purpose provided further evidence that her programme was textbook dependent.

> ... both classes had to find three words which were similar to: feed, book, sand and fall. To complete this exercise, Orla reminded them of the instructions she had issued yesterday about use of a large ruler and pencil for drawing a margin and to leave sufficient room for the numbering of questions to occupy the margin. As Orla put the word food on the board she said, 'Don't start yet,' and as they began writing appropriate words in their notebooks she warned, 'I sincerely hope I don't see a girl looking at another copy'. (fieldnote 4/9/'90)

Later in the week, further opportunity presented itself to reinforce this element of her practice. The good humour and spontaneity which accompanied the reiteration of the rule was an indication that the teacher was appealing to the better nature of learners rather than wishing to be heavy handed:

> The spelling test proceeded with Orla calling out words alternately for third and fourth class. She began good humouredly with the twin exhortation, 'Books closed, mouths closed! Jane, I do not want to see what Joan has written twice; I want to know what you know'. Even though Joan was not the guilty party in this particular episode, she too was included in the admonition which seemed to extend beyond them both, thus sending a clear signal to all concerned that copying was something which would not be tolerated. Orla began, 'Joan, if you are allowing Jane to copy then you are at fault too'. (fieldnote 7/9/'90)

The test was over rapidly and the notebooks were being collected for correction. Orla added some additional refinements to the collection process to streamline it as much as possible. As this was to be a daily occurrence for the remainder of the year, it was important to ensure, from the outset, that it worked with maximum efficiency. These and the following structures and routines seem to resonate with some interpretations of traditional teaching, though the formal and informal communication routines through which they were negotiated seemed oriented towards commonly held beliefs about progressive ideology. Perhaps this was evidence that child-centredness, contrary to popular belief, could embrace both structure and informality. The additional burden of working with two age groups is an important contextual constraint which puts pressure on Orla's use of time so that routines must be established for maximum efficiency.

Orla pointed out, in response to a draft of her case study, that rules, routines and structures appeared to be overemphasized and that when her teaching was in full flow later in the term a quite different picture would emerge. Conducting fieldwork during the first week of the school year was rather like observing the foundations of a building being poured. However, foundations do have a bearing on the ultimate shape of a building. Consequently, the pedagogical scaffolding that she erected would have a significant shaping influence on learning during the year. Nevertheless, such routines retain a degree of flexibility and they are open to some alteration. The following extract indicates that not only are routines not cast in stone, but their very malleability may be their strength. The imaginative deployment of rules and routines as well as setting them aside sometimes, may enhance rather than detract from them. Orla had brought the senior classes together for choir practice.

> It was obvious that all concerned were enjoying the experience. Orla's competence in singing and conducting readily communicated itself to the learners. The style was relaxed, yet thorough and it was lunch time far too soon. In all this movement and general excitement, neither the Angelus nor the grace before meals were included in the day's proceedings. It was as if Orla, having spent the early part of the week being very insistent on creating routines, could now afford to relax the regimen a little. Schools, it seemed were humanized when rules were disregarded sensibly. (fieldnote 6/7/'90)

While structure was an important element of teaching for Orla, lending flexibility to that structure through skilful deployment of formal and informal communication routines animated the process and provided flexibility as a means of accommodating individual needs.

Jane

Jane had a tendency to teach the basic subjects as separate entities, though she structured many learning tasks to integrate aspects of content also. For example, craft activities were based on work from the history programme on our Stone Age ancestors. In the vignette which follows, it was Friday afternoon and the learners had been in their 'PE gear' since lunch time in anticipation of going to the yard for the final lesson of the day. However, they were also very keen to finish the seventeen crannogs[3] which they had begun to make earlier in the week. Jane had made it very clear at the outset of this craft session that the longer it took the class to tidy up, the less time they would have for PE. She gave the learners greater responsibility for organizing their time and their learning tasks, which was consistent with more typical interpretations of child-centredness. At the time that this vignette occurred, Jane had already signalled, almost ten minutes earlier, that it was time to tidy the classroom. The episode also indicates the extent to which communication routines have impact on the manner in which content is mediated and learners engage with it.

> It was getting closer to the tidy-up deadline and it was obvious that Rose and her partner were not going to get all the intricate weaving of rushes done to complete the wall of their construction. Jane and Rose were discussing the manner in which the project might be completed by using straw for the roof which would speed up the process immeasurably: 'I don't want to rush you into doing something you don't want to do.' 'You have done a good job girls,' I said, somewhat speculatively, to which Rose replied, 'I don't like this side,' meaning that one side of the weaving was better than the other. Jane, as always, ready with her sense of humour, suggested, 'You will only photograph your house from one side'. At this point Jane moved away quite deliberately to allow the girls to decide for themselves . . . I noticed some moments later that Rose was frantically selecting lengths of straw which she placed on the structure in an attempt to complete it. She soon realized that this was a futile exercise and quickly began stripping away the straw she had already piled onto her Stone Age dwelling. I felt that this vignette was all the more significant because Rose was oblivious to the organized chaos which was going on around her. It displayed a great deal of empathy and understanding on Jane's part, particularly when the class was already clearing up. It seemed also to bring together the qualitative dimension of an 'educational encounter' (Eisner, 1985) and the notion of 'reflection-in-action' (Schön, 1983) except that here, in the enabling environment created by the teacher, reflection-in-action was a concept which applied to learner and practitioner. (fieldnote 21/9/'90)

This was a task to which the learners were highly attuned: its structure provided for considerable variation, the learners worked collaboratively, and Jane provided advice and assistance while not dictating in a manner that would run counter to popular interpretations of progressive teaching. The final comment in the fieldnotes concerning these episodes was that 'Jane found the time to be sensitive to the needs of the individuals involved as well as valuing the qualities inherent in the educational encounter' (fieldnote 21/9/'90). Her practice seemed highly consistent with her image of the teacher as 'someone who is there for the children' (transcript 10).

As an integral element of structuring the learning in her classroom, Jane tried to ensure that learners made connections between various content: a form of incidental integration that she regarded as important. For example, the painting, which each group had undertaken while their peers were grouped for mathematics, was of a factory. Emphasis on its possible impact on the local environment arose out of discussions on industry in the local community. It also reflected the teacher's concern for environmental issues. Building of the crannogs had emanated from the history text but provision of additional resource materials (photographs which she had taken during her summer holidays) and informal communication brought their past to life in a very real manner for the class.

> Jane circulated photographs of crannogs which were at various stages of construction and these proved an excellent stimulus to discussion and the practicalities of building such a dwelling. When these photographs had been thoroughly discussed, the history textbook was produced and individuals read sections as a summary to the discussion which had taken place. (fieldnote 17/9/'90)

The photographs she had introduced to stimulate discussion were later displayed and labelled at the back of the classroom. Though the learning task and its essential content were chosen by the teacher, thus suggesting a traditional approach to structuring learning, the manner in which the task was mediated seemed highly consistent with axioms of child-centredness.

Similar encouragement was provided to connect geography content with science. While Jane conducted a demonstration of the colours of the rainbow, learners moved freely to gain an intimate view of the proceedings and thus increase their passive participation in the process. Only when the demonstration and its attendant conversation had been completed did they turn to the text. In the following fieldnote extract, Jane recalled previous references to the rainbow and light.

> She attempted to make further connections with work they had done the previous week about what the world would be like without light. This led to mention of Newton, light, prism and rainbow. One of the pupils was able to add that Newton is also remembered for the concept of gravity and his insistence that the world is round. With a bowl of water, a large torch, a piece of card with a tiny hole, a magnifying glass and the assistance of a few members of the class, she set out to demonstrate that by bending light it was possible to show that it contained all the colours of the rainbow. These were written on the board, complete with acronym to aid memorization of the colours. The class gathered around the top of the room while this demonstration was in progress. It was repeated a number of times so that all could get a ring side seat at the experiment. (fieldnote 19/9/'90)

Jane was conscious that with more resources she could give learners more hands-on experience. In the absence of such materials she structured the learning as best she could and tried to maximize the flexibility of this to accommodate individuals' needs by skilful deployment of her formal and informal communication routines.

Ian

Ian's metaphor of the teacher as 'magician' has some superficial resonance with popular interpretations of progressive rhetoric, while his practice was dominated by class teaching, extended periods of teacher talk, and an emphasis on memorization as part of his basic approach to structuring learning opportunities. The following extracts are illustrative.

Every pupil had been provided with the class reader but Ian also procured thirty additional texts with funding from the school principal and parents as a means of providing reading enrichment. His intention in formally introducing these books to the class was to stimulate and foster a love of reading. As he introduced these texts he stated that 'as he was still in the process of getting to know the class . . . he could only make an educated guess as to what their reading interests were' (fieldnote 26/9/'90). Many of these books were beautifully illustrated and Ian's interest in art was apparent from his enthusiasm for these illustrations. He also advised on appropriate care for books, as well as expressing the pleasure he derived from 'giving books to children'. These books had been selected 'because they are lovely to look at' apart from the story or because they could be a 'source of ideas for doing your own drawing and colouring' (fieldnote 26/9/'90). Ian continued to speak about these books for more than thirty minutes. He distributed them to individuals who expressed a willingness to take good care of them.

When a minor crisis arose, Ian indicated how the structures he was putting in place were intended to function:

> Josh, who had received a book earlier, now complained, 'I can't read it . . . it is too hard'. Ian, a little taken a back with this announcement, took the book and inquired, from no one in particular, 'What is so difficult about it?' He then gave the book to Mick. (fieldnote 26/9/'90)

When each member of the class had been given a library book, ten minutes were allocated for perusal of these acquisitions. Ian chose this time to explain to me how he intended the library books to function in relation to the class reader, as well as within his overall language structure:

> Ian assured me that the introduction of these texts so soon after the primary English text for the year did not indicate any diminution of the central importance of this text. The library books were something like parallel lines rather than aspects of a complementary programme. (fieldnote 26/9/'90)

Within the whole class approach that Ian adopted towards the teaching of reading (and other subjects) there is a basic tension between his enthusiasm to promote a love of reading through good story (such as the class reader), attractively illustrated library books, and learners' needs for materials which are suitable to their reading attainment and ability. This tension was implicit in his recommendation to less able learners in the following extract:

> Ian encouraged those who attend the remedial teacher in particular, to watch their 'Mammies' as they read some of the text, as it is important to be 'able to see the words that she is reading . . . very important that you see how the words are read'. (fieldnote 25/9/'90)

Another prominent element of Ian's structuring of learning was an emphasis on memorization of poetry which is embedded in the minds of many as a routine of traditional schooling. However, he attempted to ameliorate this by attempting to make it a fun exercise. The class had been given some English poems to memorize and individuals were asked if they were ready to 'make a spell' by standing in front of the class and reciting a poem of their choice. This routine was applied flexibly, depending on the context. If the poem was one which the class had been learning for some time, then the individual who volunteered was expected to be a 'spell-maker' without assistance. This routine was, to some extent, an extension of Ian's image of teacher as 'magician', weaving spells for his audience. When an individual faltered, the class chanted 'spell-breaker' and the pupil returned to his or her seat. However Ian could request that this routine be relaxed.

> He [Ian] went on to allow three individuals to recite the poem and rather than allow the class to be vigorous in invoking the 'spell-breaker' approach to the child in the hot seat, he asked that they give 'all their support'. (fieldnote 25/9/'90)

Giving support involved prompting the individual if he or she forgot the lines.

Ian's basic structuring of learning was to treat subjects in isolation and to deliver them to the whole class; this was particularly so in relation to Irish, English and mathematics. In the areas of music and PE, in particular, a more informal structure was adopted. The following extract, which details the introduction of rounders to the class, is illustrative. The rudiments of the game were explained at some length. The class then proceeded to a green area adjacent to the school where three games were organized, two for the boys, one for the girls. When the three games eventually got underway, Ian had some moments to surface his reasons for his general strategy. His initial intention was to get them going and refinement could be added later. Adopting an informal approach to constructing the learning environment is itself a definite approach to structuring learning situations that may turn out to be more rigid than more overt formal planning. In this way, intended informal structures may, in practice, be quite rigid to the extent that they do not resonate readily with what is commonly thought to be child-centred.

> While there was some dissent about rules among the boys, in general the games progressed as planned. Ian confided that, in so far as possible, he

allowed them to sort out any difficulties, as he found that they were more capable of doing this than he. He also indicated that his approach at this stage in the year was 'holistic' and that when the class had some experience of the game he would hone in on particular skills that he identified as being weak in individuals and he would get them to coach each other. (fieldnote 24/9/'90)

During the initial interview Ian indicated that he regarded scaffolding as a prop for practitioners who wished to play safe. As we discussed issues of structure, which were documented in the fieldnotes, Ian began to articulate his own tacit understanding of striking a balance between what constituted enough, too much, or too little structure.

Ian went on to say that 'I wanted art to be the highlight' but the experience left a lot to be desired because it sort of grew out of the English reading and he did not deal with the issues he wished to be central to the art experience for the class. 'I did not devote enough time to it,' he went on. I mentioned at this point that in the transcript of his interview he had said that he didn't place a great deal of store on timetabling and planning as this tended to segment and interrupt the learning process and, as a consequence, the learners never got to what he called 'critical mass'. He recalled this but went on to say that 'yesterday a timetable would have provided the space . . .' which he felt was necessary to give the class the art experience he wanted them to have. (fieldnote 28/9/'90)

These extracts reveal planning and structuring as inescapable issues for practitioners even when they wish to distance themselves from such concerns. Taken in isolation, the evidence from Ian's case suggests much that resonates with common understandings of traditional schooling, though aspects of his communication routines appear homologous with common interpretations of child-centredness also.

Paula

Paula planned her work thematically and spent at least ninety minutes each evening preparing for the following day. The concrete evidence for this degree of attention to detail was apparent each morning as she simultaneously pressed photocopier and spirit duplicator into action to deliver materials for the day as thematic planning diminished the importance and usefulness of textbooks. It became apparent, as the week progressed, that it was this level of attention to detail as well as her dedication that enabled Paula and her class to pursue learning in a structured, integrated, thematic manner with exemplary rigour; evidence perhaps that child-centred ideologues underestimated the high concentration of imagination and creativity, energy and dedication required to transform ideological sentiment into classroom actions. The fieldnotes recorded my response to Paula's manifest dedication.

I don't think that I have ever seen this degree of planning and attention to detail except during teaching practice. I was beginning to understand what Paula meant when she said in the initial interview that she spent an hour and a half preparing work each night. (fieldnote 1/10/'90)

It is difficult to provide a comprehensive picture of a thematic approach to structuring the learning environment in a manner which captures the pervasiveness of the connections that practitioner and learners make while participating in the process. The thematic experience Paula constructed included mathematical calculations about the length of various television programmes, investigation of the amount of broadcast time devoted to different categories of programme, to discovering the amount of time that peers spend watching television, in addition to learning something of the medium's history. This kind of experience is qualitatively different from presenting disparate information in an unconnected fashion. The contractual nature of the communication process with its emphasis on teaching and a high degree of interaction, as well as her thematic structuring of content, seemed to combine successfully features of didactic teaching with assets of child-centred ideology.

All of the components mentioned already — as well as writing, poetry, the creation of advertisements, reporting on various events, doing book reviews for an imaginary children's television programme — were integral elements of the learning experiences in Paula's classroom. Towards the end of the week, it seemed as if the attention to detail in terms of planning, and the purposeful nature of the activities, combined with Paula's judicious use of questions, were willing the learners on to make more and more connections between seemingly disparate aspects of the theme. During the initial interview, Paula suggested that, through her teaching, she strove to enable learners to learn how to learn. In the following extract, Paula was drawing the learners' attention to a chart made by her the previous evening to display some of the television advertisements they had designed. The extract illustrates that it is Paula's commitment to a high degree of structured preparation combined with sophisticated communication routines that generate challenge, engagement and enthusiasm on the part of learners: a classroom buzz rather than a hum!

Angus inquired as to what they would do with these colonies [of micro-beasts] now that they were growing, and his query facilitated further discussion. This discussion gave Paula the opportunity to draw attention to the chart on the TV ads, and the manner in which advertisers tended to put the best possible face on the product being promoted. It was for this reason that she put the caption 'Does it grab you?' at the bottom of the chart. She was delighted when one of the girls suggested, in answer to Angus' question, that the micro-beasts could be put in vinegar. The pupil was making connections between information in the video that was viewed two days previously about medieval villagers (in Eyam) who found an ingenious means of paying for goods while they were isolated due to an outbreak of plague. They put their coins into little pools of vinegar in a rock at the edge of the village for collection by those who delivered food. (fieldnote 4/10/'90)

Paula's case suggests that planning in an integrated, thematic manner facilitates and encourages learners in constructing their own conceptual frameworks to cope with the volume of information which assails them thematically. This carries the implication that it is less demanding cognitively on the learner to deal with subject matter content in discrete elements within subject boundaries. Another possible interpretation is that without detailed planning a thematic approach may well end in a conceptual muddle that confuses rather than enlightens (Alexander, 1984; Dearden, 1984; Peters, 1969). Consequently, it may be the absence of the kind of detailed planning and pedagogical skill manifest in Paula's practice that has given rise to the belief that there is more rigour attached to teaching subjects as discrete disciplines (Hirst and Peters, 1970; Hirst, 1974).

From observing the pace and frenetic engagement of the learners in Paula's classroom, the most appropriate metaphor which constantly came to mind was attempting to put a litre into a pint bottle: an analogy to which Paula readily assented (fieldnote 3/10/'90). While planning and teaching were teacher driven in a manner that appears homologous with aspects of traditional teaching, Paula was very sensitive to emergent suggestions from learners which she subsequently incorporated into the planning process. The next extract is illustrative of her attempt to lend flexibility to the planned structure. Paula had already indicated that the class was to have a debate later in the week. As part of the television theme there had been some animated discussion about a particular advertisement featured on national television. The fieldnotes take up the story.

> In recognition of this manifest enthusiasm, Paula decided to go with the flow and immediately announced a debate, proceeding to write the motion on the board as follows: 'The Power of TV'. The class was invited to agree or disagree with the motion and she emphasized again the civilized manner in which this debate should take place. Tara, Orla and Olga all spoke against the supposed power of TV, and Paula summed up the contributions by saying that, 'Ultimately it is our own free choice that decides on a product'. Paula then directed the debate to the issue of the educative power of television and the class were forthcoming once more. (fieldnote 2/10/'90)

There is much in Paula's practice that suggests a januform approach to structuring teaching and learning. It would require a more prolonged period of observation to determine the extent to which such structures met all learners' needs and interests or were eschewed towards the more able.

Noel

Noel had to prepare his class for entrance examination; a strong focus on the basics was necessary to ensure that as many as possible reached the appropriate *standard*, and this necessitated a teacher-driven didacticism. This basic structure was rein-forced by a marking system to provide additional encouragement to learners. This combination of structure and communication routines was intended to show the learners what standard was required; a notion that rests uncomfortably with common interpretations of child-centred ideology. The school context suggested a certain urgency about the need to communicate its future orientation to the learners. This extract records correction of homework.

> The total number of marks awarded on this occasion was 12. Noel pointed out at the end of correcting this exercise that the purpose of the work at this stage in fifth was to begin to stretch them mentally and that if they did not work now they would be 'left behind' when the pace heated up later in the year. He went on to say that some of the behaviour in the class was 'unacceptable' and that he was 'fed up telling' people. (fieldnote 9/10/'90)

This general structural approach was identifiable across the basics and embraced homework also. Because it was early in the school year, and it would not be until the following school year that entrance examinations would be taken by the learners, elaboration on the routine as a means of orientating and initiating the learners into the structure was an important element of the process at this point:

> When the entire exercise had been corrected there were 30 marks to be allocated and the pupils were instructed to award a mark and to pass the copy back to its owner. When this had been done, Noel asked those who got full marks to stand up. He continued in reverse sequence [from 30] and by the time he got to 27 about two-thirds of the class was standing and he did not proceed any further. He did point out, 'It is very interesting to see some of those who are sitting down' because 'I know if they pushed them-selves they could do it.' The whole emphasis in this approach seemed to be that the tasks could be completed if only there was maximum concen-tration and dedication. (fieldnote 10/10/'90)

When Noel inquired about marks received by individuals, he tended to ask about the highest marks available as the extract above indicates. The excerpt also demon-strates that the majority of learners typically performed in the categories about which he inquired. This particular strategy also became a subtle means of reminding learners that there was a standard to be maintained by those who already found themselves in that category, and to be attained by those who fell short of that level of achieve-ment. In a written reply to a draft of his case study, Noel commented, 'I would like to stress that I see a marking system as providing children with information which challenges them to improve their performance in class rather than grading themselves on a surreptitious ladder of achievement' (Letter, 23/4/'90).

There were occasions also when the structures were more collaborative, altru-istic and less competitive when more able learners were requested to provide assist-ance to less able peers in Vygotskian fashion. It was a routine intended to overcome some of the limitations of class teaching while enabling the teacher to reduce the burden of corrections.

> The more able learner examined the incorrect sums and wrote a brief description of the errors that had been made. This enabled the teacher to get through corrections relatively quickly and to provide individual feedback to all who required it. Noel had spoken of this earlier in the week and he indicated that as an additional measure he could take these identified errors and deal with them on the board with individuals, groups or the entire class. It certainly keeps up the productivity. When the errors had been identified by peers, the owner of the copy returned [to the teacher] with it. This encounter could result in having 'Take more care' written on the copy or a more elaborate consultation ensued if deemed necessary. (fieldnote 12/10/'90)

Noel did initiate a fieldtrip and a project on transport during the fieldwork, where several groups would work collaboratively on a particular aspect of transport arising from work in history and based on the local environment. However, the dominant structures of teaching and learning were as outlined above and these carried the redolence of traits commonly associated with traditional teaching. These structures led to persistent dilemmas with which Noel wrestled constantly; the need to cover the prescribed programme and to ensure that as many as possible of the thirty-seven learners reached a standard set by entrance examinations while trying to remain sensitive to individual's needs and abilities.

Theme Three: Balance

Terms such as whole child, whole curriculum, more rounded, broadly based, full and harmonious development, full life as a child, implicitly, explicitly and simultaneously call for attention to learners so that their potential is identified, nurtured, challenged and developed. The achievement of this end is commonly sought through a balanced programme provision which goes well beyond the narrow confines of traditional (3Rs) schooling. The term balance itself suggests productive tension and compromise between competing demands and concerns. The social and cognitive development of learners becomes an organizing metaphor for practitioners as they construct their practice around these dilemmas while seeking to balance the weight of competing traditions of teaching, their own biographies and the contexts of their work. The evidence for this theme indicates that context has a significant bearing on these tensions. However, regardless of context, social and cognitive development is a dilemma with which practitioners' teaching constructions seek an accommodation. Looking at practice through the lens of balance becomes an important means of understanding how the social and cognitive needs of learners are dealt with as teaching is structured and brought to life through the formal and informal communication routines of practitioners. In this second phase of the inquiry it was more a question of recognizing that balance was an issue for practitioners rather than providing a sophisticated and detailed analysis of what it entailed. Balance as a cultural theme focuses attention also on the essential unity of practice. There are instances, therefore, in the following extracts when two or all three cultural themes are simultaneously evident, though some will be more overtly apparent than others.

Orla

Orla was particularly enthusiastic about music and she communicated this enthusiasm to the learners, while hinting that her subject expertise enabled her to have clear cognitive goals for the programme. The inclusion of music and (later) physical education was important for providing balance in the curriculum.

> During the practice that followed, Orla also gave some signals concerning the nature of the task in hand and her expectations for the programme and the children. 'If you are fixing your hair and stretching' she intoned to two of the girls, then you are not 'learning to read music'. The purpose of the exercise is to learn to read music 'not just get a tune off by heart'. The follow-up exercise which began shortly afterwards reinforced this programme aim. They began the task by drawing three lines in their new copies and proceeded to copy the notes of the little ditty they had been singing. (fieldnote 7/9/'90)

The learners had been informed of the need for appropriate dress for physical education. This requirement was role modelled by Orla herself as she came to school dressed in a tracksuit. By having the rule established from the outset, Orla was able to concentrate on setting expectations for the subject. Her approach to the subject matter maximized participation, interaction and encouraged enjoyment, all of which contributed to a more balanced curriculum diet for the learners.

> After the warm-up activities I became involved with Orla and the pupils in a large circle to practice three folk dances. This practice was preceded by discussion on a variety of dances. The purpose of this discussion was to set an agenda for part of the programme. A large cassette recorder supplied the music and we all had great fun attempting to keep time to the patterns in the music with the steps that Orla had skilfully demonstrated. (fieldnote 7/9/'90)

Orla also sought to balance the need, as she divined it, for a relatively rigid set of routines that are task oriented, and the need for flexibility to foster good relationships and promote the social development of learners. Structure and pedagogy are intimates while the latter is deployed as a means of lending flexibility to the process in an attempt to accommodate both cognitive and social needs.

> Orla suddenly noticed that two of the girls in the back row had swopped places. On inquiring good humouredly as to how this had come about, she

admitted, 'I only noticed now ... it's for today anyway ... provided it works, we'll allow it to happen'. There had been surprisingly little discussion earlier in the week about seating. Orla was sending signals that if pupils were not disruptive, friendships could be accommodated in the seating arrangements. (fieldnote 7/9/'90)

This accommodation gained further significance from knowing that Orla had already relocated two learners for being too talkative. When she determined that a particular individual needed more support than provided by rules she had recently introduced, she did not hesitate to bend the rules. Formal and informal communication routines are an important means of humanizing structures to accommodate both the social and cognitive needs of learners.

This rapport, as well as sensitive to individual needs, became apparent again when Maria was asked to read an extract from the religion text. Three things came together in this vignette. Maria was the third class pupil who was having difficulty locating her reading glasses earlier. Despite the reappearance of the glasses she was not paying all the attention that was expected. Orla had also (at various stages) expressed her displeasure at pupils' becoming engaged in the work of peers. Nevertheless, when Chloe, Maria's immediate neighbour, indicated where she should be reading from in the text by placing her finger under the word, Orla ignored this assistance. When Chloe whispered a word to get Maria started on the reading, this was also ignored, despite the general rule. (fieldnote 7/9/'90)

Balance, therefore, is not just about a broadly based programme but includes meeting the social needs of learners as well as providing appropriate cognitive challenge.

Jane

Jane displayed a significant reflective bent during the initial interview and subsequent fieldwork. This reflexivity had significance for her practice as she continuously demonstrated a capacity and a willingness to see things from learners' perspectives: an 'empathy' which encouraged her, perhaps, to give adequate recognition to the 'emotional intelligence' of the learners (Goleman, 1996). This commitment was apparent even when there was pressure to complete the tidy-up process on Friday afternoon prior to a PE lesson. Making time available for art, craft, and PE was an important means also of providing a balanced programme. For some time the class had been collecting straw, rushes and twigs from the floor and tables. In similar circumstances many practitioners would have been happy to seek immediate asylum in the school yard! While the experience of building crannogs was still fresh in the learners' minds, she wanted to hear them reflect on the experience as an extension of the learning encounter. The fieldnote extract is illustrative of Jane's commitment to learner's social and cognitive development while simultaneously demonstrating a capacity to elevate their cognitive understanding to a different plain.

'I don't think I'd be good at making houses . . . I wouldn't be able to survive,' remarked one of the girls. Sensitive to the pupils self-confidence and self-image, Jane responded that if she had lived in the Stone Age 'instead of going to school you'd be . . . learning to build houses'. 'Even a raindrop would come through the roof on my house . . . it must have been hard on them.' 'Mine kept falling down,' said another, which drew the retort from a neighbour, 'It is still down'. Jane immediately offered to lend a hand with the re-building. When another remarked that she made a 'mess', the ever-vigilant Jane was on hand again to support that self-image with consoling words: 'I don't think you made such a mess.' At this point Jane introduced the photograph which she had shown to a smaller group earlier. This photograph showed how Stone Age people built a fire tunnel over which they smoked, and thus preserved, their food. (fieldnote 21/9/'90)

The dialogue in the extract reflects Jane's concern for social and personal development, the integrity of the learners, as well as cognitive gains from the learning experience. The learner's comments indicate that the educational encounter of making the dwellings, opened their minds to the possibility that their farming ancestors had developed a range of sophisticated skills which could not be emulated as a consequence of one craft lesson. Reflecting on their activity had been significant in developing their understanding. Jane's own reflective bent created a particular classroom environment which extended the structured learning experiences she provided to encourage thoughtful responses from the learners, thus challenging the learners to think beyond the boundaries of the learning task. The classroom climate she cultivated indicated a commitment to process: commonly identified as an important feature of child-centredness (Blenkin and Kelly, 1981).

A very similar extract dealing with an aspect of the same episode was quoted when discussing the theme of structure. From a methodological perspective the impact of both extracts demonstrates the essential unity of practice, while indicating also that the cultural themes provide different interpretive lens through which practice is understood and reconstructed.

Ian

Ian indicated very clearly during his interview that he was vehemently opposed to the tyranny of the 3Rs. Consequently he was especially keen to cater for the whole child by promoting art and music particularly, instrumental as well as musical appreciation. As the learners ate their lunches each morning at break time, 'serious' music was played and they were invited to dance. As the week progressed, introduction to the orchestra was replaced by Russian bells.

After some educated guessing and a replaying of a piece with the sound of bells there was a suggestion that it was Santa. Ian wrote the word Troika on the board and explained that it was a type of sleigh drawn by horses. The excitement of this guessing had about twenty-five pupils on their feet with the result that Ian shouted 'OFF' and all had to return to their places at once or the whole process would be abandoned. Four boys and four girls were selected to dance to a replay of the music. Ian took two of the boys by the hands to encourage them to dance more expressively in response to the music. (fieldnote 26/9/'90)

Ian was highly committed also to introducing the learners to art and art appreciation. During the first days of the fieldwork he spent a significant amount of time introducing his own paintings to the class. As he displayed a variety of watercolours, he introduced useful vocabulary with which to develop the learners' awareness of various dimensions of art work. A sense of standard and expectation was also being established, even if the learners were growing a trifle impatient to get their hands dirty.

Ian reminded the class that he had shown them his art work the previous day and on recalling that Ann had not been present, he proceeded to show his paintings again quickly for her benefit. The class wanted to know . . . if they could do a picture. Ian replied that all he had at present were crayons. He would, he said, 'bring in my own paints and I'll show you how to get paint out of a tube without wasting the whole tube'. At this point he introduced Lisa's painting of a bird, which she had done the previous evening (at home). She had also provided some information about the bird. Ian praised her initiative and there were further queries from the class as to when they would be allowed to do some art work. 'Next week', suggested Ian, they would work on the Zoo and also write some information about what they would paint. (fieldnote 26/9/'90)

Immediately after the presentation of his own paintings, Ian continued with a discussion of Origami craft work. This again raised the prospect for some learners that they might get hands-on experience:

Having attempted to get the class to follow the instructions in the text for making a simple bird-like figure, he took a piece of paper to set about making it himself while the class watched closely. When Ian suggested that he would photocopy some simple and some difficult designs from the text, Josh began hopefully, 'Will I go . . .' thinking that he could be the messenger to the secretary and that he might get to do some craft work that day. He seemed to realize that this was not to be, at least not then, as he did not finish the sentence. (fieldnote 26/9/'90)

Ian's approach to meeting learners' social and cognitive needs was prefaced on a particular interpretation of child-centred ideology, namely, responding to learners' needs while attempting to observe carefully what fired their enthusiasm. In this particular instance Ian responded to the learners by making provision for them to draw charcoal pictures the following day. While being responsive to learners' needs is an important axiom of child-centred rhetoric, Ian remained in control, particularly in the sense that learners' responses were to his initiatives, his agenda, something which resonates with a central tenet of traditional teaching. Ian's commitment to balance may be regarded as januform.

Paula

Paula, in common with all other participants, demonstrated a concern for the whole child in her attempts to establish rapport and to forge relationships with learners through classroom interactions. These episodes are typically identifiable around the fringes and informal moments throughout the school day. They are rarely the sole focus of attention during more formal interactions. This, say Piagetians, is because 'the school can work on the child's developing intellect in a more direct way than it can on the child's affective or social relations' (Furth and Wachs, 1975, p. 41). Yet, these important interactions are frequently present in unobtrusive ways during formal communication routines. Paula's capacity to care is particularly evident in the following vignette. The self-esteem, the social self of the particular learner, is key when the local police sergeant makes a visit to the classroom and the fieldnotes take up the story as Tommy is summoned from the classroom for questioning.

> Teacher confided that Tommy, along with another member of the class, had attempted to break into a van the other night. Further conversation revealed that Tommy had a rather complicated background which did not provide him with the stability he required. I could detect a note of concern in Paula's voice as she spoke of all this ability which he undoubtedly had and the danger of its misuse through circumstances beyond his control. When Tommy returned to the classroom some minutes later, he heaved a big sigh as he resumed his seat. Just as he did so, the teacher was there reassuringly at his side and opened his copy for him and clued him into what the class was doing. She told me afterwards that she did not approve of inquisitions being conducted in the school about matters that occurred in the community. Consequently, she wished to demonstrate in a tangible way that she was still there for this pupil even if other adults had lost faith in him. It is these simple but important gestures that have significance among the normal routines of school which enable many adults and parents to say that schools are happier places today without their being able, very often, to articulate what they actually mean. If we are to talk meaningfully about the quality of education in our schools we would be foolish to ignore the many interpersonal exchanges between teacher and pupil that nurture and protect some of the most fragile self-images. (fieldnote 3/10/'90)

The significance of the incident is enhanced, I think, as it occurred without interrupting the flow of the lesson. Yet gestures of this nature are remembered long after the worksheet which was being discussed is any longer even a memory (Rutter, Maughan, Mortimore, and Ouston, 1979; Ben-Peretz, 1996). The point is that the social development of learners is of concern to the teacher even if cognitive matters overshadow its significance. Consequently, practitioners may underestimate and undervalue the importance of the attention given to these concerns, even in an incidental manner. In a very tangible way, the vignette about Tommy focuses attention on the importance of good communication and relationships as the basis for a more balanced approach to learner's social and cognitive needs, thus demonstrating also the essential unity of practice. The degree of subtlety with which Paula embedded this in her routines seems to resonate with many aspects of child-centred ideology.

Paula indicated during her initial interview that balance for her included grounding mathematical problems in the everyday experience of learners. As part of this general strategy, the class was exploring the amount of time spent looking at a variety of television programmes. Apart from the cognitive skills required, Paula added a social dimension when she suggested that 'maths is part of your life' and you should 'never be afraid' to have a go at a problem (fieldnote 2/10/'90). The same encouragement was repeated some time later after she had outlined a series of four steps that should be taken in systematically approaching the problems on the worksheet. If these steps were taken, she suggested, 'they would be less likely to panic and more likely to adopt the attitude "yes I can and I'm going to try"' (fieldnote 2/10/'90). It is also a clear indication that these structured steps were intended to scaffold the learners (Tharp and Gallimore, 1993). However, though this structure was essentially cognitive in emphasis, Paula's intention was that the learners' affective response to the challenge inherent in the learning would be adequately cushioned within the carefully structured process.

Another fieldnote extract, and subsequent correspondence and dialogue with Paula, revealed that, when she structured learning tasks, cognizance of learners' needs were integral to the planning process. Seven less able learners had spent ninety minutes completing a worksheet while Paula taught Irish to the remainder of the class. The length of the period and the isolation of the learners, which I commented on, elicited the following correspondence from Paula.

> By the time weak pupils reach me, I feel that they lack self-confidence and the belief that they *can* actually achieve. The tasks which I have set have been carefully selected with a specific purpose in mind [improving self-confidence]. I must readily admit however, that lurking underneath the aforementioned is the realization that this group has been usefully deployed to enable me to take on the task of teaching 'Gaeilge' [Irish] to the more able pupils. (Letter, 4/10/'90)

In addition to demonstrating her concern for the whole child in terms of her classroom actions, Paula's thematic approach to structuring her programme included art, PE, science, music, with significant participation by learners. The cumulative impact of extracts in this theme suggests that a broadly based programme alone is not sufficient to ensure adequate attention to the social dimension of education; how that programme is structured and mediated is critical also.

Noel

Noel's class had thirty-seven learners, and making provision for art, PE and a 'nature walk' (all of which were documented in the fieldnotes) was highly problematic as space, materials and organizational skills were taxed to the hilt. However, as Noel had indicated previously (see theme one), 'keeping the lid on things' while meeting social and cognitive needs can be trying as the following episode illustrates. Groups of four students were working on mathematical problems. The fieldnote extract demonstrates how the social needs of learners are present and when teacher control is ceded to the group, street corner and school states are temporarily aligned, thus indicating the learner's growing (pre-adolescent) awareness of gender difference — at least at the anatomical level! They trade on the ambiguity of language and the fact that the teacher was out of earshot.

> The group nearest to me did a good deal of tittering as one suggested, 'Everyone get their whole'. The following response was elicited from another member of the group, 'I don't have a whole,' while one of the girls in the group came to the rescue with the retort, 'I have another whole,' as she reached into her school bag. (fieldnote 8/10/'90)

This episode suggests that when structures facilitate social interaction among learners their own agenda may surreptitiously be added to the learning process. Practitioners, therefore, are constantly faced with making judgments as to where the balance lies between social needs and cognitive goals: retaining control and giving learners responsibility for learning. These are tensions which have resonances with the grand narratives of teaching, as well as arising from classroom dilemmas.

It is at the individual level particularly, as demonstrated by Paula above, that practitioners attempt to nurture the social while frequently focusing on a cognitive task. For example, when Laura indicated that she had difficulty with a mathematical problem, Noel attended to both her cognitive and social needs.

> Noel said to Laura, 'I'll do this with you.' Some minutes later Noel drew my attention to her first independent attempts to do these sums with great success. By drawing my attention to this success, so that the entire class could hear, Noel was attempting to boost her confidence. (fieldnote 11/10/'90)

Similarly Noel was on hand to provide support and encouragement for Tim when his confidence betrayed him. The learner's group was in the process of presenting its Irish drama to the class as part of the conversational Irish programme. Despite the competitive element which existed through the awarding of marks to each participating group, Noel came to Tim's assistance. A delicate balance was achieved between individual and group needs, though something of the competitive edge to the classroom atmosphere can be gleaned from the muted complaints by some individuals who suggested that Noel's intervention conferred unfair advantage on Tim's group. The context, if not the extract, suggests that it may be more difficult to balance social and cognitive needs in a competitive environment.

> When it came to the piece in the drama where the group was in MacDonalds, Tim was reluctant to play the part of [shop] assistant. After some verbal prodding from the others in the group, he opted out altogether. Noel realized what was going on and suggested, '... don't opt out ...'. He stepped in immediately and with a little encouragement and a jump start with a sentence for Tim he was involved and participating again. (fieldnote 11/10/'90)

This extract, in addition to illustrating how the cognitive and the social are inextricably linked, underlines the essential unity of practice also.

Summary

The purpose of this second phase of the inquiry was to narrow the substantive focus, to identify common threads of practice for closer scrutiny through a major case study in the third phase. The three themes of communication, structure, and balance are, themselves, summaries of the commonalities, complexities and variations of these cultural themes which were demonstrably influenced by practitioners' biographies and the contexts of their work.

It was clear that elaborate communication rules and routines are a critically important aspect of practice: the informal and formal glue that give meaning and coherence to practitioners' constructions of teaching. While informal routines resonate most readily with popular interpretations of child-centred practice, it was evident also that the informal imbued the formal with a character that has importance for the quality of classroom interactions, and positive classroom climate. Yet, more formal, set-piece, communication routines seemed, in several respects, to be homologous with typical interpretations of traditional teaching.

Structure, when discussed in isolation from the other themes, suggests a much more traditional approach to teaching as much of practice appears to be teacher driven, though there was evidence also of thematic planning, integration of subjects, incidental integration, as well as attempts to respond to individual needs within programme frameworks espoused by practitioners. In every instance, there was evidence of implicit or actual planning and structuring of content.

Finding an appropriate balance between the social and cognitive needs of learners was a persistent dilemma for practitioners also. There was recognition that a broadly based programme contributed towards that end but in all areas of the curriculum practitioners attempted to protect, nurture and develop learners' well-being and self-efficacy while simultaneously providing cognitive challenge.

Finally, the essential unity of practice has substantive and methodological importance. By abstracting elements of the mini case studies and presenting them in isolation there is a danger of presenting a distorted picture of individuals' practice.

While the themes do have the merit of focusing attention on common threads of practice, they should not be misread as adequate representation of, or commentary on, any participant's practice. However, they do provide a cultural lens through which a comprehensive picture of one practitioner's teaching is reconstructed in a major case study.

Notes

1   For those who do not know, Jack Charlton was a member of the English soccer team which won the world cup in 1966. He has been manager of the Irish Republic's soccer team for close to a decade during which time the national team has had unprecedented international success. Alas, in the same manner that empires have their day, Jack's reign came to an end in December 1995, thus closing an unrivalled chapter in the history of Irish soccer. It was announced at the beginning of 1996 that Jack is to be granted Irish citizenship, a Presidential prerogative.

2   Craic or crack, has nothing to do with drug abuse. It is essentially gaelic in origin but it is frequently used in English. It has also found its way into popular folk songs. Essentially it conveys the notion of bonhomie, of having good natured fun. It is one of those intangible things to which the Irish 'diaspora' frequently refers when asked what is missed when being away from Ireland. The craic, is the usual reply.

3   Crannogs are lake dwellings constructed by our Stone Age ancestors who were also probably the earliest farmers. Some of these have been reconstructed in various theme parks around the country.

Chapter 5

A Major Case Study: Participant, Context and Substance

Introduction

Through the cultural lens of structure, communication and balance, the third and final phase of the inquiry becomes an in-depth investigation of one practitioner's teaching to illuminate understanding of child-centredness and to articulate these grounded insights in an inclusive manner. Though the substantive lens of the inquiry has been set by the emergent cultural themes from the first two research phases, it is appropriate at the beginning of the third phase to address a number of issues as part of the necessary scene-setting for the major case study. These issues are: a biographical sketch of the participant; the context of the teacher's work; a typical day for the participant; the metamorphosis of the cultural themes in the major case study; the presence of the substantive themes in the participant's practice; along with some methodological comments, as well as criteria for selecting a collaborating teacher.

It is an unfortunate artifact of the inquiry's structure that the selected participant's work has not been reported. Consequently, there is an element of trust that the choice was particularly suitable. However, as trust alone is an unwarranted imposition which threatens the rigour of this inquiry, it is necessary to provide evidence that the three cultural themes were prominent features also of the teaching constructions of the sixth participant (in phase two). In the interest of economy, however, fieldnote extracts from the participant's practice are combined with comments on the metamorphosis of these cultural themes which also reflect the intrinsic merits of a case study, the idiosyncrasy of practice, as well as indicating the substantive orientation of the major case. The related issues of the participant's biography, the context of her teaching and the substantive focus of the inquiry are combined to situate and contextualize the major case study's substantive themes which are documented in detail in the three subsequent chapters.

A Biographical Sketch

Helen (a pseudonym) had been teaching for more than fifteen years, the majority of which were spent in her present context. In the last decade, she has been awarded a Bachelor of Education degree, which she pursued on a part-time basis. She was keen to further her own professional growth but experienced difficulty in locating appropriate inservice courses due to their limited and infrequent availability (Coolahan, 1994).

For more than a decade, Helen had been teaching third, fourth and fifth grades in a girls' school, though she recently had the experience of teaching a first grade. At the time of the fieldwork, she was teaching a fifth grade with twenty-one female learners; a very small class by Irish standards. It was a mixed ability class and Helen had taught approximately two-thirds of its members during the previous school year. This class had earned the reputation throughout the school of being 'slow'. When I spoke with Helen by telephone the evening before the initial fieldwork began, she expressed delight at the number of learners in her new class. However, the first set of fieldnotes recorded that 'her ambition for the year was not to have an easier time but to be able to do more for less pupils' (fieldnote 10/9/'90). The full impact of Helen's intention to do more for the twenty-one girls in her fifth class cannot be fully realized without situating her teaching constructions within the physical and socio-cultural surroundings of the school and the community she served.

Barrytown

The case study's title has been appropriated from the much acclaimed fictional writings of Roddy Doyle (1988, 1990, 1991), all of which are set in Barrytown. Apart from the ethical expediency that the title affords, the particular social circumstances in which Helen taught were evocative of many features that Doyle captures so readily in the Barrytown Trilogy. The Barrytown of the case study was an area officially designated as disadvantaged. It was generally accepted in the community, that 60–80 per cent of adults were out of work. The staff of Barrytown school estimated that between 50 per cent and 70 per cent of its learners came from homes with one parent. The people of Barrytown were disenfranchised, forgotten, ignored by mainstream society. This growing 'underclass' was a distinctive sub-culture and one of its few links with mainstream society was through the nameless, numbered hatches through which welfare entitlements were dispensed (Smith, 1992). Barrytown residents were the human fodder for reports produced by a variety of organizations (Combat Poverty Agency, 1989, 1990; Reynolds and Healy, 1988; Whelan, Hannan, and Creighton, 1991; Hannan and Shortall, 1991). These reports corroborate the commonly held belief that one-third of Ireland's population lives below the official poverty line with a disproportionate amount of the burden falling on women and children (Callan and Nolan, 1988). However, the vast majority of people in Barrytown were poor, honest, poorly educated, and unskilled, trying to do the best they could with the meagre resources at their disposal. For all the reasons given above, they were psychologically vulnerable, their self-esteem was low, their horizons limited by their context; by what officialdom describes as the 'poverty trap' (Reynolds and Healy, 1988; Kellaghan *et al.*, 1995).

Barrytown School

The learners were pale, thin, undernourished and many looked younger than their years (Watson, 1990). They stayed up late and watched television programmes that many regard as unsuitable material for impressionable minds. They frequently wore clothes out of season so that flimsy Summer tee-shirts and canvas shoes were still being worn in December. Many came to school without breakfast because they got up late and there was often no one to provide food, even if it was available. Many eagerly awaited the milk and buns provided by the Corporation which were distributed during the morning break (10.50 am). Though they were chatty, smiling, humorous children, their eyes frequently betrayed a knowing and a maturity beyond their tender years. These were the children of Barrytown, the learners who occupied the places in Helen's fifth grade.

Irish primary schools are seriously underfunded by international comparison (OECD, 1995). The poverty and deprivation of Barrytown was all too apparent in its school. There was an obvious lack of care and maintenance for the building, made more apparent in places by discoloration caused by dampness. Stairwells were dank and the drabness of the walls was accentuated by the faded pock-marked paint, chipped away by the sellotape which suspended the displayed project work of former years. Art material was almost invariably in short supply so that Helen and her colleagues constantly subsidized the system by purchasing basics such as thumb tacks, blue-tack, as well as resource books, just to keep their heads above water. As a consequence of persistent vandalism, glass in all the classroom windows had long since been replaced with non-breakable macrilon, a substance which is not quite as translucent as glass and impossible to clean. This phenomenon added significantly to the school's dilapidated appearance. Consequently, when adults and children, in the school yard and beyond, were viewed through the macrilon lens of a classroom window, they became surrealist versions of Lowry's matchstick characters. This general contextual picture imposed enormous practical and psychological constraints on Helen and her colleagues.

Despite the graffitied greyness of school and community, on my first visit to the school, I was conscious that the learners crossed a threshold in a number of ways when they entered its precinct:

> Barrytown school was fairly typical as a genre of disadvantage in the greater Dublin area. The building was surrounded by a metal perimeter fence (about 8 feet high) in an attempt to protect it from local vandals. . . .
> I wondered what was in the minds of children as they passed through these metal railings on their way to the classroom each morning. Did they become oblivious to these icons of education in disadvantaged areas after some familiarity or were these provisions some subtle means of socializing them into entering the factory gates or into places of detention in an uncertain adult life.[1] As I entered the administrative area of this large urban school, the barbed wire strategically placed to prevent nimble and adventurous limbs from negotiating their way on to roofs, prodded further thoughts along

these lines. However, all such thoughts were quickly dispelled when I meet some of the staff, but particularly the school principal and Helen herself. (fieldnote. 10/9/'90)

Classroom

Helen's classroom had an informal layout which made it difficult to say with certainty that it had a particular focal point. Its bare tiled floor gave it a Spartan appearance. However, this was more than compensated for by the ever-expanding display of learners' art, craft and project work which detailed the progress of her planned themes of sea and rainforests, giving the classroom a lived-in, comfortable, at-homeness. This was the immediate context in which the inquiry's three themes were investigated in depth.

A Typical Day

The school day began officially at 8.55 am but the number present at that time varied significantly depending on the weather and on the day of the week: Thursday was 'payday' from welfare so, for many, Friday was not a legitimate workday! The opening 20 minutes of the day were spent in informal conversation, homework copies were collected and corrected, written work was returned and the rhythms of the day were cranked up gradually. At approximately 9.15 am a few short prayers marked a formal beginning to the day's routines. From then until 10.50 am the routines of the morning proceeded at a rapid pace. They included 20 minutes of 'oral maths' for which an array of flash cards and concrete materials ensured that all concerned were involved in mental gymnastics of a mathematical nature. This gave way to a similar period for conversational Irish conducted with remarkably similar structures and routines. This pattern was interrupted briefly at about 10.15 am for just long enough to call the roll. Some 'rounds' were sung to provide variety and respite from the rigours of rapid oral work. The period from 10.20–10.50 am typically followed the pattern of two ability groups doing mathematical tasks of a practical nature such as weighing items and recording their weights. Helen gave much of her time to the weaker of the two groups where she consolidated the oral work done earlier in the morning with the whole class.

There was a ten minute break at 10.50 am but teacher and learners remained in the classroom. Learners formed various social groups at this time which I observed with interest. Immediately after break, mathematical work was resumed for a further 15–20 minutes. Copies were collected for correction after school and the focus of attention then shifted to language. This focus typically began with oral work and new vocabulary was continuously introduced, spellings were examined, sentences constructed and lists of words recorded in specially designated copies. At about 11.55 am the learners consumed the remainder of their lunches and went to the toilet before proceeding to the school yard for 30 minutes.

The period from 12.30 pm to 2.30 pm had a somewhat different rhythm than the earlier part of the day. There was more work on language which was invariably theme related, and poetry was used frequently as an integral element of the process. The routines included oral and written work as well as some formal English reading which was interspersed with periods of time spent on music with more formal music lessons on occasion. These procedures involved class teaching, two ability groups for reading, while as many as four mixed ability groups were formed to do mini projects before individuals completed their own written work on an element of the theme. Painting and craft work also formed part of the programme's mélange. The day usually came to a close with homework being assigned, copied from the blackboard, and a prayer was recited before the learners departed (2.30 pm).

Despite the importance of contextual constraints for practitioners' intentions and actions, it is the cultural themes which provide the substantive focus of the major case study.

Substantive Focus: Cultural Themes

The purpose of this element of the scene-setting for the major case study (as already indicated above) is to provide evidence that the three emergent cultural themes were indeed features of Helen's practice while simultaneously renaming them to reflect the particularity and idiosyncrasy of her teaching without distorting the emergent focus of the study. This approach orients the reader also towards the substantive detail of the major case study. I begin with the theme of structure as this is presented first in the major case study. Fieldnote extracts included in this section were compiled during the second week of the school year when fieldwork for the second phase of the study was conducted in Helen's classroom.

Structure

Planning her work thematically, because it did not 'make sense' to do it any other way, was an integral element of structuring programme content for Helen (transcript 8). However, she admitted to having difficulty finding ways of integrating mathematics and her oral Irish programme with her chosen themes. In the following extract. Helen and her class were working on the theme of the sea. The group in question had been working with the ubiquitous coffee jars and Dienes blocks, when she indicated how the learners were to be given some ownership of the teaching–learning process and the theme of the sea could embrace the mathematical concept of weight. This structuring includes a close alignment of oral, concrete, task-oriented group work also that is both child conscious and teacher directed:

> The concentration was on work with the Dienes blocks and other concrete materials in the form of the coffee jars. They explored the relationships between 1kg. and 1gm. and they could show examples of these as well as everything in between. Helen sat among them as she had done the previous day, and the same intimacy was apparent within the group where making

errors was seen to be merely a further opportunity to learn and to clarify through interaction with each other and with the materials. This group was also asked to write the names of their sea creatures and the creature's weights in their copies so that . . . this information could be transferred to flash cards. This, in its turn, would become part of the fabric of the work in mathematics for the following day. (fieldnote 12/9/'90)

Before the fieldwork for the major case study began, I conducted a second interview with Helen to re-establish field relations, and to discuss her planning for the remainder of the Michaelmas term. When I had been in her classroom at the beginning of the school year, she had structured content around the theme of the sea. This work had been completed and the new thematic structure was the rainforests. Though this was the organizing focus of her teaching, it emerged from the interview, in addition to further data analysis and fieldwork, that the anchoring thread of her structure was an emphasis on language. Developing the learners' language was the skeleton of Helen's teaching constructions and the rainforest theme was the content which she chose to put flesh on those bones. Her consistent intention was to improve the language competency of the learners and this thrust provided the very vertebrae of her structure.

During the second interview, I asked Helen to indicate the impact that the social context of the school had on her teaching. She unhesitatingly suggested that it was most apparent on learners' language. After Helen had commented on an earlier draft of the major case study, I asked her how she would communicate her sense of the learners' limited language fluency to someone unfamiliar with her context. She was reluctant to provide the kind of detail I sought as she thought that other practitioners might interpret this as an excuse for tailoring her teaching constructions in particular ways. Part of her reluctance stemmed from her own tacit realization that having grown accustomed to language deficit, it had become the norm, and therefore no longer noteworthy.

Other practitioners in Barrytown were approached for corroborating evidence in relation to poor language, and the most commonly recurring phrase which they (and Helen) used was: 'you can take nothing for granted'. Consequently, practitioners must begin, they said, from a much 'lower base' (transcript 8). Though familiarity ensured that Helen and her colleagues were no longer consciously aware of language deficit as a problem because it was embedded in their practice, nevertheless its presence had significant implications for Helen's classroom constructions. The particulars of her case, continuous data analysis, and the evidence of others in the site, suggested that the theme of structure would more accurately reflect her practice if it were renamed. Thus structure metamorphosed into: *Language, The Leitmotiv of Helen's Practice.*

Communication

Structure without vitality is unlikely to have a significant impact on learners. Helen animated her programme structure and roused her learner's minds to life with a series of communication routines that had been honed in response to context and learners.

Helen's initial interview revealed that she did not want the learners in her class to be 'afraid' of her and that mutual respect enabled her and her class to enjoy the attendant *'repartee'*, an indispensable element of the Dublin character (transcript 8). This intention was given practical expression through the rapport, relationships and respect for individuals which were important elements of the informal as well as the formal communication routines in her classroom. The following extract gives implicit recognition to issues of importance for advocates of child-centred ideology such as individuality, and cultivation of a positive classroom atmosphere.

> Helen took some time to correct copies which contained the assigned home-work for the previous evening. She invited one of the girls to come up to her table saying, 'You did your homework carefully and neatly,' and gave her a sticker with a smiley face which said 'good work'. 'If you try hard and get the wrong answer, but did it carefully, you still get a badge,' Helen told them. 'You didn't call me up,' said Trish. 'Was it sloppy?' [inquired Helen]. 'Come up and I'll show you why you didn't get a badge,' responded Helen. 'Oh you did,' she declared as she opened Trish's copy. With that, many others were also awarded badges . . . These served to encourage everybody. The little episode with Trish also indicated that she was not afraid to ask how she had got on, and Helen did not attempt to make any cover-up of her own error. Rather, she went on to present the badge in a very positive and magnanimous manner. I overheard one of the girls as she spoke to her immediate neighbour while putting a sticker in her copy, 'Me Ma is going to think that I'm great'. It is hard to put a price on this reinforcement. (fieldnote 11/9/'90)

Helen's more formal communication routines included a judicious mix of class and group teaching. In the following extract, she had done oral work with the entire class and, having assigned weighing tasks to the more able group, she began further work with the less able learners. This work was given a very practical orientation by using a whole range of coffee jars with different capacities that concretized and consolidated their grasp of the concept of weight. This practical focus for their mathematical work connected with the concrete operations stage of Piaget's developmental theory. The atmosphere was informal and the relationships between learners and teacher spilled over into the pedagogical exchanges where individual needs and abilities were respected by all.

> They were building on the oral work done that morning and the coffee jars were pressed into action again. Additional material was provided in the form of Dienes blocks and these were used to good effect by the pupils to explain the relationship between tens, hundreds and thousands in decimal terminology. This time they were all seated around a nest of tables, nine pupils with Helen seated among them. The atmosphere was informal and

business-like, they all participated, everyone contributed and additional help was provided by both teacher and pupils as required. Though the atmosphere was very informal the programme was teacher directed. (fieldnote 10/9/'90)

The manner in which Helen combined structure and communication took on a unique quality in the setting in response to her perceptions of learners' needs and their context. As a reflection of the particular quality of her communication routines, this theme was renamed: *Conversational Style*. It became apparent also that the structure and communication themes were intimately connected and that some distortion of the essential unity of practice was unavoidable in presentation. The communication theme not only provided additional insights into her practice, but it shed light also on matters of central concern to child-centred ideology such as individuality, the needs, interests and abilities of learners, their social development, and the entire communication edifice, interpersonal and pedagogical, that facilitates the teaching–learning process.

Balance

Due to the poor socio-economic circumstances of her fifth grade class, Helen was faced with the constant dilemma of finding the appropriate balance between the social and cognitive needs of learners. Just how finely tuned this balance needed to be was hinted at in the following extract. It also gave some insight into the impact which the contextual constraint of poverty has on teaching when the most basic requirements for an art class have to be accumulated by foraging. This was necessary as the raw material for their sea creatures.

Helen had sent one of the girls to the school secretary some time earlier to get a large cardboard box which would hold all the 'odds and ends' that would be useful in constructing sea creatures. She had a book of the same title with very colourful examples of things which they might like to make. The language potential was again exploited so that the large cardboard box had four different labels written on each side: 'odds and ends', 'bits and pieces', 'bric-a-brac' and 'recycles'. A different pupil was asked to do this inscribing with a large felt marker. 'I can't do this, I'm no good at this,' protested one of the girls as she wrote. 'Go on, you're doing fine,' came the encouraging reply from Helen. Suddenly it became apparent how vulnerable these learners were. Any task outside their normal routine and the basic confidence to 'give it a go' was lacking. (fieldnote 11/9/'90)

Because of the ever-present need to provide support for the self-image and confidence of these learners, much of Helen's energy was directed towards responding to individual needs in a way that enabled the social and cognitive development of learners to progress in tandem. As happened repeatedly during the fieldwork for the second phase, fieldnotes became a catalyst for dialogue: an important means of revealing practitioner's reasons for their established routines. My conversation with Helen surfaced issues about balance relating to contextual constraints and individual learner's needs.

> When I spoke to Helen after school this issue [balancing the social and cognitive needs of learners] became a topic of conversation. Knowing what she did about the backgrounds and family circumstances of these children, she was at pains to protect whatever equilibrium and stability they had achieved within the classroom context. Challenging them in a rigorous intellectual sense or, as we say, 'stretching them', might be sufficient to provoke major confrontation with a child and/or its parent(s). (fieldnote 14/9/'90)

The approach that Helen adopted towards the dilemma posed by simultaneously promoting the social and cognitive needs of learners taxed her programme framework and her conversational style in a unique manner. Its particular characteristics suggested a more appropriate title for this theme: *Scaffolding and Shepherding*. This particular cultural lens became the substantive framework through which these tensions in Helen's practice were documented. This theme relates in significant ways to the principle of individuality and the full and harmonious development of learners; both axioms of child-centred ideology.

Selecting a Participant

Though the emergent themes were present in complex and various ways in the classrooms of all participants in the second phase, the overriding consideration in selecting a participant was substantive: to select a teacher and a context particularly suited to in-depth investigation of the inquiry's problem through the lens of the three cultural themes. There were a number of reasons that Helen's classroom was chosen as the most appropriate site for in-depth investigation of the substantive issue. Her class was unusually small by Irish standards and, with twenty-one learners, it would be easier to investigate the entire communication network constructed within the classroom. Furthermore, the communication theme appeared to be particularly prominent in that classroom. Similarly, due to the background of the learners themselves, Helen thought that it was necessary to pay particular attention to structuring and sequencing curriculum content. As part of her strategy in relation to structure, she was also very committed to planning thematically. The disadvantaged social and economic circumstances of her school appeared particularly suited to examining tensions between social and cognitive development in a way that would not be as striking in other contexts. She had enjoyed participating in phase two, field relations were very positive, and she was more than willing to invest the time which was necessary for a more in-depth investigation. These were the substantive and methodological reasons for choosing Helen as the participant who would enable me to increase further my understanding of child-centred teaching, through in-depth, interpretive accounts of her classroom constructions.

Though each of the three themes is presented individually, and in separate chapters, they should be understood as contributing to a comprehensive picture of child-centred practice. The initial focus on *Leitmotiv* detailed in Chapter 6 is relatively narrow, while the other two themes, in Chapters 7 and 8, gradually pan out to reveal further layers of meaning in the complex process of classroom practice. Helen has read earlier drafts of the major case study and she has corroborated my reconstruction of her teaching as being accurate in spirit, substance and detail. Mention of the particulars of the case is a timely reminder to focus briefly on pertinent methodological issues.

A Note on Method

The fieldnotes that were written during phase two were added to the documented evidence accumulated during an additional thirteen days spent in Helen's classroom during a period of six weeks. Eighteen days in all were spent in the site, providing in excess of 200 pages (A4, single-spaced) of fieldnotes which became the raw material for the next three chapters. These data were accumulated, therefore, over a total period of seven weeks. A continuous presence in the site was avoided during the fieldwork for the major case study. This strategy allowed ample time for data analysis, as well as for writing more reflective fieldnotes than was feasible or appropriate during the second phase. In general, I planned to be in Helen's classroom for three days each week; I could be present on consecutive or alternate days depending on what was happening in the classroom. This flexible arrangement enabled me to provide Helen with a copy of the most recent set of fieldnotes on the evening prior to my next visit to her classroom. Consequently, we devoted 45–60 minutes after school to reflective dialogue on the data. This arrangement proved to be an invaluable means of gaining insight into the 'why' of her teaching constructions which were incorporated into subsequent fieldnotes. This practice increased the 'trustworthiness' (Lincoln and Guba, 1985) of these 'insider' accounts (Erickson, 1986; Hammersley and Atkinson, 1983).

Chapter 6

Theme One: Language,
The Leitmotiv of Helen's Practice

Introduction

The term leitmotiv conveys the idea of a 'leading theme', which owes its original meaning to orchestral work where it was regarded as 'a kind of musical tag that identifies a particular character or idea that recurs . . . at appropriate moments, often with subtle variation' (O'Donnell, 1990, p. 139). The term is particularly suited to describing Helen's intention to improve the language capacity of her learners. It also communicates a sense of the pervasiveness of this structure to all aspects of her practice. This theme documents the various stages of this linguistic-curricular structure that she created.

When language development is mentioned within the boundaries of the case, the English language is the focus of attention. There are six distinct phases or *cognitive steps*[2] identifiable as part of Helen's structured approach to providing language experience for learners that effectively encompass the entire framework of her teaching. With a view to exposing the backbone of this structure, details of the first theme have been stripped to a minimum. In addition to the desire for clarity, this approach avoids unnecessary duplication as embellishments of the theme occur through investigation of the other two cultural foci: communication and balance.

My description of the six cognitive steps remains close to the nature of Helen's practice and can be described in the following terms: feeding, regurgitation, consolidation, transition from oral to written language, group written work, and finally, individual independent writing. In addition to these six steps, intermediate stages were added also to facilitate particular individuals or groups of learners. They were sequentially ordered to provide maximum support for learners initially, while gradually encouraging greater independence in their use of language. Within the structure of Helen's teaching, these stages are not highly differentiated so that transitions are not immediately apparent. This is an intrinsic element of the structure, thus enabling learners to move back and forth on this linguistic platform as their confidence, competence and independence allow.

Cognitive Steps One and Two

Helen indicated that one of the frustrations of her context was: 'They are always feeding off you,' meaning that learners were dependent on the teacher (transcript 8).

Consequently, the cognitive structures she created were intended to wean the learners from dependence to more independent learning. She had begun to work on the rainforests theme immediately after the Hallowe'en break but she had lost the rhythm of the work due to an additional and unexpected closure because the school's heating system had broken down. These were the circumstances in which she was attempting to re-establish the first two cognitive steps in the programme's structure.

> She began by asking individuals in the class to provide various sentences of the story about the jaguar. They responded that he had been sleeping in the forest, lying 'limply' on a branch. Leaving this location, he headed for the village and 'jumped over the fence'. He 'grabbed a little kid by the scruff of the neck' and proceeded to 'scramble carefully' back to the forest to devour his prey. This language was virtually verbatim what Helen had 'fed' to the class some two weeks earlier. If the earlier phase of the process of language development can be described as 'feeding' them, then the present one, which I had just witnessed, could be said to be the 'regurgitation' phase. (fieldnote 26/11/'90)

This structuring, and the process of interaction which it promotes, underlines the social nature of language acquisition and has striking similarities with what Bakhtin (1981) termed 'ventriloquation': 'the process whereby one voice speaks through another voice' — in this instance, the voice of the teacher (Wertsch, 1991, pp. 59–61).

Because of the importance attached by Helen to language development, she required all subject matter to contribute to that process and the structure reflects this emphasis. However, the prominence and pervasiveness of language was also more visible due to her thematic approach to planning: these cognitive steps permeated every aspect of her teaching. Thematic structuring and sequencing of content to dovetail with learners' needs seemed particularly homologous with popular interpretations of child-centred ideology, yet it was teacher directed. Even learners' work in music was linked to the theme of the rainforest. The integrated cocktail which resulted might be legitimately described as jungle music with a difference!

> Each of the three [mixed ability] groups were asked to put together a song, a rhythm and some movement that would deal with the sub-plot of 'The Hunt of the Jaguar' by the villagers. This attempted to capitalize on the work done on rhythm earlier in the day, as well as on the language of the poem which had been presented, and the language just written on the board. (fieldnote 13/11/'90)

Though the approach to language development was almost exclusively oral at this point, the structure had a future orientation as lists of words being compiled became the basis for work in spellings and written exercises at a later stage. As subsequent details revealed, structure, content and pedagogy were intimately connected, thus drawing attention to the essential unity of practice. The benefit of an integrative, thematic structure is apparent when the medium of music becomes a means of refining learners' understanding of descriptive words for rainforest creatures. This structure appears to provide additional pedagogical possibilities not available in a rigidly subject-differentiated curriculum. Nevertheless, if subjects such as music or art are continuously used in this supportive role, learners may internalize the hidden curriculum which, in this instance, may perpetuate 'the basics' and 'the frills' dichotomy. Such a distinction suggests that subject areas which are additional to the 3Rs have been grafted to a well-established root system rather than having a distinct identity in their own right; they play a role that is supportive and lend variety to traditional fare. The following extract marks a transition from cognitive step two to three where ownership rather than mere regurgitation is being encouraged through learners' active participation.

> As if playing with the very notion of language itself, Helen invited the three groups to 'do the story using the drums . . . no words'. She asked them to do this after each of the groups had presented its story as requested earlier. Now they were being asked to interpret the key words of the story through the use of drums and tambourines. This promoted some interesting conversation on the more precise meaning of words such as padding etc. Paradoxically, banning the use of words facilitated the exploration of a more precise understanding of the language. (fieldnote 13/11/'90)

Cognitive Step Three

Spending intermittent time in the classroom had the paradoxical effect of making it easier to unearth Helen's programme structure which enabled the pupils to progress. The third cognitive step (consolidation) was apparent, though the learner's capacity to avail of these steps varied. Helen had given me the task of identifying the best book that the learners had produced as part of the final phase of their work on the sea theme, and this task enabled me to identify her structures more clearly. The following extract also reveals that the more able learners were already benefiting from the structure. They were using language in the present thematic context (rain-forests) which had been learned during work on the sea theme earlier in the term. This process resonates with interpretations of child-centred ideology which suggest that individual initiative should be fostered and supported so that transfer of learning can occur.

> I noted when reading the material they had written . . . that they tended to give back the language which Helen 'gave' to them, when she was developing the theme of the sea, without any embellishment that would indicate a degree of ownership or initiative on the part of the learner. Helen was in agreement with this general thesis and as we spoke, the phrase 'always

feeding from you' and getting so little back seemed to take on a new meaning. Through the experience of language — via poetry and drama — Helen attempted to create a classroom climate in which the learners experienced new language at first hand. They entered, through the development of the rainforests theme, into a linguistic world that helped them to understand, explore and to acquire new information about the tropical forests. This was conducted through the communicative process that Helen had constructed in her pedagogical style which I had identified as being conversational. It was noticeable that the more able in the class made connections between the language which they acquired while exploring the theme of the sea . . . and the language of the present theme. (fieldnote 26/11/'90)

Helen's intentions, as revealed through the cognitive steps she constructed, enabled learners to 'internalize external knowledge and convert it into a tool of conscious control', thus fostering their independence (Bruner, 1989, pp. 24–5). Structuring learning to foster learner's ownership and independence has been identified as an important dimension of teaching though it is less frequently associated directly with popular images of child-centredness. My fieldnotes recorded the following at the time.

. . . there was a need for the scaffolding to enable the learner to experience the language and the manner in which Helen actually succeeds in doing this was admirable. . . . What I had called ownership earlier, Bruner (1983) refers to as *handover*. The process is described as follows: 'The essence of the process is that learners do not remain for ever propped up by the scaffolding of adult assistance, but come to take control of the process for themselves.' (Edwards and Mercer, 1987, p. 23) (fieldnote 26/11/'90)

This perspective has remarkable similarities with the idea of assistance through the Vygotskian ZPD which is followed by independence (Vygotsky, 1989; Cole *et al.*, 1987; Wertsch, 1989, 1991; Tharp and Gallimore, 1993; Woods, 1993a; Woods and Jeffrey, 1996).

The cognitive steps, which have already been identified, were designed to enable the learners to move back and forth within the framework depending on their level of confidence and competence. This flexibility is commonly regarded as an important asset of child-centredness so that individual needs and abilities can be accommodated rather than everyone marching in step. The steps interrelate and overlap quite deliberately to facilitate learners' relatively painless movement from the dependency end of the continuum towards greater independence. In the following extract, the quiz, as a prominent feature of Helen's conversational style, is evident also. The routine is intended to promote greater understanding and ownership of new vocabulary by playing games. Play, too, as a means of imaginative engagement has many associations with the rhetoric of child-centredness and is often anathema to critics of progressivism who regard it as trivial and time-wasting. Despite the apparent child-centred features of the encounter, the process was orchestrated, if not entirely directed, by the teacher: a factor which resonates with perspectives on traditional schooling.

> They began to read the poems which Helen had distributed before the break. This time there was the additional exercise of using the language of the poem in addition to the 'riddles'[3] which had been used earlier, to develop oral competence and to encourage greater precision in thought and sentence construction. Individuals provided sentences (for the next 10 minutes) so that the others could decide what forest creature they had in mind. Three clues were provided such as reptile, slithers, swallows its prey whole. Another example was — stench, nocturnal, eats anything, scuttles along. The responses to these were a snake and the moon rat. The final set of clues Fran provided was primate, leaves, and is often captured by poachers when very young and taken from its mother. The class did not have any difficulty deciding that this was the orang-utan. While there was fun, activity and involvement here, there was also very serious intent to enable the learners to be more comfortable and secure in their oral use of the language which they had earlier experienced. It also encouraged precision and refinement in their understanding of the language to enable them to provide adequate clues in the riddles they compiled. (fieldnote 26/11/'90)

The first three steps of this cognitive structure seemed straightforward and unambiguous. However, due to the context and social background of the learners in Helen's classroom, the process frequently seemed like 'one step forward two steps backwards' as she struggled to consolidate gains in linguistic competence and independence. The evidence provided in the following extract indicates the frustration experienced by Helen while she attempted to maintain progress. It illuminates why she placed such emphasis on language, while it exemplifies also one of the frequently cited hallmarks of child-centredness, namely, responsiveness to context and to learners' needs. Helen's structures needed to be watertight to provide adequate support for the learners. Yet, too much structural rigidity creates dependence rather than facilitates independence, which was her intention. The routine itself was typical of her oral work.

> Some moments later, when a learner identified the shape being concealed by Helen as a 'right angled triangle', Maeve was asked to repeat the answer. She had great difficulty getting her tongue around the words and on the third attempt she succeeded. Some minutes later, Marge experienced similar difficulty when attempting to say the word trapezium. The latter child was far from being dull. She was very lively, helpful and cooperative in class, with more confidence than many of the others. I am deliberately drawing attention to these little episodes in order to highlight the apparent poverty of language which exists among the majority of the learners in Helen's class. It is only when this context is understood that the *modus operandi* in terms of purpose and approach to teaching construction makes sense. (fieldnote 28/11/'90)

Cognitive Step Four

One of the threads that linked the first three cognitive steps of Helen's structure was oracy. The variety of pedagogical routines she employed was designed to maximize language use, thus promoting ownership and more independent use of new vocabulary. For the remainder of the language process there was a very gradual attempt to encourage learners to write with as much independence as possible. The fourth step fostered greater independence through a combination of class, group and individual work: it was a transitional stage between the oral and the written word. This transition was not something which happened suddenly. Rather, there was a build up, in a continuously structured manner, making the process almost imperceptible to the observer and, I presume, to learners also.

> The primary concern at this point in the process was to give the learners confidence in handling language with a minimum of involvement on the part of the teacher. This was one of the interesting elements of written exercises that the conversational style of communication underlined. The teacher was always on hand when the work was oral so there was a continuous safety net. When it came to written work this safety net was less obvious to the learner. The pupil had to take the initiative in seeking the assistance of the teacher. Was this part of the process . . . that Bruner referred to as 'handover'? As if to emphasize this transitional dimension to the task and the process, Helen provided a series of flash cards which she placed on various ledges around the room to assist those who experienced difficulty. When some of the class subsequently asked her for specific responses to particular questions, she indicated the location of these flash cards . . . that would answer the question for them, and [she also told them] that they had to take initiatives for themselves.
>
> The flash cards in this context served two functions. They helped the teacher to put some distance between herself and the learners, and thus encourage the learners to look elsewhere (other than to the teacher) for assistance in solving their problems. However, in doing this the teacher was also recognizing that this was a daunting task for some of her class, thus necessitating the provision of a halfway house between dependence and independence. In this sense there was a tension between the need to develop ownership and independence while at the same time providing sufficient support for the learner to enable her to take that vital step. The cognitive steps that Helen created in the stairway to independence for the learners were influenced by her perception of the learners themselves. Her understanding was that their confidence was fragile so that the cognitive steps needed to be relatively short to facilitate a corresponding growth in the social and emotional confidence of the learner which go hand in glove with the cognitive steps which Helen had mapped out in her structured approach to linguistic independence. Attempting to build-in success at each step in her teaching was an important element of the programme she constructed. (fieldnote 26/11/'90)

Nevertheless, despite her best intentions, plans and actions, the uncertainty of practice remained, which was both its challenge and its frustration. The practice of rehearsing language orally was an important element of the structure that nudged the learners towards independence. The structure simultaneously attempted to increase their confidence while encouraging them to appropriate the new words for their written work: a process that was consistent with interpretations of child-centredness which suggest that responsiveness to learners' needs and cultural context is critical to classroom routines.

'We will be writing a poem today,' she announced and proceeded to produce a scrapbook from which she read two poems which, she informed the girls, were written by former pupils some years previously. The intent at this point . . . was to indicate, through the presentation of these two poems, that if former pupils could do it, so could they. It was to make the next step to independence seem less daunting. She read the first poem, 'How Bats Fly', followed by 'Flying Mice', which was read twice. The learners were clearly impressed and one of them inquired, 'What class were they?' There was an air of disbelief when Helen informed them that the young poets were in fourth class, a grade lower than themselves. Suddenly, from being a source of encouragement, these poems, for some at least, were an intimidation. Helen, as always, sensitive to their needs, responded, 'Aren't they good? You'll be just as good,' in a reassuring tone. (fieldnote 28/11/'90)

Further bridge-building between the cognitive steps was introduced when one of the more able learners was asked to read a poem she had written the previous evening. Helen was rewarding her for her efforts as well as signalling to the others that if one of their own could do it, then so could they (fieldnote 28/11/'90). This sensitivity on Helen's part resonates with important elements of child-centredness as one learner's need for praise is simultaneously accommodated with provision of encouragement for less able members of the class. This is the kind of sophistication and complexity that increases the quality of practice where structure and flexibility are employed simultaneously to meet different individual's needs.

Further evidence of the ongoing tension between the need for structure and flexibility was apparent as the emphasis shifted from oral to written work. It is difficult to maintain a clear distinction in this context between teacher control and direction, on the one hand, and the apparent need to structure teaching and learning opportunities in ways that facilitate and encourage greater independence in learners, on the other. As emphasis shifted from oral to written work, pedagogical routines needed to be tailored in ways that fostered independence, while Helen remained in command.

When it came to determining the composition of the three groups, Helen indicated, 'I'd prefer to divide myself'. Her intention was to provide three mixed ability groups to ensure a degree of cooperation and cross fertilization within each group. When the three groups were seated she suggested that one member of the group act as a recording secretary while the others concentrate on getting the language right. None of the groups bought this suggestion and every member, regardless of ability or extent of contribution, wrote the same words as were suggested by the group. I noted with interest their enthusiasm to write as this implied that they were keen to establish ownership of the language, that they were exhibiting a keenness to take the cognitive step which Helen had so carefully contrived over a period of days and which was about to culminate in this poem. The right ambience was created when Helen indicated to Maeve that a tape of Grieg's music would be appropriate in the background. (fieldnote 28/11/'90)

The pervasiveness of structure and the degree of control that Helen exercised over the process seemed consistent with notions of traditional schooling though it resonates also with the conclusion that 'when pupils were given a high degree of choice as to the content and nature of their work activities, the results tended to be poorer pupil progress', thus reinforcing the benefits of highly structured learning experiences (Mortimore *et al.*, 1988, p. 230).

Helen had spent a considerable amount of time, at an earlier period, discussing the content of the poem which each of the three mixed ability groups were being encouraged to prepare and write. Several phrases were rehearsed as possible means of describing images which could be included. When the three groups were instructed to actually write the poems, it became apparent that the more able took the initiative thus, in Vygotskian terms, they provided a model for their less able peers. In some instances, they resorted to actually writing some of the lines for the less able, particularly those who had been called away by Helen who was correcting homework. The beginnings of the three poems produced by each of the groups are reproduced here (fieldnote 28/11/'90). Each individual in the group wrote the same lines, as dictated by the more able. Despite the initiatives, structures and encouragement by the teacher, there remained a remarkable degree of dependence, by the learners, on the language of the teacher.

The Hunt (1)

Ink black night,
rain pouring, moon shining,
jaguar stalking,
owl monkey chattering,
chatter, chatter, chatter,
snakes hissing,
gorilla and baby kissing ah!
tiger padding,
alligator snapping, leaves
crunching, moon rat
munching,
all of a sudden white eye
staring;

The Hunt (2)

Ink black bandaged night,
rain falling,
wind howling,
leopards stalking,
parrots squawking,
cobra hissing,
tiger growling,
big white eye suddenly
appears;

The Hunt (3)

Ink black bandaged night,
rain pouring, moon shining,
noisy howler monkey howls
loudly,
staring owl monkey peers
cautiously,
mother Orang Utan feeds
babies, peers down cautiously
from tree sees white eye
gleaming brightly;

Those familiar with the achievements of fifth class pupils may not be particularly impressed by this poetry. Consequently, it is important to put the present process in context. Apart from attempting to communicate how hard both teacher and learners had worked through these four cognitive steps, it is important to communicate the pupils' and teacher's responses to the formers' written efforts. The interpretive piece which follows was written immediately after the poems in the fieldnotes.

... these poems represented the very best attempts of the three groups to construct their own poem out of the language that Helen had fastidiously taught to them over a period of time. She recorded her appreciation of their efforts in successfully negotiating a further step towards more independent use of language. She invited each of the groups in turn to the top of the class, where they read their creations together. This was quite deliberate so that no matter how minimal the input of a particular individual, all could take pride and some credit for the effort. Each of the three groups was also asked to nominate an individual who read the poem a second time after the group performance. The other groups applauded ... enthusiastically. Helen had suggested at various stages during the composition of the poems that she was not overly concerned with spellings. She informed them now that this was being regarded as a first draft and a second would be written into their copies tomorrow. Asking individuals to read was also a subtle means of recognizing the leading role played by some individuals in the process. Helen instructed them to put their pages in their folders and pronounced, 'I'm very pleased with that'. (fieldnote 28/11/'90)

The evident provision of feedback and positive stroking to learners resonates with the conclusion that 'time spent on praise or neutral feedback . . . was related to positive effects' (Mortimore *et al.*, 1988, p. 230). Subtlety and sophistication were also evident when the groups were given the opportunity to nominate the most able to read their work a second time, thus rewarding individuals as well as providing positive feedback to the groups. Such sophistication resonates readily with particular assets of child-centredness such as responsiveness to individual needs.

Helen recognized that without the support of the mixed ability groups, some of the less able learners would not be capable of writing a poem on their own at this stage. Nevertheless, several days later, with many additional hours of oral work, some of which had been conducted in ability groups, each individual was asked to write her own poem. This additional element of the fourth step attempted to foster greater independence by making the task an individual rather than a group one. The poem which follows was intended to mark the completion of the transition from oral to written work as an important point in the structured journey towards greater independence. The poem was written by one of the more able learners. (fieldnote 6/12/'90)

> At night the jaguar stalks through the jungle,
> Its silent figure creeps and crawls,
> Then it pounces on its prey
> And munches its prey happily, Then it grooms itself,
> Shadowy hunter that kills at night.

Cognitive Step Five

There were similarities between steps four and five as the mixed ability groups planned a mini project to which each individual contributed. These final stages on the continuum, towards more independent use of language, were concentrated in group and individual work, while some preparation was done on a class basis. The cognitive skills necessary for group work proved their usefulness also in the final element. It became apparent that each component was preparatory to the next: taking one cognitive step anticipated a subsequent move on the stairway to greater autonomy. It is necessary to realize also that this cognitive stairway was built over a period of six to seven weeks, so that there was regurgitation and consolidation associated with every step of the process. Four mixed ability groups were formed for this particular phase of the language programme.

... they were instructed to 'get into groups for the mini projects' which were formed the previous week. This was one of the final stages in the spiral of language development which Helen incorporated into her curriculum. It was an activity where each group was expected to report on some aspect of the rainforest theme. Helen indicated to them that she did not want masterpieces or detail at this point. Rather, she required the outline of a plot. The connection between doing a project and the need for a similar structure in writing a story was obvious. The project was preparatory also because it gave practice in the cognitive skills of organizing material in a logical, sequential fashion. It was preparatory therefore to the final stage in the language spiral, which required that each individual write her own story. (fieldnote 12/12/'90)

There were intermediate stages that the different groups were expected to pass through such as putting an outline of their plan together, and discussing this with the teacher. When plans had been revised and amended to measure up to the exacting standards Helen attempted to uphold, there was still an oral dimension to the process which owed something to the context. The presence of the oral dimension at this point was also indicative of the continuing tension in the learners themselves (and Helen's cognizance of it) between their desire for security and their struggle to gain additional independence, both of which were provided by the language edifice she constructed.

The four groups involved in the preparation of the mini projects on the rainforests were asked to give an oral presentation. What they said obviously had been revised with a tighter structure than was evident two days earlier. Helen had already indicated that a considerable amount of time had been spent on this the previous day, as the standard of work in earlier drafts was unacceptable to her. This too was a source of frustration to Helen. Having done so much work over the last several weeks, she did not feel she should have to push so hard to extract the amount she did from the class. Each member of the group was to be responsible for a page or sometimes two pages of the book. The individual in charge of a group introduced the theme: 'The theme for our mini project is "Death of the Rainforests" and the first page will be contents followed by where they are' [meaning where the rainforests are located worldwide]. Each individual in the team stood in line at the top of the room to tell her part/page in the sequence. (fieldnote 18/12/'90)

The oral dimension that persisted through this stage of the process also ensured that the eventual outcome might still be influenced by the teacher. If Helen was unhappy with the outline of the work given by each of the groups, she could intervene and negotiate additional refinements. The process of having all the learners stand in front of the class also derived significance from the context. Although the priority at this point was completion of written work, the oral presentations served the further additional functions of clarification while reinforcing social gains. The following extract indicates that though the structure was highly teacher directed it was also child-centred to the degree that it was responsive to learners' needs, thus retaining some flexibility.

> While Helen granted autonomy during this phase of the theme process, she had no hesitation in intervening when she thought that the group was capable of doing more. Also, given that the study of the theme had been largely teacher driven until now, the content element of the projects was already reasonably well known to many of the learners. This stage of the process was concerned primarily with the logic of presentation, with sequencing ideas and material to facilitate the process of moving from oral presentation to written work. (fieldnote 18/12/'90)

Further differentiation was added at this stage in the process as negotiation between teacher and learners became more individualized and Helen encouraged greater effort from those she thought were not doing their best. This approach suggests that Helen was not applying some arbitrary standard to the learners' work. Rather, the norms applied to individuals' work were shaped by her expectations of them. There were further consultations, redraftings (for some learners as many as four and five times) which became quite a frustration for teacher and learners, as patience became frayed here and there. The brief extract below conveys something of the atmosphere during these sessions. This work was being completed only days before the Christmas holidays when it was difficult to encourage the learners to concentrate on completing their tasks.

> The poor quality of some of the work which Helen was scrutinizing was a source of frustration. This frustration was sometimes audible in the exchanges she had with various individuals. This was part of a general pattern to which Helen frequently made reference. It was that *déjà vu* sense of 'after all the work that I have done . . . this is all they are capable of doing on their own . . . what have I been killing myself for'. This seemed to be a permanent feature of the context in which Helen was a practitioner. (fieldnote 18/12/'90)

When Helen commented on the permanent tension in her work which derived, in part, from her perception of learners' lack of progress, she insisted that it was necessary to 'keep after them', otherwise they would not perform to their ability. However, even in these trying circumstances there were moments when all the effort suddenly seemed worthwhile, and all the accumulated frustrations along the way evaporated in a feeling of well being that said; 'Yes, even for just some learners, significant progress had been made.'

As indicated earlier, it had been my practice to deliver fieldnotes to Helen before returning to the field, on alternate days, so that our ongoing dialogue could be sustained. On this particular evening, the more usual feeling of frustration had been replaced with a sense of satisfaction.

> When I called to Helen last evening with the most up-to-date set of field-notes she commented that they had spent about two hours drafting and redrafting pages for the mini projects yesterday and this resulted in work of a quality in which she took some satisfaction. She had collected it all for scrutiny on the previous evening and obviously the feedback was constructive and helpful. The books that each of the four groups had completed were visible on the tables when I entered the classroom the following morning, and the quality of the work was impressive. While one of the groups had indicated [some days previously] at their oral presentation that they would have a page as a surprise; neither I nor Helen anticipated a short little drama. It was an impressive, sensitive dialogue between a logger and a rainforest inhabitant about the cutting down of the trees. It indicated a reasonably sophisticated internalization of the moral problem. (fieldnote 20/12/'90)

The presentation had all the hallmarks of a 'critical incident' in teaching (Woods, 1993a, 1993b) or what is described by McLaren (1986, p. 236) as a 'great moment of teachability'.

Cognitive Step Six

The mini projects were primarily a group exercise. The sixth and final cognitive step in this complex structure shifted from group to individual independent work in the form of a written story: the culmination of several weeks' work. After a long and, at times, arduous journey, the independence end of the language continuum had been reached. All the elements of Helen's teaching were building towards the act of independent writing. The following extract illustrates the subtle interdependence of the leitmotiv of language and theme of rainforests: as dependent as creepers are on trees. Although the inclusion of this lengthy extract is intended primarily to indicate the elaborate structures Helen constructed, it also focuses attention on the complexity of these structures when pedagogical routines are woven into the fabric of the teaching–learning process. From a methodological perspective, there is greater awareness of the importance of complexity and detail for constructing a more sophisticated and more inclusive understanding of child-centredness. When this occurs, a januformity of teaching traditions becomes more apparent, where teacher direction and learner autonomy, programme prescription and student independence are perceived as persistent dilemmas rather than ideological posturings. Nevertheless, getting the synergy right becomes critical to the quality of these learning encounters.

> Helen began to prepare the class for the final phase of the rainforest theme. This task required each individual to write a story. She drew the entire class into a circle around her by moving some of the tables to one side. She began this process by inviting them to enter imaginatively into the early morning life in the forest and to begin to tell her the various chores

that they completed before having breakfast. This approach served the dual purpose of setting the context for constructing the story as well as revising material already encountered. They responded that . . . they had collected pineapples, gathered sticks for the fire so that mother could put on a vegetable stew, cultivated the vegetable patch, watered and grazed the buffalo, and some had also milked these animals. Into this tranquil scene Helen introduced noisy chain saws with triangular teeth and groups of men, armed with these, were felling trees at the rate of one every 10 minutes. There was even a little computation thrown in as they were asked how many trees could be cut down by six men in 30 and 60 minutes. As Helen presented this scenario in dramatic fashion, she invited the group to comment on what they saw transpiring before their very eyes. She reminded them of what they had learned from their elders about not picking fruit from the same trees all the time, in order to ensure renewed growth. To lend greater reality to this process, Helen invited some of the group to lie on the floor in imitation of the newly felled trees and she began to lay them across each other. Extending the imaginative process further, Helen announced, 'I am going to talk to these trees,' and she began by asking, 'What kind of tree are you?' and followed with others such as, 'What lived in you?' 'What happened to the animals?' 'What will happen to you?' Helen elicited a variety of responses before she moved on to the next phase. She introduced two poems, 'The Steam Shovel' and 'The Cement Mixer' and when all had a copy to peruse, she read both and they discussed the first one in particular [detail]. A great mechanical device, very similar to the mechanical shovel, was introduced into the forest to grab the trees and load them on the back of a truck. Further dramatization was added to this developing story when five individuals were invited to stand in the centre of the circle and to hold hands so as to represent the food chain. The first individual was invited to state, 'I am the tree that grows in the rainforest' and to show off its buttress roots and canopy layer. Next was the fruit eating bat who lived in the canopy layer of this tree and ate its fruit. Next in the chain was the jaguar who would devour a monkey if he could catch it. The human link in the chain said that he was a man trying to stop all this madness of felling trees and that his father, Mendes, had already been killed in his efforts to prevent this destruction. It was obvious from their familiarity with this procedure that they participated in a similar exercise at another time. They enacted the process of decline by beginning with the felling of the tree. They no longer held hands and each in turn explained what would happen as a consequence of severing the links in this chain of life. Only when this had been enacted were they ready to discuss possible stories in more detail. They suggested four different possibilities under the general title. These were 'Deforestation', 'Poachers', 'Hunting for Food' and 'The Jaguar Hunting for Food'. [When] the discussion was completed, they were encouraged to think of a plot for their stories and to begin a first draft. (fieldnote 20/12/'90)

The extract reveals that an adequate account of teaching constructions requires paying attention to the sophisticated nature of the process in addition to its structure. It also suggests that, though this was the final stage in the process, the oral element of the structure was still a prominent feature of supporting and encouraging more independence. Comment on the oral dimension of the process is a timely reminder that structure without communication is unlikely to result in the development implicit in the former. Consequently, focus on the theme of communication becomes an essential means of increasing understanding of teaching practice and child-centredness. The substantive theme of structure shows that content and process are intimately connected through classroom routines. This runs counter to the received wisdom that progressive teaching is preoccupied with process while traditional schooling is overfocused on product (Blenkin and Kelly, 1981).

A subsequent conversation with Helen revealed that the food chain idea had originated with the learners during the theme of the sea earlier in the term. During their morning break, they had spontaneously begun to experiment with the idea of making a chain. She had forgotten where it had come from until mention of it in the fieldnotes jogged her memory. This recollection indicates the significance of the research process for stimulating reflective recall and, thus, revealing further insights through reflective dialogue. However, without the stimulation of outside help this element of practice would have remained hidden as it had become embedded in her routines, no longer accessible to reflection. It lends further credence also to the conclusion that classroom routines are a response to practical dilemmas rather than 'belief in a set of abstract propositions' (Berlak *et al.*, 1976, p. 88). It suggests that the thinking-on-your-feet or 'reflection-in-action' (Schön, 1983) element of practice is what enabled Helen to incorporate the food chain routine into her teaching. However, her experience, and the logic of Berlak's insight, may also suggest a less desirable implication. When practitioners' structures and routines become almost exclusively a response to contextual constraints through thinking-on-their-feet, their practice runs the risk of becoming 'moribund', cut off from any shared vision or common understanding of the process usually inspired by collegial dialogue or through sustenance from a set of principles or ideology. In the same way, therefore, that Schwab (1969, p. 1) suggested, 'the field of curriculum is moribund' because of an 'unexamined reliance on theory', teaching practice may also become unhealthy from exclusive reliance on the immediacy of thinking-on-one's-feet. There is a need, therefore, to extend the dialectic of the practitioner beyond intentions, actions and context, to embrace a wider concept of the teaching process (Goodson, 1992a). It is this more encompassing dialectic that is both implicit and explicit in the problem statement of this inquiry.

Summary

The first theme of this in-depth investigation reveals the critical importance of structure, as illustrated by the various cognitive steps Helen constructs to mediate content in response to learners' needs. This structure provides challenge and continuity to learners while remaining flexible to accommodate individual difference. This first theme also hints that structure retains its flexibility and responsiveness through the adequacy of its communication rules and routines. This general perspective resonates with the analysis in Chapter 1 that structure is a necessary but insufficient condition for child-centred practice. The sequence of cognitive steps was intended to promote cognitive development while fostering independence.

Nevertheless, despite the apparent importance of structure, it is necessary to recognize what a particular structure excludes as well as what it facilitates (Eisner, 1991a, 1995). Structure and content can be the exclusive domain of the teacher or they can be mutually agreed in a spirit of collaboration between teacher and learner. In Helen's case, content appeared to be entirely her decision while structure was flexible and responsive to learners' needs. This theme reveals that structure, far from being inimical to popular conceptions of progressive teaching, is one of its essential elements. However, the extent to which structure facilitates, challenges and fosters independence is critically dependent on informal and formal communication routines.

To continue to gain insight into Helen's teaching constructions, it is necessary to widen the focus of the investigation and to look at her practice through the lens of her conversational style. Documenting the detail of this cultural theme indicates how the cognitive steps were used: a use which was critical to the teaching process. The details of the communication theme provide additional insights into Helen's practice while simultaneously increasing understanding of child-centred teaching. Superimposing the detail of her conversational style on her structure also indicates the essential unity of practice and the cumulative intent of the major case study by gradually documenting the complexity of the most significant themes of child-centredness as constructed by practitioners. It is in this way that the details of her conversational style fulfil the dual role of increasing understanding of her practice as well as illuminating the problem of child-centredness.

Notes

1   These comments suggest (with McLaren, 1986) the notion of transition from community to school, a kind of demarcation: in Giroux's (1993) terms a kind of 'border crossing', in the work of Clandinin and Connelly (1995) the notion of 'crossing boundaries'. There are similarities, too, with Willis' (1977) classic work where working-class kids, in resisting transition from street corner state to student state, consign themselves to working-class employment opportunities. At the time of writing, an evening paper headline caught my attention. It read: 'Concentration camp' playground makes residents see red' (Cox, 1995, p. 15). These irate parents were complaining about having a newly established playground surrounded by a perimeter fence almost identical to those which surround many schools. One parent was reported to have said, 'I feel as though my child is going into a prison everytime we visit the park' (p. 15). I have yet to hear a similar complaint about entering schools!

2   What I have identified as cognitive steps have much in common with what Tharp and Gallimore (1993) describe as 'cognitive structuring' as a means of providing 'assistance' to learners. For further details see pp. 63–69.

3   The 'riddle' was a prominent pedagogical device that Helen employed as part of her repertoire which she also required the learners to use as part of the process of promoting 'ownership' as well as fostering independence. In Vygotskian terms, she was modelling a particular technique that she expected the learners to internalize.

Chapter 7

Theme Two: Helen's Conversational Style

Introduction

Although this second theme is concerned with documenting details of the informal and formal communication rules and routines of Helen's practice, it is important to realize that they are the animus of her programme structure also. Therefore, the accounts illuminate her practice as a whole as well as the more general issue of child-centred teaching.

Several features of this general theme are foregrounded for particular scrutiny. At the informal end of the communication process the importance of relationships is apparent as is the mutual regard between learners and teacher, which has respect for the individual at its core. Consistent with this respect for the individual there was a positive, supportive classroom climate which encourages learners to be secure in themselves and to take the cognitive steps that the structured learning environment provides: all of which resonate with popular interpretations of child-centred ideology.

When the focus shifts to more formal communication routines of Helen's conversational style, the extent to which the informal imbues her pedagogy is remarkable. Consistent patterns in her class teaching, ability groups, and mixed ability groups reveal a set of rules and routines that are highly consistent across the communication continuum. The communication mélange of rules and routines is altered with subtle variations to meet the needs of individuals as well as the specific requirements of different subject matter areas. The general climate is deceptively informal, cloaking a highly structured programme with a concentration on basic skills in keeping with Helen's own intentions. Yet, many of the factors which contribute to Helen's conversational style resonate with particulars of child-centred ideology. However, without the details of how they function and the 'practitioner's reason' for 'the understandings already built into the skilful actions of everyday practice' they are unlikely to illuminate the inquiry's problem of child-centred teaching (Schön, 1991, p. 5).

Conversational Style

The particulars of Helen's teaching constructions suggest that the term conversational style is a suitable means of encapsulating the blend of formal and informal communication embedded in her practice. Conversation is characterized by individuals taking turns at talking without much formality about who speaks next. However, some element of formality is required depending on the number of people involved. Kilbourn's (1988, p. 100) identification of 'Green's (1968) notion of "a conversation of instruction"' is particularly relevant in this context. The former anticipates many of the nuances of Helen's conversational pedagogy when he identifies 'flow, intensity, active participation and smooth interaction' as important elements of a conversation of instruction (1988, p. 100). However, he is also concerned with identifying the core of this process as having an 'underlying intelligibility', a rational foundation. Understanding Helen's conversational style in this way, enabled me to document its actions while also seeking its underlying intelligibility through reflective dialogue with her.

The term is indicative of a general 'pattern' in Helen's practice which reflects an 'underlying structure' that is neither 'inflexible' nor 'totally open to change' (Kilbourn, 1990b, p. 13). This pattern suggests that 'radical change would be difficult' but it is also indicative of a 'mode of teaching with which . . . she has become comfortable' (p. 13). The cognitive steps of the first theme provide a relatively rigid structure, while Helen's conversational style introduces a modicum of flexibility into the process. Thus, the rigidity of structure may be offset by the degree of flexibility, subtlety and sophistication of the practitioner's system of communication. This blend became apparent during the fieldwork for phase two of the study and the following episode captures some of its prominent features.

> The atmosphere was informal and individuals contributed out of turn without causing any disruption. Comments such as 'a take-away sum' or 'it was real easy' were relatively commonplace. The eight or nine girls who had made these comments, stood in a line at the blackboard and they were asked to arrange in sequential order, from the largest to the smallest, the 'weights' [written on flash cards] which they held, in as short a time as possible. While the teacher counted the seconds, there was great excitement before the line reformed in the desired order, in less than ten seconds. The group whose flash cards had been in use earlier in the week, swopped places with the present group and these learners were asked to get in sequence also. This they accomplished in a much shorter time than the first group, causing a little friendly rivalry to creep into the proceedings. When asked to reverse the sequence beginning with the smallest, it was interesting to see the problems this posed for a short while. The fun/activity element of the exercise came to the fore when the entire class (seventeen that particular day) was asked to get in sequence . . . Later that morning I began to call this a conversational style. (fieldnote 13/9/'90)

Helen's intention of creating a 'fun/activity' climate so that the learners were participating in the process, meant that many of her routines were simultaneously informal, active and participatory, while retaining a formal didactic edge. This complexity reinforces a point acknowledged by Bennett (1976) and his colleagues that, except for the extremes of the twelve categories of teaching style which they framed, practice was far too complicated to regard such classification as accurate. This detail suggests that a more inclusive conceptualization of child-centred teaching is required which seeks to build on the strengths of practice and has the potential to identify commonalities between grand narratives rather than to perpetuate their alleged opposition and incompatibility.

The introduction in the previous chapter drew attention to the starkness of the school environment with its metal defences. In contrast to this forbidding exterior, I began to see the classroom as an *oasis*: an image that Helen was happy to embrace. The atmosphere remained informal, characterized by the fun and activity which Helen intended, while the cognitive element of the process was rigorously pursued.

> When an individual was invited to put a shape behind her back the others were asked to close their eyes while the shape was being selected. Gina put a hexagon behind her back and provided a sentence in relation to it. 'Oh teacher I know what it is but I can't remember the name of it,' said Wanda excitedly. This spontaneous outburst drew some smiles and laughter from the rest of the class. Almost instantly Wanda announced triumphantly, 'Hexagon,' and Helen responded by requesting a 'buala bos' [applause][1] for her in recognition of her achievement. I began to think of Helen's classroom as an oasis, a place that stood in stark contrast to its surroundings; a place that provided structure and organization in the learners' day. (fieldnote 13/11/'90)

The classroom as oasis has much in common with what Woods calls 'communitas' which is characterized by 'a state of undifferentiated human kindness' (1993b, p. 362; 1993a).

Though the teaching process gained in malleability through communication routines, this flexibility was within limits set primarily by the teacher. During Helen's initial interview, she indicated that:

> . . . you have to give them the confidence to realize . . . learning isn't that hard once you get into it . . . there's an awful lot of teacher input, you need an awful lot of energy . . . I'm always very concerned that they have the basic skills. (transcript 8)

This combination of social development and basic skills was most evident during the morning. There was emphasis on activity, dialogue and involvement to keep the class tuned-in. The subject matter content rarely varied during this period, and typically included oral Irish and mathematics with some discussion on the theme topic — the rainforests. Helen's perception was that the learners required structure as this was absent in their lives outside school. This point (reported in Chapter 3) was echoed by other practitioners who taught in similar social circumstances. Collectively they had indicated that communication routines, as well as programme structures, were a response to contextual issues. Kutnick indicates that there are many such contextual details on which teachers make judgments which affect their teaching:

. . . teachers are under great pressure to handle a mass of information about their pupils. Teachers must make quick judgements concerning simple actions such as seating and more complex actions such as appropriate curricula, pace of work and future opportunities for pupils. (1988, p. 155)

Responsiveness to contextual constraints, particularly as they relate to the needs and interests of learners, is regarded as a significant element of child-centred ideology. Discussion of the ideology in Chapter 1 suggested that this responsiveness was a worthwhile asset of child-centredness so that it could be distanced from the rigidity, uniformity and lock-step methodology of traditional curricula. This responsiveness will vary, therefore, according to local context.

Flexibility in Helen's conversational style derived, in part, from her capacity to accommodate individual needs within the structures she created. The following vignette is illustrative of the extent to which she was protective of her relationships with each individual. It is indicative also of a supportive, cooperative, rather than competitive, classroom atmosphere. There was implicit recognition that good relations were vital for the communicative approach she adopted (Woods, 1993a). As already indicated, Helen had invited me to examine the 'books' that each learner had produced as the sixth cognitive step of their work on the sea theme.

I returned the books . . . and deemed Vera to have produced the best. Helen immediately offered her a prize of a packet of markers which she would purchase that evening. On immediate reflection Helen thought that perhaps Vera herself might have something else in mind, or might have some markers already. When Helen realized this she asked Vera if the markers would be to her liking or perhaps she might prefer coloured pencils? She went on to say that it was immaterial to her as she had not yet purchased the prize. Vera was dumb struck. Not only did she not respond but she seemed to indicate that the choice was posing difficulties for her . . . One of the girls responded, 'She's afraid to answer teacher.' Helen sensed this and asked her if she would prefer to think about it for a while and she could let her know later. Another pupil piped up and said, 'She can tell me and I'll tell you teacher.' A short while later when they were lining up at the top of the stairs to go to the video room, Wanda returned to the classroom with the message, 'She'll have the pencils teacher'. Wanda was not a bit shy about asking Vera once both of them were outside the classroom door. Helen thanked her for delivering the message and that was the end of the affair. I was keen to record this vignette for two reasons. It is difficult to communicate the fragile nature of the self-confidence and self-image these children have to someone who has not taught children in a similar social context. They can frequently give the superficial impression of having plenty to say for themselves and be quick to respond with a witty turn of phrase. Nevertheless, it is extremely easy to intimidate them or to put them on the defensive. I was delighted to be able to award the accolade of the best book to Vera as I knew that she could do with the boost more so than her two main rivals. She was not accustomed to being in this position, and her confidence betrayed her when the teacher offered her a simple choice . . .

The other point of interest is how some members of the group came to her aid with various suggestions as to how she could arrive at an answer via intermediaries . . . Helen sensed Vera's dilemma and rather than force her to make a choice, there and then in front of the whole class, she was prepared to defer the issue to take the pressure off. This was another example of the sensitivity with which Helen related to these girls and the degree of respect she had for them as individuals. (fieldnote 28/11/'90)

Within these relationships, which Helen fostered, there was a degree of mutual respect and support which is characteristic of communitas and from which 'the individual . . . gathers strength from the support of the group' (Woods, 1993a, p. 363). However, there was a cognitive interest in fostering these relationships also because they facilitated the teaching process. It was as if sharing hearts was a means of rousing minds to life, thus facilitating the creation of a 'common-knowledge' between learner and teacher (Edwards and Mercer, 1987). Informal communication structures became the foundation on which more formal pedagogical communication routines were established; getting on with teacher becomes an important gateway to cognitive and social development. Due to the background of the learners, it was necessary to win their social confidence as cognitive issues were being addressed. Even in the tough arena of 'rapid-fire' questioning (Perrott, 1984; Brown, G., 1985; Dillon, 1988), associated with a very competitive classroom climate, Helen combined successfully this competitive edge with meeting individual needs.

Learning tables was an important element of Helen's routines — a practice that enjoys much favour in Irish schools generally — which demonstrated her own expressed concern that they needed to know the basics. This apparent preoccupation with the basics has its origins in 'elementary' schooling (Alexander and Contributors, 1995). The nature of the relationships were such that Helen treated individuals differently in terms of the amount of time allowed to respond, the level of difficulty of questions asked, and assistance provided, without being accused by the learners of being unfair. Even in learning situations that seemed tailored to promote competitive individualism, they were tempered to provide a climate more conducive to altruistic individualism and consistent with a cooperative classroom climate (Watt, 1989). Consequently, in an aspect of her programme, which many identify with traditional schooling, her conversational style resonated with popular interpretations of child-centred ideology as she balanced the need to challenge learners with being flexible and responsive to individual's needs.

Given the weather [snowing and bitterly cold], the fact that it was Friday and there was the build up to doing the tropical fruit salad today [as part of the rainforest theme], there was a certain reluctance in both learners and teacher to begin the regular morning routines. It was as if the elements were aiding and abetting in the planning decision which had already determined that this was not just another school day. Helen encouraged the class to begin by initiating counting in 90s. All the usual routines were in evidence. They counted up to and including 1080 and then backwards from that number, with an individual providing just one number in the sequence. After one individual had said 810, Trish was asked to provide the next number. She responded with 90. 'Ninety, Trish,' repeated the teacher with a mixture of surprise tinged with alarm. Trish repeated the answer and as the doubt conveyed by the teacher's gaze met Trish's eyes, the latter said, in her own defence, 'We're countin' in 9s teacher'. 'We're not, we're counting in 90s,' replied Helen in the same matter-of-fact tone in which she had been addressed. 'Oh 900,' replied Trish immediately as she strove to recover her unstable equilibrium. As Helen moved on rapidly to another individual Trish smiled that smile of relief and embarrassment at her friends around her table. While the questioning could certainly be described as being of the rapid-fire variety, Helen, as usual, was sufficiently caring to find accommodation for Trish's needs so that this rapidity did not always have to mean shooting first and asking questions afterwards. This episode was all the more important as it was Trish who had been moved by the teacher earlier in the week for talking. Helen was mending her relationship fences as well as being patient and supportive towards a weaker individual in the class. (fieldnote 7/12/'90)

The same concern for individual needs was manifest in other aspects of Helen's conversational style. When discussing the cognitive steps in language, which were intended to promote independence, the extracts indicated that the routines of providing riddles and clues were a conversational means of attempting to promote more refined and accurate use of language. Helen extended this strategy by including the mode of popular TV quiz programmes. It may be suggested also that inclusion of the quiz was a response to the learners' environment in which game shows feature prominently on the multiplicity of television channels which were available to them. Helen was connecting with their everyday experience of 'popular culture' to extend her pedagogical routines while adding a further dimension to her conversational style (Giroux and Simon, 1989). In the process, she was connecting also with prominent elements of child-centredness. The quiz was essentially the same strategy as that used in the language setting, but with subtle modifications. When these strategies were used in the context of mathematics, there was the same concern for precision in the use of language, plus the additional concern for refining and honing learners' grasp of various mathematical concepts.

The next extract captures many facets of these routines. One advantage of the good relations Helen cultivated was that she could take risks in breaking the rules of the teaching game. This was acceptable as there was an implicit understanding of its permissibility to accommodate the learning needs of individuals. Apart from the relationships which were cultivated, the learners may have been happy also to collude with the teacher's rule-breaking so as to prevent the classroom climate from becoming too competitive. There was an implicit recognition on their part that, if it were too competitive, many would not participate as the fun/activity element of routines would be swamped by a more egotistic individualism. Additionally, the extract indicates the pervasiveness of the routine across subject matter boundaries. Although the subject matter was not always closely related with the theme, the routines provided common ground rules that made it easier for the learners to participate: subject matter varied while communication routines remained constant with subtle variations. It was apparent also that Helen did not stick rigidly to a timetable despite planning her day in great detail. These characteristics of flexibility and responsiveness resonate with popular images of child-centred ideology and promote a positive classroom climate that has many features of communitas.

> Helen switched the focus of attention to the quiz on shapes and solids which, she had indicated, they were going to have on Friday last, but the planning of the tropical fruit salad took more time than was anticipated. Individuals were brought to the top of the class, shown a flash card with the name of a solid or shape, and invited to give two clues as to its identity. There had been much practice of this the previous week as a lead up to the planned quiz. It was as if all this preparatory work had somehow evaporated over the weekend. Laura, normally an eager and able participant in such affairs, could 'not give us even one clue'. When another girl gave a clue that said, 'A solid with 8 faces,' the groups were slow to respond, so much so, Helen had to tell them, by way of additional help, 'You made them,' before the clue began to make sense. Some of the octahedrons (which they had all made) were produced, and the faces counted. Helen also pointed out that it was the only solid they had discussed that had 8 faces. What had begun rather poorly, warmed into a full-blooded competition between the two mixed ability groups [for mathematics]. Helen used the old ploy of deducting marks from one of the teams for challenging the 'referee', thus keeping the competition alive right up to the final question. The fate of the competition hung on the final question and Gina provided the following clue, 'It has three sides and a right angle'. This final piece of information clinched it, and every hand in the group to which she belonged shot up. Even Ailbhe, who had been reduced to tears earlier as a result of an incident in another classroom, was in there with the best of them. Helen was now faced with a decision. It would be a wonderful boost to Ailbhe's deflated ego if she was allowed to save the day for her team. What would happen if she got it wrong? The group erupted in a chorus of joy when Ailbhe timidly answered, 'A right angled triangle'. Helen was quick to spot the opportunity to restore Ailbhe's flagging fortunes and immediately suggested a 'buala bos' (applause) as Ailbhe had won the day for her team. Even the members of the opposition sensed the import of this occasion, and clapped as loudly as the others. 'You did very well today, Ailbhe. Good girl,' said Helen, as the applause died away. (fieldnote 10/12/'90)

Because her conversational style was highly interactive and participatory, Helen was able to challenge the learners while simultaneously conveying the feeling that the teaching process was not just about mastery of facts but about real people, their feelings and emotions. This complex routine juxtaposes individual needs with the need for challenge, both of which are frequently cited as being important elements of child-centred ideology.

Communication Routines and Resources

Availability of resources is an important contextual constraint on the nature and quality of classroom climate and communication routines and structures, and is frequently regarded as a progressive imperative. Materials have particular significance when content is planned thematically with little reliance on textbooks. There were many aspects of Helen's classroom and school environments which left much to be desired in terms of basic comforts, like heat, toiletries and a whole plethora of resources which would facilitate many of the activities she organized. However, to describe all these little irritants, which had an unknown impact on morale and teaching would, I fear, run the risk of distorting the present theme and Helen's case in general. Nevertheless, a dearth of resources was a constant constraint that adversely affected teacher morale. Suffice to say that Helen's context bore an uncanny resemblance to that of practitioners in Nias' study who confided that:

> Peeling walls, leaking ceilings, broken windows and vandalism also have an adverse effect upon morale. One woman summed it up: 'At the beginning of the term you can cope with these sorts of things, but later on the pressure builds up and you begin to get ill and have to take time off . . .'
> (1989, p. 122)

Helen was able to rise above these constraints in terms of the environment she created. Her conversational style included 'coping strategies', which are a 'constructive' and 'creative' means of overcoming local constraints (Hargreaves, 1984a, p. 66). The effort involved in constructing imaginative responses to learners' needs which overcome local constraints, however, takes its toll on the energy levels of practitioners while increasing stress. This is particularly so in a school system that is protective of teacher autonomy with a tradition of professional isolation that is intuitively suspicious of a more 'collaborative culture' (Hargreaves, 1994, 1992; OECD, 1991, Lieberman, 1990; Nias, 1989; Rosenholtz, 1991; Louden, 1991; Lortie, 1975).

The following vignette is illustrative of the cumulative impact of structure and an informal conversational style which is supportive and encouraging of individual initiative, and the qualitative differences they collectively make to classroom processes. It implicity suggests that the psychological argument which favours the matching of learners' abilities to appropriate curricula should be extended also to embrace the notion that communication routines should be honed to the learners' immediate context, thus reflecting learners' inclinations in terms of preferred learning styles. The extract is a good example, therefore, of the dialectical relationship between the unique case and the problem of child-centredness whereby the specific details extend the boundaries of understanding of the problem in general. These details suggest that practitioners are active, transformative agents in the process of constructing teaching rather than passive implementers of pedagogical prescriptions.

> Another issue which I had intended to record was the behaviour of one particular group of pupils during the morning break. They stood around a large map of Ireland which hung from one of the window frames and the five of them had a quiz about the location of various places around the country that were marked on the map. As I listened to them earlier in the week they spelled out the name of a place and another pointed it out on the map. If the individual concerned was having difficulty, others assisted by providing some clues such as mention of the river on which it was located. As Helen and I chatted during break [on this particular day], the same group was involved again. I drew Helen's attention to this and she informed me that she had done some work on counties in relation to various other issues. I was keen to discuss a number of factors of importance in relation to this learner's routine. It was a regular feature of break time. Consequently, it was reasonable to assume that this interest was sparked off by work done earlier in the term by the teacher. Because the resource — in this instance the large map of Ireland — was available, the learners exploited its presence. This was something which infant [kindergarten] teachers are more likely to talk about than teachers of senior classes. Placing things where learners have access to them enables them to follow their natural curiosity. In general it indicated that a classroom environment which is well-equipped with resources is more likely to stimulate interest, even when competing with drinks and sandwiches. (fieldnote 30/11/'90)

A similar group developed subsequently around a map of the world which had been used repeatedly to locate the rainforests. This development suggested that a more relaxed atmosphere, due to a relatively small number of learners in the room, as well as the availability of the maps, was a determining factor. Helen had confided that a consequence of the smaller class was, 'I have no fear of losing control' (fieldnote 30/11/'90). While it could be argued that these groups were primarily social, there was a sense in which the social orientation of learning, which the conversational style of the teacher created, was taken up by the learners themselves. Helen had modelled this behaviour through her conversational approach and, in Vygotskian manner, the learners adopted her structure as a means of taking greater responsibility for their own learning. It is possible also that learners realized learning could be fun, thus assimilating an intention which Helen ambitioned for her practice. This pattern of behaviour strongly suggested that it was not structure per se, or Helen's communicative approach that led to this modest independent learning. Rather, it was the consequence of the combined impact of both: the sum was greater than its constituent parts. Consequently, it is possible to agree with child-centred theorists who suggest that an adequate account of practice requires that attention be paid to its processes as well as its structured content.

A major assumption of the cognitive steps (which were activated by the conversational style) was that, by travelling the route which they mapped out, handover would occur. Achieving handover would result in greater autonomy for the learner. The combination of structure and conversation was no guarantee that it would happen, but when it did occur the frustrations encountered along the way suddenly seemed to have been worth the effort. In Helen's context, this was one of the few feedback mechanisms available to her which indicated the effectiveness of her teaching routines. This constitutes a 'critical incident' which is 'unplanned and unanticipated' but 'elevates teacher–pupil interaction to a new level' (Woods, 1993b, p. 357). The following extract gains further significance because its substance received independent corroboration later from the home–school liaison officer, herself a former teacher.

> While we drank our usual mug of coffee at break time, one of the girls brought a box of percussion instruments to the classroom from the secretary's office. Some of the learners began to put various musical rhythms together while three others began 'surreptitiously painting' as Helen put it. These were individuals who had not completed their paintings [the previous day]. Although Helen had refused them permission earlier to put the finishing touches to their masterpieces, she was now delighted that they had sufficient ingenuity to 'seize the day'. As the break progressed, a definite group formed around the percussion instruments. One of the interesting things about this group was that it crossed the boundaries of the two ability groups in the class. I thought it significant that the element of the curriculum which facilitated this mingling was music. By comparison the group which formed around the map of Ireland during break was made up of people from the high ability group. As Helen was about to signal the end of the break, she was approached by this percussion group, which now resembled a troupe of wandering players, and requested if they could put on a performance for the class. Permission was granted and they immediately launched into 'The Hunt of the Jaguar'. This was a theme that the entire class had worked on earlier in small groups. However, it was noticeable . . . that various elements of the work done in rhythm had been included in the drama. Particularly good use was made of the basic rhythm, sometimes loudly, sometimes quietly, for dramatic effect. The rest of the class rewarded them with a good round of applause after their short presentation.

> There were some notable aspects to this dramatic interlude. It is important to recognize that it was entirely on the initiative of the learners that it occurred. It is unlikely that it would have happened were it not for the arrival of the box of percussion instruments in the classroom just before the break. One could argue about the impact of their arrival in the room as opposed to having them there permanently, but the significant point is that they were the catalyst that brought this spontaneous production into

being. However, it is also important to recognize that resources per se will achieve very little. A necessary prerequisite of the spontaneity which characterized this work was the amount of structured preparatory input which had been done by the teacher in language and in music. Presentation had already been encouraged with more direct involvement by the teacher. It was at the end of all this sequenced, systematic developmental work that the spontaneity of the learners came to be.

There were two other crucial structural elements that contributed to this spontaneous presentation. The classroom atmosphere was such that the kind of initiative these six learners took was appreciated and facilitated. It is unlikely that it would be possible at all if there were thirty-six pupils in the classroom . . . While all these factors play their parts . . . unless the teacher had expertise in the various aspects of the curriculum which were included in the presentation, and she placed sufficient store in them, that the learners were encouraged to take them up as part of their own agenda, then 'The Hunt' would not have materialized. To the casual visitor or observer, this drama presentation was wonderfully creative and spontaneous and a great tribute to both pupils and teacher. What is not appreciated frequently when these issues are commented on or reported, is the sheer amount of hard work that has to be put in before the learners get to the spontaneous stage which I had just documented. It is important to record that this independence and spontaneity was the consequence of a great deal of structured curriculum work which in turn was attendant on careful planning and sequencing. (fieldnote 7/12/'90)

To the casual observer, the episode above might well be interpreted as a bit of spontaneous good fun on the part of the learners which came to fruition through some momentary indulgence on the part of the practitioner. However, as already indicated, it was the voluntary response of the learners to a whole confluence of influences intimately connected with structures and communication routines that brought this particular episode to fruition. It was this timbre of Helen's practice that made it resonate so readily with that intuitive sense derived from reflection on child-centred ideology. In methodological terms, there was a certain sense of achievement at this point that 'first hand immersion in a sphere of life and action' was yielding 'important dividends' (Glaser and Strauss, 1967, p. 227). Consequently, what could only be sensed in abstract theoretical terms (when the principles of child-centred teaching were being discussed in Chapter 1), was being grounded now in the particulars of practice.

The cumulative impact of these fieldnote extracts increased my awareness that, in the absence of adequate resources, the flexibility and opportunity for independent initiative on the part of individuals or groups of learners is severely restricted. Though it is necessary to acknowledge the limited flexibility inherent in teachers' planned structures, adequate resources become a significant means of increasing individual autonomy as well as facilitating a growing diversity in learners' range of interests. The critical incident reported above draws attention also to the importance of time:

in a rigidly timetabled context, spontaneity and creativity would be sacrificed for time on-task. In the present climate of 'accountability' it is important that these incidents are acknowledged and nurtured rather than painted out of practice.

Communication and Second Language

Earlier fieldnote extracts indicated that the communication routines of language teaching (English) were similar to those employed in teaching mathematics, and these routines were similar also in the context of second language teaching (Irish). The following extract indicates the consistency of Helen's routines in addition to the persistence of her intention to construct a fun/activity, participatory programme. A number of learners had been brought to the top of the classroom and, at the point where the extract begins, the objects this group were holding were swopped and hidden so that the remainder of the class had to establish who held what by asking questions.

> The others were then invited to ask questions with a view to establishing the name of the item each individual was hiding. This seemed very similar to the approach adopted in the English lesson except that, as might be expected, a little more support was provided by the teacher in the case of the Irish language. Helen produced a flash card with the phrase 'Cad tá agam?' ['What have I got?'] . . . Helen informed the class that she expected them to provide a 'riddle but you're doing it in Irish'. One of the girls provided the following: 'Tá sé dubh. Is féidir liom scríobh leis.' ['It is black. I can write with it']. The important point here was not the detail of the responses but that Helen herself acknowledged the similarity of routine in both languages. (fieldnote 26/11/'90)

Helen indicated that she experienced difficulty integrating the Irish language and mathematics with the rainforest theme. However, experience had taught her that, as a theme progresses, something usually suggests itself, so that all the subject areas could be connected, in a tangible way, with the organizing focus of the curriculum. They had been working on the preparation of a birthday cake as the focus of the oral Irish programme. Helen combined and extended much of this language to include the preparation of a tropical fruit salad which was being organized as part of the rainforest theme. Because the focus was second language teaching, it was possible to identify the cognitive steps of the approach more readily as it required more structure than in English. In this particular instance, though the rainforest theme encompassed the Irish language, the basic structure was not subordinate to the theme: the internal structure and integrity of the subject *qua* subject was retained.

An extended period of time in the site made it increasingly more feasible to identify patterns that connected various aspects of practice. Lack of resources, as well as a poorly surfaced blackboard, were additional constraints which restricted Helen to the ubiquitous 'flash card' as the mainstay of her programme. Once the new element of language had been introduced and modelled, Helen immediately handed over the process to the learners. An additional subtlety to the routines emerged which had not been observed previously.

> As soon as possible she handed over the role of asking questions to the learners themselves. It was immediately obvious that the six girls who were asked to choose a flash card with the name of a fruit written on it, and to stand at the top of the room, were not drawn from the brightest in the class. Those who performed this function two days previously were. Now that the requirement had been modelled by them, the mantle passed to this [less able] group. By the end of the week almost everyone had this experience. They were asked a series of questions by the others and they provided as exhaustive an answer as they could. An example of this was the following. 'Cad a dhein tú leis na síolta?' ['What did you do with the seeds?'] to which the girl who supposedly had prepared the melon replied, 'Thóg mé amach iad agus chuir mé iad sa chiseán' [sic]. [I removed them and put them in the bin.] As if there were any doubt about the similarity of approach in teaching this second language to that which Helen adopted to language generally, she invited the class to provide riddles so that others could guess what fruit was being spoken of. (fieldnote 12/12/'90)

These lessons frequently ended abruptly as if Helen suddenly lost heart in what she was doing. At the slightest hint that the learners were growing tired of the routines, she switched to another aspect of the curriculum. Apart from being a valuable pedagogical strategy, as well as a response to learners, she was also recognizing that context influenced her practice because of limited enthusiasm displayed by some and open hostility by others. Implicit in the extract also is the manner in which more able learners are used to model, and therefore assist, less able peers. However, one of the likely consequences of this strategy is that more able learners cannot be challenged to an appropriate level if they continue to be taught as part of a class unit, thus leading to underachievement (Alexander, 1992; Alexander *et al.*, 1989).

Though Helen's structures and routines were sufficiently flexible to enable the learners to influence content and its direction, this influence was in matters of detail rather than substance. The rapport and positive classroom atmosphere, which were cultivated through Helen's conversational style and its attendant enabling environment, allowed the learners to exercise this influence. In this way, the teaching process was all part of a deliberate, consciously determined structure with some flexibility, rather than something which came about by chance and good fortune. There was a degree of negotiation but within routines and structures determined by the teacher. Once again, the details of practice suggested that, through its very complexity, formality and informality, rigidity and flexibility could be accommodated in its structures and communication system. This realization reinforced my belief that it is more valuable to understand practice by exposing its underlying reasons through documenting its dilemmas rather than classifying these classroom actions as traditional or progressive. This inclusive approach suggests that aspects of traditional teaching were being reconstructed within the rubric of child-centred ideology: a confluence of teaching traditions.

Grouping and Group Work

Many of the extracts included in the case so far, have been examples of class teaching, with a preponderance of oral work. As part of the more formal elements of her communication system, Helen organized ability groups for mathematics and English. Such groupings are highly consistent with practice elsewhere (DES, 1978; Alexander *et al.*, 1989; Mortimore *et al.*, 1988) and grouping is usually advocated by adherents of child-centred ideology as a means of overcoming the limitations of class teaching. Within these grouping arrangements, the routines of her conversational style remained remarkably consistent. The detail documented below is indicative of this omnipresence.

> Helen had asked the more able group to provide her with the weights of the different fruits which they had weighed during maths class the previous day. These weights had already been added to the flash cards which carried the names of the various fruits that Helen had purchased as part of the preparation for the fruit salad. Eight individuals were invited to come to the top of the class and to pick a flash card from the board where they had been placed by the teacher. Again, some familiar routines were in evidence with some variation. Helen asked various individuals to contribute to the sequencing of the flash cards in contrast with the more regular requirement of asking those who held the cards to get themselves in sequence. When individuals experienced difficulty deciding which card came next in the sequence, Helen was on hand to guide them in the right direction, through questioning. This was another example of creating a structure which was intended to facilitate the independence of the learners. When this supportive structure appeared inadequate for a particular individual, Helen was there to provide instant remediation. The class in general seemed to understand and accept the need for this individual nurturing and in many instances they contributed to it. It is as if they attempted to explain to the adult mind where the individual who was having difficulty 'was at' in a cognitive sense; to explain to the teacher the groove in which she was stuck. The supportive environment which Helen cultivated was taken up by the learners. This was something that came easily to the class anyway as their orientation in terms of learning seemed to be cooperative and social rather than individual and competitive.
>
> Helen moved the process along with a series of questions, typical of which was: '2kg. of kumquats + 10 passion fruit + 1 pineapple, what change will I have out of £10.00?' There were several such questions. In keeping with normal routines, some were asked by the teacher and this was followed

by questions asked by individual learners. As part of that usual process, when there were conflicting answers being provided, the process of calculating the correct answer was done piece by piece in conversational style. At no stage was anyone criticized or reprimanded for not being correct the first time round. In a very real way, errors and disagreements were exploited for their learning potential. (fieldnote 7/12/'90)

My interpretation of these episodes appears to agree with Galton and Williamson's finding that during such collaboration 'pupils learn from each other', they 'lose the fear and the stigma of failure', and 'improve their self-image' (1992, p. 16). Underneath the informality of conversational style, the actual computational element of the content was highly consistent with traditional curricula as well as with Helen's intention that the learners should be well versed in the basics. Nevertheless, the more casual observer might well be forgiven for recognizing the informality of the process without identifying its didactic and cognitive intent. Discussion in Chapter 1 suggested that an adequate conceptualization of child-centredness needs to recognize the intimacy of the relationship between content and process, while indicating also that such a conceptualization needs to become more sophisticated so as to embrace what dichotomous thinking suggests are mutually exclusive.

It was typical of Helen's conversational style to engage in oral work with the entire class: work which was frequently repeated with the less able group of learners while the higher ability group completed written assignments as a follow-up activity and within these routines individual difficulties were addressed. Individualization of work was not in evidence, unlike other jurisdictions where 'a laudable commitment to individualized learning' has been documented (Alexander, 1992, p. 191; Galton and Simon, 1980; Galton *et al.*, 1980). The immediate context of the following extract was that the more able learners had been asked to calculate a 10 per cent reduction on several items from the shop at the rear of the classroom while Helen turned her attention to the weaker group. The communicative pattern was highly consistent with what has already been documented.

The weaker group had been working on solids and further discussion of their attributes was the main focus of the period. Helen's routines were in evidence from the very beginning. Amy was instructed to acquire a cuboid, Maeve a cylinder, and to stand at the top of the room. Helen immediately invited Wanda to ask someone to pick a solid and to join the other two. A fourth joined this group equipped with a cube. Each individual was asked to describe all the attributes of the solid which she held. Once this had been done successfully more of Helen's routines were pressed into action to extend the practice further. Some more solids were added so that a row that included a cube, sphere, cuboid, as well as a square and triangular pyramid were lined up on the floor at the top of the room. While all the other individuals in the group were instructed to close their eyes, one individual was invited to the top of the room. Helen pointed to one of the solids and the chosen learner was asked to provide three clues to its identity. The others were invited to say what they thought it was. As a final addition to the exercise Helen provided a photocopied worksheet on which there was a series of solids arranged down the left-hand side of the page and their characteristics had to be identified under a series of headings. The group worked on this sheet in pairs with obvious enjoyment. Having done a great deal of work orally, they were more than capable of completing the task. There was a very definite pattern to this work in maths as there was in language. The emphasis was on the linguistic element of the concepts as well as the provision of concrete materials. Only when a thorough grounding had been given, did the class or groups proceed to written work. (fieldnote 4/12/'90)

When Helen worked with the more able group during the mathematics period the same work pattern was manifest. The usual orally constructed routines were followed by written work. It is probably true to say that the weaker group spent more time on worksheets than the more able group but this was more a consequence of their slowness in completing tasks rather than a tendency, suggested by Sharp and Green (1975), to keep weaker pupils busy while working with the more able. Mortimore and his colleagues (1988, p. 230) concluded that it was necessary for teachers to be 'sensitive to the varied abilities of pupils and on the need to provide work at appropriate levels of difficulty'. Helen's cocktail of whole class, group and paired activities indicated a consistently high level of interaction, implicitly recognizing a social dimension to learning, while attempting to accommodate individuals and their abilities also. This complex approach is consistent with interpretations of child-centredness that emphasize cooperation, interaction and respect for individual difference.

There was additional complexity in Helen's conversational style due to the manner in which she used ability groups for Vygotskian style peer coaching. As the language element of her programme advanced to the mini project stage (cognitive step five), Helen, as she had done in other areas of the curriculum, used the learners in the higher ability group to provide additional information for the less able. This ability grouping worked to the advantage of both groups, although it could be argued that it increased dependency in the less able. However, Helen believed that this routine had certain advantages for both groups and, from her own point of view, it enabled her to make some progress which was important for morale. As usual, in the complex world of classrooms, the strategy was a compromise.

One of the small groups, from among the more able learners, was asked to present the material they had been writing on the people of the rainforests. This was part of the general strategy of providing an audience for the more able, while providing additional time and opportunity for the less able to hear this information again, before they began the writing process. As Laura read her opening sentences it became clear that she had confused the location of the Indian and the Pygmy tribes people. Helen immediately set about rectifying this misunderstanding by dispatching Laura to the rear of the room to locate the various rainforest regions of the world. 'Show me Africa,' requested Helen, and Laura, more in hope than with any movement that demonstrated conviction, moved her index finger from Australia to the USA. As Laura realized that she was 'at sea' she became confused and intimidated. Helen, in her usual understanding manner, asked Jo to come to her assistance. (fieldnote 12/12/'90)

Despite several weeks of work with regular reference to the map of the world, it was obvious that some of the learners did not have a grasp of where the rainforests were located. This may be a function of a thematic approach where the basics of geographical knowledge are essentially subordinated to the higher priority accorded to language. It is the danger of a subject not getting its due, thus denying learners' access to the rigour of the discipline, that has provided ammunition to critics of integration: commonly regarded as one of the hallmarks of child-centredness. The manifestly slow progress of learners, in a paradoxical way, underlined Helen's need to make progress to sustain her own morale while it attempted also to challenge the more able. Though she created ability groups within the class to enable the more able to initiate further reading and research, these groups were used also to provide additional tuition for the less able. This tension in her practice was a trade-off between the former's need for further cognitive challenge and the latter's need for additional support. The process included social gains for the more able, which enhanced their prospects of further cognitive growth, and cognitive possibilities for the less able group were evident also. However, such strategies were limited by the overarching requirement of such an approach which was to advance the development of all the learners more or less at the same pace: a characteristic commonly attributed to traditional teaching.

There has been much debate about the virtues of group teaching and researchers have been careful to distinguish between 'grouping . . . [as] an organisational feature of the classroom' and 'group work . . . [as] a pedagogical feature of the classroom' (Tann, 1981, p. 43; King, 1978; Bassey, 1978; DES, 1978; Galton *et al.*, 1980; Galton and Simon, 1980; Alexander *et al.*, 1989). Helen's practice was consistent with the general finding that 'children were grouped by ability for their work in mathematics more commonly than in any other subject' (DES, 1978, p. 53). Her widespread use of concrete materials had the additional advantage of retaining a high degree of interaction through her conversational style. This was a particular transformation of child-centredness which was intended to cultivate additional interests and sustain learners' motivation.

Nevertheless, there were tensions in Helen's routines between class and group work. In mathematics, for example, the entire class was involved in the same oral work, but the two ability groups did different written work. This differentiation was an attempt to bring about the best possible match between learners' abilities and to enable them to work at an appropriate pace. However, by persisting with the same oral work for the entire class, which had benefits in terms of individuals learning from one another, there were constant limits set to the degree of differentiation which occurred within ability groups. Too much differentiation makes it extremely difficult to teach a class as a unit, too little and there is no longer a need for ability groups. It seems that many teachers will group a class to enable learners to work at a different pace but on the same topic. Working on multiple topics requires much greater organizational skill as the classwork element of a subject becomes increasingly difficult to sustain. This discussion indicates clearly that structures and their attendant pedagogical routines are invariably a compromise. It is important to remember, therefore, that there are limits to what they can achieve and such resolutions are context specific.

Helen's resolution of these tensions within her teaching constructions provided additional social development for the more able, which had positive impact on their cognitive development. The less able simultaneously received a form of peer-modelled behaviour from their 'more capable peers' (Bruner, 1989, p. 23). This general pattern of class and group teaching contrasts with the picture painted of Leeds teachers by Alexander *et al.* (1989, p. 82) which states that '23% of teachers' communications were with the whole class' while '67% were with individuals'. Helen's case, and the evidence in Chapters 3 and 4, suggests that, in so far as these data are typical, the tradition of class teaching seems more deeply rooted in Irish classrooms than in primary classrooms elsewhere. Helen's conversational style sought to maximize the strengths of interaction and cooperation without ignoring the undoubted merits of individuation. It may be suggested, therefore, that child-centredness is enhanced by a discriminating mix of class, group and individual attention rather than over-reliance on any one communication strategy. Critical to this communication matrix is a sense of the classroom as a 'learning community' more so than a place of assembly where individuals compete with each other (Barth, 1990).

Another striking feature of the fieldnote extracts has been the persistence of a conversational style within smaller group situations. Essentially, teacher input continued with the same focus on language and learner involvement with a series of routines to foster independence. There has been a tendency in recent research literature to favour guided discovery as a pedagogical device rather than discovery learning (Ireland, 1990a; OECD, 1991). Helen's conversational style would certainly belong more to the former, but it might be more accurately described as 'directed discovery' which was negotiated through the conversational mode of communication. In her particular circumstances she had to resolve the tension between providing adequate structure and support which encouraged learners, and a more driven approach that would alter the classroom climate significantly. With this more driven orientation the entire axis of her practice would likely shift from being positive and supportive to being rigid, oppressive and teacher dominated in an unpalatable way. Her *modus operandi* resonates with Vygotsky's perspective 'that passing on knowledge is like passing on language' because 'his basic belief' was 'that social transaction is the fundamental vehicle of education and not . . . solo performance' (Bruner, 1989, p. 25).

Her particular blend of structure and conversational style was intended to keep the learners 'in the zone' that, at once, holds out the prospect of challenge, motivation and escape from boredom (Bruner, 1989, p. 30). This complex process implicitly recognizes also that 'there must needs be at any given stage of voyaging into the zone of proximal development a support system that helps learners get there' (p. 32). Due to the nature of the learners in Barrytown, Helen's conversational style was a persistent attempt to extend their period of time in the zone, and, in tandem with her cognitive structure, may be understood as an elaborate, complex and sophisticated response to the learners and their context which embraces many of the assets of child-centredness while retaining a didactic edge. In postmodern terms, her teaching constructions are januform as they include aspects of traditional and child-centred practice. Dewey (1916, p. 5) would be likely to approve of her conversational style as he suggested that 'not only is all social life identical with communication, but all communication is educative'. One could be forgiven for thinking that it was Helen's practice he had in mind when he emphasized the social dimension of learning as critical because: 'it enlarges and enlightens experience; it stimulates and enriches imagination; it creates responsibility for accuracy and vividness of statement and thought' (p. 6).

Routines and Aesthetics

The case which has been advanced so far is that the structures and communication routines of Helen's teaching were highly consistent, particularly in relation to the 3Rs. Evidence for the pervasiveness, consistency and complexity of her conversational style would, therefore, be more convincing if it were visible also in other subject matter areas. Moreover, a broadly based programme is a further axiom of child-centred ideology.

Some fieldnote extracts have indicated that Helen frequently used music as a welcome interlude between periods spent on the more 'serious' subjects. However, when she spent a more extended period of time on music, a judicious mix of formality and informality included many of the same features of structure, sequence, enjoyment and participation already documented. Earlier extracts have indicated also that Helen had harnessed music to the theme of the rainforests. The enabling environment she cultivated encouraged the learners to explore additional aspects of the music programme which they had enjoyed. Further detail reveals the extent to which I was struck by the similarities of pedagogical routines which included subtle alterations to suit the particular subject matter.

She began on this occasion by writing a tune on the board in solfa and in notation. I have reproduced this here in rhythm and in solfa.

ta tete tete tete/ tete ta ta ta_/
m mm rr rr/ rr r r d_/

tete tete ta tete/ ta ta ta_/
mm mm r rr/ r r d_/

The class began by clapping the rhythm of each line separately. This was followed by a combination of singing and clapping of the tune. Individuals were then invited to sing part of the music text to Noo and to stop wherever they chose and another was asked to come to the board to indicate the precise note on which the singing had stopped. The manner in which the lesson had so far unfolded and continued to be developed by Helen, was highly consistent with her general pedagogy of advancing in a series of carefully graded cognitive steps which, in conventional language, were hierarchically sequenced. They were invited to sing the rhythm to Noo and to clap the rhythm at the same time. The class was then divided, and one half was asked to clap the beat while the other half clapped the rhythm. When this had been done a number of times, and after a good deal of re-mediation . . . on the first bar of the second line, both groups were invited to sing the solfa as well as clapping at the same time. Some of the class were beginning to recognize the tune at this point and Helen requested that they keep their counsel. After some further practice she asked for the name and many recognized it as 'I know a woman'. They were all asked to stand in their places and they put words, actions and notes together as they sang. (fieldnote 28/11/'90)

The informal, participatory, interactive process belied the structured, didactic and cognitively oriented nature of the teaching in a highly charged encounter which seemed to merge, with accomplished ease, particulars of child-centredness with a traditional didacticism, thus providing additional evidence that complexity frequently embraces what previous research has habitually categorized as mutually exclusive. Further pedagogical continuity and consistency were revealed as Helen included some additional activities leading to a subtle blending of musical rhythms and pedagogical riddles.

The lesson was extended with the inclusion of what Helen referred to as 'pass the rhythm game'. The class was organized into three groups of equal size (six in each). Each group was given a set of three flash cards with different rhythms written on each. The groups were essentially working in pairs. An individual from one pair began by clapping the rhythm which she had in front of her. This was then passed on by her partner to one of the pairs next to her. The action proceeded in a circular direction until all participants were busy receiving or transmitting a rhythm which all were obliged to do alternately. It required a high degree of concentration and necessitated everyone sticking to the basic beat of a four beat bar; otherwise the transfers got out of sync leading to breakdown of the system . . . Finally, each group was invited to perform for the others. This introduced a note of friendly rivalry which added to the enjoyment . . . The most striking feature of this lesson, given the themes being investigated, was the persistence of the pedagogy which Helen employed in this and other subject matter areas. (fieldnote 28/11/'90)

Helen was enthusiastic about the potential of music, both for its contribution to learners' development as a distinct subject, and for its contribution to the rain-forest theme. She was keenly aware also that the context and background of the learners commended music as a means of expression that came spontaneously to them. Awareness of this increased her own intent to improve her expertise in the subject matter. She discussed this openly when she said, 'I have a need for a music course' (fieldnote 6/12/'90). Helen informed me that she had searched in vain. Because Helen perceived her musical expertise to be limited, there may have been a tendency to use the discipline as an adjunct to the content theme only rather than having a distinct contribution to make to learners' development. Such an approach gives rise to important questions about the impact of integration or thematic planning in areas of a programme where practitioners' expertise may not be particularly strong. The cumulative impact of the inquiry's evidence suggests that thematic planning, which includes the strengths and the integrity of the various subjects, requires an uncommon level of expertise combined with significant conceptual and planning acumen.

Not surprisingly, there was a strong thematic influence on the art work of the children. Restriction on the availability of materials was a significant constraint on activities. The classroom walls had accumulated much decorative material associated with the theme of the sea since the beginning of term, thus reducing the drabness of the room significantly. However, the following is important because it underlines further Helen's persistence in boosting the confidence of the learners, while reinforcing the linguistic gains they had made. The 'conversation of instruction' has significance also because it reveals Helen's own implicit valuing of the subject matter, as well as 'the place of reasons' in her practice, and the importance of 'sincere interaction' in the teaching process (Kilbourn, 1988, p. 110). Nevertheless, the work, though valued, is constantly in the service of the curriculum's theme and leitmotiv, more so than an opportunity for self-expression and development of artistic talent. Such a balance may be determined ultimately by practitioner's intent and level of expertise. The interactions between teacher and learners seek to extend the potential of dialogue for further meaning-making, a process which resonates with common understandings of child-centred teaching.

The class had obviously been painting [the previous day] as the learners' work was left to dry on the tables. After Helen had begun the day formally by asking the class to recite the Ár nAthair, Sé do bheatha a Mhuire,[2] [Our Father, Hail Mary], followed by the singing of 'Be not Afraid', she directed their attention to the bundle of paintings which some minutes earlier she had asked one of them to collect. What follows was another commonplace of Helen's practice. Though she was providing positive feedback on their paintings of the jungle, she availed of these emergent contextual opportunities to reinforce, revise and improve the learners' understanding of some of the content area of the curriculum. This was evident from the comments Helen made as she held up each painting in turn. Behind her on the board was the sketch she had done the previous day in preparation for individuals' efforts. So it was that she commented on buttress-roots, the forest floor, fungi growing, height of trees, forest canopy, evidence of wild life, etc. This was all done in a positive constructive manner . . . One painting was different from the others in that it was an obvious night scene with an eerie quality conveyed by the flight of a bat across the face of the moon, resulting in partial eclipse. The owners of these works or anyone else who chose to do so, were free to provide comment as their response to the work. (fieldnote 30/11/'90)

The cumulative impact of this and the previous theme is to create a strong sense of a fusion of informal communication with formal framework. What emerges from the details of Helen's teaching constructions is an understanding that these two cultural themes of child-centredness are complementary, creating a classroom climate that is tolerant and respectful of individual needs and abilities though cognitively oriented. Her conversational style animated the structure so that it was a highly interactive, inclusive and positive process intended to motivate and enthuse rather than to coerce and circumscribe. Within this complex and varied communication pattern there was a dynamic community that encouraged initiative while respecting individual difference through personal relationships.

Summary

Helen's conversational style appears as a unique response to her context. Its patterns, consistencies, complexities, responsiveness, and subtle variations provide a stimulating, humane, though always purposeful, learning environment: a process that adds significantly to her relatively rigid structures. Her mélange of class, group and individual interactions contrive to motivate and direct the learners towards greater self-confidence and independence, particularly in the use of language. Many of these details resonate meaningfully with assets of child-centredness in ways that do not *a priori* exclude aspects of communication and structure more usually identified as being traditional or didactic. Persistent tensions and dilemmas were evident between the teacher's need for progress, thus sustaining morale, the strengths of and necessity for structure and routine as an integral element of practice, and the realization that these necessary ingredients may imprison, inhibit and infantilize learners rather than foster independence, initiative and insight.

Thematic planning or integration is attractive as a means of providing a broadly based programme but it may reduce the degree of cognitive challenge presented to students while taxing the subject matter expertise of practitioners as it demands a capacity to think and plan within and between disciplines simultaneously when much of the teacher's socialization has been within the boundaries of particular disciplines. Structure and communication combine to foster learners' independence but observation of end-product only may create simplistic understandings of the extent to which secure independent learning and performance have been fostered by the very structures and routines which facilitated their development becoming invisible as a consequence of becoming embedded in the teaching–learning process. In-depth investigation reveals that structure and communication routines may be much closer to imaginative and independent activity beloved by advocates of progressivism than modernist, dichotomous thinking has commonly allowed. Post-modernist spaces create opportunities to move beyond paradigm wars and colonization to a reconstructed, grounded and more inclusive narrative of practice.

Notes

1 It is commonplace of infant classrooms in the Irish context to have the day punctuated with rounds of applause (buala bos) for the class as a whole or for groups and individuals. However, it is rather unusual to find this routine in use in a fifth class. It emerged in conversation with Helen at a later stage in the fieldwork that she had taught infants three years earlier and the content of the fieldnotes had made her realize that many of her communication routines were rooted in that experience.

2 This practice focuses attention on two additional commonplaces in Irish classrooms. Due to the fact that all but a few primary schools are vested in the local Bishop as patron, and are, therefore, denominational, the school day typically begins and ends with a prayer. In this particular instance the prayers are recited in Irish — a strategy which is frequently encouraged to increase the use of the language ('incidental Irish'), to cultivate an Irish atmosphere and to increase learners' contact with the language.

Chapter 8

Theme Three: Scaffolding and Shepherding

Introduction

The central dilemma of the third cultural theme — balance — is that of simultaneously scaffolding learners in a cognitively challenging manner while paying attention
to their social and personal needs in ways that adequately safeguard and shepherd
their social development, self-confidence and self-esteem. Due to the particular social
circumstances of Barrytown, the dilemma for Helen (and her colleagues) of finding
an appropriate accommodation for learners' social and cognitive needs was particularly acute. Though the dilemma was a constant source of tension in her practice, as
the investigation progressed it found particular focus around the issue of promoting
and maintaining standards while remaining sensitive to individual needs and cultural
context. Through this cultural lens, the manner in which contextual constraints, including policy and structures, influenced Helen's intentions and actions, were thrown
into high relief as she struggled to harmonize the national norms of schooling and
attainment with the learners' needs for security, self-esteem and social development.
The notion of a broadly based programme becomes subordinate to promoting and
upholding standards, particularly in basic subjects. Balance is reduced to a persistent tension between learners' needs for shepherding and a system's apparent need
for controlling challenge by setting and seeking to maintain standards.

Scaffolding and shepherding are not only axiomatic to teaching, they emerge
as important requirements for teachers, too, if their morale, personal and professional self-esteem and lifelong learning are to be sustained throughout their careers.
To understand this is to recognize that 'the [teaching] profession is itself a major
element of the curriculum', of everyday life in classrooms (Purpel, 1989, p. 141).
Through this cultural lens, therefore, a more wide-angled perspective on practice is
provided where classroom actions are contextualized, situated and reconstructed
within the broader school community; the social context of Barrytown; and national
educational norms and traditions. This complex dilemma focuses attention on the
tension between important aspects of child-centred ideology and more traditional
practice such as the dilemma posed when simultaneously seeking to minister to
learners' needs and interests and the social requirement for continuity through
cultural transmission. Through the lens of scaffolding and shepherding, additional
insights are gained into Helen's practice and, through these particulars, into the
general problem of child-centredness.

Scaffolding

Scaffolding is a term which has much in common with the idea of building a framework or structure which was documented in detail in the first cultural theme. However, Vygotsky's distinctive use of the term suggests that '*human learning presupposes a specific social nature and a process by which children grow into the intellectual life of those around them*' (Cole *et al.*, 1978, p. 88). This approach is said to go beyond the merely interactionist theory of Piaget to provide a more 'interactionist–dialectical' account of development (John-Steiner and Souberman, 1978, p. 124). Polanyi (1958, p. 207), too, recognizes the essentially social nature of learning through the importance he attaches to the quality of the relationship between 'the apprentice [and] . . . the master'. The potential of this dialectical relationship between learner and practitioner is maximized within 'the zone of proximal development', while appropriately structured programmes and 'good learning' are always 'in advance of development' (Cole *et al.*, 1978, p. 89). Scaffolding, is a means of providing a framework which challenges or stretches learners beyond their 'actual development' (Cole *et al.*, 1978, p. 86). However, the process is inherently risky and destabilizing so that 'what a child can do with assistance today she will be able to do by herself tomorrow' (p. 87). There are obvious similarities between the concept of scaffolding and the cognitive steps that Helen constructed as the mainframe of her teaching. Moreover, her conversational style was essentially social in orientation with an obvious emphasis on the acquisition of language as a centrally important ingredient of the meaning-making process. However, in addition to scaffolding learners to bring about their intellectual development, Helen was also very conscious of the need to 'shepherd' them and, thus, to ensure their adequate social progress.

Shepherding

Shepherding is the opposite side of the scaffolding coin. The concept of scaffolding or creating appropriate structures implicitly includes the idea of adequate support. While the cognitive steps constructed by Helen stretched the learners to the point of destabilizing their conceptual frameworks, her conversational style provided a positive, supportive, nurturing environment which facilitated risk-taking that also possessed potential for social development and enhanced self-esteem. Kutnick discusses social development in a more general sense and he identifies common agreement among developmental psychologists that:

> . . . the child moves from an initial state of non-effectiveness or autism towards a state of autonomy, self-knowledge and self-assurance. Not all individuals reach the higher stages, but they all have the opportunity of exposure to relationships of dependence upon adults and involvement with peers. (1988, p. 52)

It is obvious from Kutnick's comments that structure and support are essential requirements for social as well as cognitive development: that scaffolding and shepherding focus attention on different aspects of a single process. This unity in practice becomes more obvious when the distinction which Kutnick (1988, p. 166) makes between 'academic and social self-concept' is elaborated further. He indicates that the former 'has to do with one's self-image in relation to school success', while social self-confidence 'has to do with one's self-image in relation to interpersonal relationship'. Similarly, he argues that the relationship between the academic and social self is not a symmetrical one because '. . . a good self-concept will not necessarily mean academic success for the child: but poor self-concept will stop the child from performing to the best of his/her ability' (1988, p. 167).

Scaffolding and Shepherding in Practice

The tension in Helen's practice is the constant one she describes as not being able 'to take anything for granted' (fieldnote 20/12/'90). The details which follow reveal how she deals with this dilemma and illustrate its pervasiveness also.

> Each member of the blue group [less able] was encouraged to acquire a Geo board as well as some elastic bands and to create several shapes, all of which had been dealt with earlier that day or earlier in the week. These were triangle, rectangle, square, hexagon, octagon and rhombus. It was interesting to interact with this group while Helen worked on percentages and fractions with the more able group . . . In conversation with them, as they attempted various shapes, I was keen not to solve their problems for them, while at the same time offering help and encouragement, frequently through asking what I considered were pertinent questions. Their lack of confidence again became manifest. It would be nicer if I would complete the task or tell them how it was done. This would mean they would not have to do the thinking. Making a hexagon seemed to pose a particular challenge. It was after I had tried to make one without too much success that the pair with whom I was dealing actually tried it for themselves. One of them succeeded very quickly and announced this triumphantly to me. Her partner was immediately prepared to imitate her efforts. My interpretation of this was that my faltering attempts were enough to bridge the gap between their original lack of confidence and their ability to take the initiative themselves. It is also possible that my lack of success took the pressure off them so that the climate was more encouraging. I would be less likely to castigate for not completing the task, when I had been unsuccessful myself. There was also a sense in which they jettisoned my assistance once they realized that by trial and error, with the benefit of a hexagon shape beside them, it would only be a matter of time before they cracked the problem. The persistent thread in these various interpretations

is a lack of confidence in tackling the problem until it seemed to them that it was possible to complete the task. At worst, if the task remained incomplete, there would not be any repercussions from me. Given the basic lack of confidence which seemed to be the permanent mental state of these learners, they took risks of a cognitive kind, only when the stepping stones were sufficiently close together to ensure that they did not come in contact with the water. (fieldnote 28/11/'90)

Further reflection suggests that my attempts to solve the problem provided the learners with sufficient additional scaffolding to enable them to seek a solution to the problem independently. However, the critical point is not whether this encounter can be categorized as guided or directed discovery, but whether or not handover actually occurred. The details above suggest that one of the learners benefited from the additional scaffolding I provided to the extent that she found a solution herself. In the case of the learner who solved the problem, therefore, handover may have occurred, and in the process some 'principled' understanding of the hexagon was acquired; while her partner, who imitated the solution, is likely to have remained at a 'procedural' understanding of the task (Edwards and Mercer, 1987, p. 130). If, as Kutnick suggests, a poorly developed sense of social self retards academic achievement, then it is necessary in the context of Barrytown, to reduce the level of cognitive dissonance inherent in a learning task, so that learners' self-confidence will allow them to take up the challenge. It also presupposes that content is tailored to meet the social as well as the cognitive needs of learners. However, structures and communication routines may become sedimented in ways that inhibit rather than support and enhance learners' capacity to think. When this occurs, the propensity to spoon-feed rather than stimulate risk-taking may be increased. Nevertheless, their intended impact seems isomorphic with commonly expressed interpretations of child-centred ideology.

It is frequently suggested that middle-class children come to school with 'cultural capital' (Hargreaves, 1989). In contrast with this, there is a growing volume of evidence which suggests that the stress associated with poverty, unemployment and poor social circumstances results in significantly higher levels of 'psychiatric disturbance' among adults who suffer such indignities (Whelan, Hannan, and Creighton, 1991, p. 134). With unemployment in Barrytown estimated to be 80 per cent, it is reasonable to assume that its children were not immune to the consequences of anxiety, depression and low self-esteem. Adults who have low self-esteem and have a fatalistic outlook are unlikely to instil a great deal of security and confidence in their children, despite their best intentions. It is against this general backdrop that Helen's comments about taking nothing for granted are most adequately understood. Precisely because her learners lacked 'cultural capital', her teaching constructions, more so than practitioners in more favourable social circumstances, needed to find the 'golden mean' between scaffolding and shepherding through the teaching process.

Chapter 1 elaborated on the importance of cognitive dissonance as a means of advancing conceptual development. This dissonance is facilitated when a stable social self-concept can be taken for granted, thus enabling teachers to concentrate on promoting conceptual instability. The vignette which follows is illustrative of the tensions that arise in Helen's classroom as a consequence of the destabilization she created.

Helen moved Trish from alongside her pal Amy as they were talking a great deal. I had skipped out to the toilet and had missed the actual occurrence. On my return, I immediately saw what had happened as Trish was then sitting very close to me, and alongside Ailbhe who was probably the weakest learner in the class. It was as if Trish felt her presence on the side of the room on which we were located needed some explanation for me. As soon as she caught my eye she began, 'Teacher's mad she is. I'm not talking to teacher again'. I did not respond to this, and when we severed eye contact she went back to her copy. Some minutes later she repeated her earlier statement with the forlorn addition, 'She took me away from me best friend'. She lay back in her chair, folded her arms and gave every indication that she was going on strike . . . Some moments later she threw caution to the winds. She had been restless, looking around for some inspiration. Ailbhe's copy in particular did not seem to provide the kind of assistance she required. Suddenly I realized that much of her anger was directed at teacher because her relocation was making it much more difficult for her to complete her story. . . . She took herself and her copy back to Amy, and when she had garnered the next sentence in the story, she returned to her place of relocation. I did not hear any more verbal outbursts from her after that.

This was the first occasion I had seen such a verbal outburst against the teacher. It can be regarded as a tribute to the democratic nature of the relationships Helen cultivated that Trish did not feel intimidated into keeping her emotions to herself. It also drew my attention to how well behaved this class was generally, which was also a commentary on the quality of the relationships between pupils and teacher. This quality was effected by the relatively small number of learners in the class, allowing more time for contact with individuals . . . Trish was probably embarrassed by being moved and felt that some explanation was due to me. She lashed out verbally at the teacher because her confidence and social cohesion were undermined. Now it could be said that this was a minor issue that Trish was seemingly beginning to blow out of proportion, but, I think, it was an indication of the reason Helen felt so strongly about being positive, constructive and supportive in her practice. Otherwise, there would be many more outbursts of a more turbulent kind than the one being discussed. This would have devastating consequences for the quality of classroom relationships and the classroom atmosphere. It gave some indication of the fragility of the social foundation on which Helen had to build a cognitive scaffolding . . . A great deal of artistry was required to conduct this cognitive destabilization on a social foundation which was at best uncertain and at worst extremely fragile and/or volatile. (fieldnote 30/11/'90)

Helen indicated that when conflict occurred between herself and a learner, it frequently resulted in a very angry parent arriving at her classroom door: an adult who was frequently all too willing to vent his or her frustration on the teacher. She had learned from experience that social cohesion between practitioner, learners and parents, was an important consideration when determining the degree of challenge provided in the classroom. Our dialogue revealed that it was reflection on her practice which enabled her to refine the relationship between scaffolding and shepherding in her teaching rather than reflection on any abstract theoretical concept of child-centredness. As the inquiry progressed, it became more apparent (as Helen's intentions became more transparent: an intelligibility which resulted from more sustained dialogue and extended time in the field) that it was precisely because Helen sought to pay attention to social and cognitive needs that sometimes resulted in scaffolding and shepherding having a neutralizing effect on each other: the latter became an antidote to the former.

Helen asked the class to draw an area of six square units on the squared paper she provided. As they were about to draw this . . . she asked Kirsty to remind the class what they had learned about a rectangle. Kirsty [an academically able learner] seemed to have forgotten all she knew, and she began by telling the class that a rectangle had three sides. When this was instantly refuted by a number of voices, Kirsty was struck dumb. The task was then handed over to Laura to complete. Helen recognized the malaise and asked Sadie to repeat the details which Laura had supplied with some assistance from herself and others. Gina was dispatched to the box of shapes so that a rectangle could be displayed, thus leaving nobody in doubt as to what it looked like. Not for the first time, I was taken aback at the lack of retention among the learners. The same thing had occurred two days previously when Helen began to ask questions about solids and shapes. Since I had observed the amount of systematic work that had been done over the last number of weeks, I found it difficult to believe that there was a significant number that could not respond with any degree of competence when asked a question. The teaching routines seemed to lead to a kind of reductionism which compounded the contextual reality influencing teaching decisions. Allow me to explain.

I attempted in previous sets of fieldnotes, to provide evidence that Helen's practice, across the curriculum, involved a series of carefully constructed cognitive steps. These steps were mediated to the learners in a conversational style which involved a series of well-defined routines that began with the major input being provided by the teacher. This teacher input was gradually reduced to allow learners maximum participation and independence, bounded by the limits of the task. This was part of a well-developed strategy which was intended to promote ownership/independence in the learners at every stage of the learning process. Care was also taken in the sequencing of these steps to ensure that social development was enhanced (particularly as it related to self-confidence and self-esteem). Cognizance of this social context was very prominent in determining the size of the steps and the manner in which they were approached. Yet, it seemed that when learners were challenged by these carefully constructed steps they were very apt, like a horse at a fence, to take fright and refuse if they perceived that they might have to struggle to gain understanding, and to attain the next level. These refusals usually took the form of looking for assistance from the teacher or increasingly for my assistance as I became more a part of the culture of the classroom. I have had to struggle to resist the temptation to succumb to this 'learned helplessness' (Holt, 1970). Providing assistance in these situations where help was sought, almost inevitably meant providing intermediate stages between the already carefully constructed cognitive steps. In another context this assistance which was demanded constantly by the learners might be described as unnecessary 'spoon-feeding'. In Helen's context it was as much a part of the established routines as many other aspects of her practice. The net effect of this on the teacher's practice, over time, was, consciously or unconsciously, to smooth the way between one step and the next. (fieldnote 12/12/'90)

Providing balance implicitly suggests bringing about a state of equilibrium, while intellectual development requires dissonance and destabilization. For scaffolding and shepherding to work effectively they need to synergize rather than synchronize. When synchronization occurs, learners are more likely to remain at a procedural level rather than advancing to principled understanding, and this results in 'ritual knowledge' rather than 'principled knowledge' (Edwards and Mercer, 1987, p. 162). Cognitive theory has tended to emphasize 'high-level thinking' as the most sure-footed means of intellectual growth (Forman and Twomey Fosnot, 1982; Furth and Wachs, 1975) while more recent refinement stresses that 'all students should be challenged with problems requiring "higher order" thinking, given their current level of understanding and skill' (OECD, 1991, p. 104). However, if learning tasks which are designed to challenge are 'based solely on concreteness' to the extent that 'everything associated with abstract thinking' has been excluded, then development is most unlikely to occur. Consequently, 'concreteness is . . . a necessary and unavoidable . . . stepping stone for developing abstract thinking' and not an end in itself (Cole *et al.*, 1978, p. 89).

Helen's conversational style, in addition to widespread use of concrete materials, attempted to add this abstract dimension to learning tasks through her interactions with learners. In the process, the fault line between cognitive and social development is reduced to the extent that what demanded a significant cognitive stride for principled development to occur becomes a social stroll that preserves (but also retards) self-efficacy. Her ongoing dilemma enables me to highlight the general point that advocates of child-centred ideology have made one of its hallmarks, namely, that programme provision must pay adequate attention to social as well as cognitive needs of learners. Creating cognitive dissonance while promoting social development is inherently problematic and the degree of challenge will vary significantly according to context.

Smoothing the way between the cognitive steps designed to scaffold learners, had the additional effect of slowing the pace of progress, which became a further source of frustration for Helen. Nevertheless, she felt obliged to construct her teaching in response to learners' needs and not to impose a structure that would be more likely to alienate them, thus making classroom relationships and communication more problematic. This reflexive approach seemed to resonate with the tradition of child-centredness, though being aware of this did not diminish the underlying frustrations for her. However, when scaffolding and shepherding synergized, the resultant pleasure momentarily dissipated the quiet despair, thus providing 'job satisfaction' (Nias, 1989) as well as vindicating her commitment to 'communitas' (Woods, 1993a, 1993b).

> In a more general manner, the opportunity Helen provided to many of the class to read the poems they had written yesterday, was another example of her regard for the individual and for positive reinforcement which she provided as often as feasible. I was struck on this occasion — unlike the writing they completed the previous week — by the much greater variety in the creatures around which the learners chose to focus their poems. Consequently, it can be argued, there was a greater degree of ownership in terms of the language they utilized. While each got a 'buala bos' (applause) as they finished reading their poems, some were encouraged to display their illustrations also. Amidst this generally positive climate it would have been easy to impose demands on individuals that they did not want to meet. When Maura was asked to read her poem, she replied, 'I won't read', as she approached the teacher with her copy. Helen did not say anything but proceeded to read Maura's poem. She identified a few phrases as being particularly attractive. Maura got her applause, as did everyone else, without fuss. I remarked earlier [in this set of fieldnotes] that Vera had been reading about the Osprey when the roll was being called. Now she stood before the class to talk about the Osprey and its prey. I recorded that several weeks earlier . . . when Vera was asked to read her story to the class she had declined . . . Nevertheless, Helen coaxed her into getting on her feet and reading without leaving her place. It was encouraging to note the confidence with which Vera strode to the top of the room today. I know of no test that will even attempt to measure this kind of individual (cognitive and social) progress. (fieldnote 6/12/'90)

Through the detail of the fieldnotes, and further reflective dialogue with Helen, it emerged that a significant dimension of the ongoing dilemma of finding an appropriate balance for these learners was the external imposition of standards. Consequently, the issue of balance is nested within a wider concern for the promotion and maintenance of national norms of attainment: a concern which, when taken to the extreme, hankers after the payment by results era and its attendant lock-step didacticism, and militates against the legitimate aspiration of progressives to develop individual's potential through a broadly based programme without losing sight of civil society's goals (Goodson, 1994; Ball, 1994).

Scaffolding, Shepherding and Standards

Primary school curricula in Ireland were (as elsewhere) traditionally controlled by the twin forces of prescription (in the form of syllabi) and public examination. This resulted in a highly didactic, oppressive and competitive pedagogy that made little or no concession to individual difference with tragic consequences for the self-confidence and self-esteem of many (Holmes, 1911). Child-centred ideology reacted against this rigidity and competitiveness so that decisions regarding curricula and attainment were devolved to the level of the school. However, in a school system which has traditionally been highly centralized, practitioners such as Helen, despite many local constraints, tend to look to the centre for a yardstick by which to determine success or failure as part of a 'dependency culture' (Coolahan, 1994). Helen remarked on several occasions that she did not wish 'to ghettoize' the learners, and strove to prepare them for the mainstream. Scaffolding and shepherding in this wider context suggest that learners' needs and interests are tempered by reference to society's norms and expectations.

This concern is also closely associated with the transmission argument which suggests that certain elements of knowledge are essential, more worthwhile and, therefore, more critical for cultural continuity (Young, 1971; Apple, 1981; Eisner, 1996). The dilemma to which these concerns give rise is exacerbated in the Irish context by the fact that the calibre of entrants to primary teaching has been particularly high by international comparison (Greaney, Burke and McCann, 1987). Consequently, there has been an expectation on the part of practitioners that pupils should measure up to the exacting standards attained by teachers themselves with the insinuation that anything less somehow reflected unfavourably on their work (Sugrue, 1996a). Though not a particularly popular point to pursue, it may be postulated also that the combination of traditional curriculum requirements and the calibre of entrants to primary teaching in Ireland created a classroom climate that was generally unsympathetic to the less able. The resultant strain between the weight of this tradition and the context in which Helen taught, meant that the ongoing tension between scaffolding and shepherding was exacerbated, and encouraged a concentration on the basics: she struggled to meet learners' needs as well as to measure up to standards set by others.

Helen understood child-centredness to include responsiveness to learners and their context, without losing sight of the bigger picture of general societal needs. How much latitude this affords practitioners differs according to the prevailing socio-cultural climate. For example, the optimism of the 1960s was much more tolerant of difference and contextual variation than the more stringent conformist (and politically correct) demands of the 1980s and early 1990s (Lawton, 1992; Ball, 1994; Smyth, 1993). This has been particularly obvious in England and Wales since 1988 as successive Tory governments have centralized and prescribed curricula and attempted to institutionalize national testing. What both periods signify very clearly is that there is no ideal, no holy grail that resolves these tensions once and for all. Rather, it is through the transformative actions of practitioners that these dilemmas are momentarily resolved. By contextualizing these issues through the particulars of practice, therefore, insights are gained and understanding increased as to an appropriate synergyzing of the grand narratives of teaching: empty rhetoric is no substitute for a clearly articulated version of 'what really counts in school' that leaves room for interpretation in response to context (Eisner, 1991a). Within the particulars of this case study, the question becomes: What standards and who decides?

In the emotionally demanding, morale sapping context that Barrytown represents, my ongoing reflective conversation with Helen revealed that she developed various coping strategies which enabled her to find a balance in her teaching. However, it became apparent that the more successful these strategies were the less incentive there was for local management or policy-makers to pay attention to contextual constraints or the provision of support for teachers. One of the legacies of the tradition of schooling in Ireland is a sense of heroism, of overcoming adversity by rising to the challenge. In these circumstances, to complain about insurmountable contextual constraints is to risk being labelled 'a moaner' and the power of such labelling conveniently results in those who wear the badge being ignored. The power of labelling is further exacerbated in the setting (and the site) by the tradition of autonomy, isolation and individuality and the lack of collegiality which characterizes the system. Failure in the face of adversity would also suggest neglect of one's moral responsibility to care and this would be unacceptable to many practitioners (Noddings, 1992; Ben-Peretz, 1996). The following extract provides an insider's perspective on these tensions which centre around standards and how they can be promoted.

> Helen had suggested to me (during the coffee break) that I should ask some of her colleagues in the staffroom at lunch time how their Christmas tests were progressing. She also suggested that the likely response would be that they wouldn't give any as 'it's too depressing'. In Helen's context, the avoidance of tests seemed more deep rooted than sensitivity to the need for family unity at this festive time of year which was a reason for test avoidance cited by a number of practitioners in phase one of this study. It was a wish not to be confronted by the lack of significant progress after a term of hard work. While there was considerable progress in which she and the learners could take pride, much of it would be unlikely to register on standardized tests. I took it, therefore, that her comments about tests and the attitude toward them among her colleagues, had much more to do with the nature of testing and reporting as commonly understood. The traditional tests which many teachers would be giving in the 3Rs as well as in history and geography . . . [immediately before Christmas] would be poor indicators of progress in Helen's classroom as the process had been oral in orientation, with little attention to textbooks. Different

approaches to teaching require different modes of assessment and evaluation. If new and imaginative approaches to appraising the progress of children were devised, there would still be a question, given contextual constraints, about the progress made by individual learners. It is important not to fudge this issue but the kinds of approaches which have not been articulated would eliminate some of the 'frustration' of which Helen spoke. One of the consequences of this frustration she said was that 'you stop challenging at a certain level'. The frustrations about which Helen spoke were manifest in the tension she experienced in her attempts to construct appropriate classroom experiences for her learners. The demands of the learners for help, support and encouragement, were being constantly buffeted against her own recognition of the need to challenge and to stretch them in a more cognitive sense. To return to the analogy used earlier in these notes: this daily tension certainly takes the edge off the cognitive steps which Helen sought to maintain. It is an issue that adds significantly to the frustration of the teacher and diminishes morale. This is a serious issue which effects the quality of practice as it is constructed by teachers. The individual teacher as she goes about the daily grind of meeting the needs of the learners must suspend issues of constraints to enable her to get on with the job. When professionals do this repeatedly (and well), management [and government] assume that these problems don't exist, or even if they do, they are of no real import. By subverting the constraints, for ethical and professional reasons which orient the practitioner to empathize with the client, those who man the classroom barricades, so to speak, deny themselves a voice. That those who are silently manning the chalk face are [primarily] women, is an additional twist in this complex web. It is this constant tension between the need to construct a curriculum that is socially meaningful and cognitively challenging, that is at the heart of the cycle of frustration to which Helen was giving voice. (fieldnote 12/12/'90)

Helen felt obliged to 'stop challenging at a certain level' so that learners' social and personal developmental needs could be accommodated. Her responsiveness and sensitivity to learners' needs resonated with important aspects of child-centredness, while side by side with an officially sponsored policy of child-centredness was a growing demand for testing and accountability that ignored contextual constraints. The more successfully she promoted and enhanced the full and harmonious development of the learners the less likely she was to meet national norms on standardized tests, though in principle they are not mutually exclusive. Her sense of frustration suggested that it was increasingly difficult to serve both masters. It was difficult enough to juggle satisfactorily the cognitive and social needs of learners, but to do this while keeping a watchful eye on predetermined standards seemed to make the burden unbearable and unfair. As Stake (1990, p. 15) suggests, '. . . to evaluate on the basis of any single instrument or to rely on only one single authority is mindless.'

Recent research on teacher narrative suggests that the natural rhythms of the calendar year insinuate their way into the school curriculum (Clandinin, 1986; Connelly and Clandinin, 1988; Clandinin and Connelly, 1991). However, as the term began to 'wind down' towards Christmas, Helen was reluctant to allow the season of goodwill to become too prominent a part of the curriculum. She was more interested in finishing the theme of the rainforests so that a new theme could commence in the new year. She was also aware of the extent to which Christmas had become a commercial exploitation of people through the promotion of consumerism. She was particularly sensitive to this given the impoverished circumstances of her class. Her intention was to shepherd the learners by not raising their expectations or even their thoughts of expensive gifts by avoiding discussion of impending festivities. Previous experience had taught her also that once celebratory aspects of the season were discussed, the class was inclined 'to be hyper'. The learners' interest in the approaching festivities appeared to be subverted to preserve Helen's image of the classroom as an oasis and to shepherd them against the harsh realities of their own social circumstances. The short vignette which follows indicates how this general concern circumscribed classroom interactions in a very real sense, while it also touched each individual, and one individual in particular. It also reveals Helen's guilt and frustration for having opened a can of worms when her intention had totally unanticipated consequences.

Helen informed me while at assembly today that there were only thirteen present the previous day. She began the day with them all standing around the table where they had prepared a crib and decorated a small tree. After they had said some of the usual prayers she instructed them to close their eyes and to make a wish for Christmas. One of the girls 'burst into tears'. As she told me the story she could not hide her embarrassment and said, 'Talk about putting your feet in it'. Of course Helen's intentions were very laudable, but she was reprimanding herself for not being more aware of individual sensitivities. Her sense of guilt was heightened by the knowledge that on Christmas day last year, the mother of this learner had nothing other than a tin of beans with which to feed her family due to the drinking habits of her husband. This was another example of how social context influenced Helen's morale, her relationships with the learners, and the curriculum she constructed. (fieldnote 18/12/'90)

Despite Helen's best intentions to shepherd the learners, the realities of their social context intruded into the classroom oasis. In these circumstances it is possible that teachers '*can* care too much' (Hargreaves and Tucker, 1991, p. 498). This commitment to care needs to be 'balanced with other goals such as ones directed to providing focused and intellectually challenging work' (p. 497). Such a balance ensures that teachers are 'committed . . . *to* care' and not '*by* it' (p. 498). While Helen and her colleagues were committed to care, the yardstick by which success within the system was measured was academic achievement. There were no tangible means, therefore, by which her achievements could be recognized, acknowledged or celebrated. Excluding the possibility of interrogating the consumerism surrounding

Christmas celebrations from her programme, displayed Helen's propensity to care, yet it can be legitimately argued that this well-intentioned shepherding set limits to the programme's horizons, thus narrowing the meaning-making potential for the learners and making it more difficult to provide a broadly based content that is environmentally based. In a circuitous, unintended way, Helen's shepherding narrowed the cultural horizons of the learners though her intention was to avoid ghettoizing them. In these circumstances, norms were established in response to an ongoing dilemma shaped by her reaction to local constraints as well as internalization of nationally imposed standards.

Hargreaves (1984a) makes the general point, in relation to the setting of standards through formal systems of assessment, that:

> The further away any group of children is from the *formal* point of selection and examination, the less specific are the knowledge demands made upon the children and the more diffuse are the criteria for achievement. (p. 76)

The tradition of central control, as well as the many ways in which practitioners are encouraged to achieve certain standards, suggested to Helen that despite official endorsement of local autonomy through child-centred policy it was also necessary to look beyond her immediate context for 'real' standards. Though this may well have had its virtues, it contributed further to her sense of frustration. Homework is a commonplace of the Irish educational system and its focus, content, degree of challenge and duration are shaped significantly by context (Burke *et al.*, 1991, 1992). Helen's practice in this regard provides further evidence that in the interest of shepherding the learners, when doing their homework, the degree of challenge to the learners was curtailed.

> As usual, sum copies, in which homework had been completed the previous night, had to be put in two separate bundles on the teacher's table. Copies which contained corrected versions of the Irish story which had been written some days earlier and had already been corrected by the teacher, were also collected. Only five of the class had done these corrections the previous night, even though this task had been written down as part of assigned homework. The five who had done the homework were rewarded with a concession and all the others were warned to do it that night. Helen indicated after school that this was the reason she did not give as much homework as she would like. The class simply would not do it. This would lead to constant conflict which was not worth the hassle. It was better to give a little and insist that it was completed, was her rationale. (fieldnote 6/12/'90)

Her perceptions on homework routines corroborated comments from other practitioners who taught in similar situations (and were participants in phase one); that it was necessary to limit the amount of homework she assigned on any one night. She also realized the impact of this over a lifetime of schooling. However, her frustration did not end there. The context also imposed restrictions on the developmental potential of the work she assigned. Her responsiveness to learners' needs moved her further away from what she knew to be the standards which operated elsewhere. The inherent logic of Helen's persistent dilemma seemed to suggest that the more she responded to the cultural context of the learners, thus acting out a common interpretation of child-centredness, the more her frustration grew as she became more alienated from standards of the mainstream, while in a perverse and unintended manner she focused more exclusively on a narrow range of skills. When Helen assigned homework on the day in question, she talked the class through it to reinforce the seriousness with which she expected them to approach the work, particularly the less able group.

> Helen informed me later that she always gave computational questions to this group and never problem-solving questions. She avoided the latter as there was no one to provide help and it would only cause problems all round. She stuck with the basic mathematical processes and gave plenty of practice in these. (fieldnote 6/12/'90)

One of the unintended consequences of this strategy was a narrowing of content, of the basics even, thus reducing the degree of challenge and potential for development while redefining balance in terms of aspects of the 3Rs. Finding an appropriate balance between the social and cognitive needs of learners, something which is encouraged by popular images of child-centred ideology, eroded the potential for development. Thus, progress was much slower as the balance between scaffolding and shepherding shifted in favour of procedural rather than principled knowledge. This interpretation is strengthened by international comparative research which suggests a focus on basic skills in the Irish context to the detriment of higher cognitive processes (Martin and Morgan, 1994; Elley, 1992; La Pointe, Mead, and Askew, 1992; La Pointe, Askew, and Mead, 1992). Helen's very success in achieving a balance was tempered by the knowledge that colleagues in more favourable circumstances took for granted learners' social needs, thus enabling them to accelerate their cognitive development. Helen's sense of frustration was increased rather than diminished by her transformation of the principles of individuality and full and harmonious development into her structures and routines as she felt it less likely that standardized tests (which continued to be the 'real' measure of appropriate standards) would be an accurate reflection of learners' progress.

There are many insidious contextual means by which a teacher is demoralized which, over a period of time, may have profound effects on professional well-being and teaching quality (Nias, 1989; Connell, 1985). This demoralization is exacerbated in the Irish context by a lack of mobility in teaching, of adequate resources, and adequate inservice structures to ensure lifelong learning opportunities for practitioners (INTO, 1993, 1994a, 1994b; Coolahan, 1994). The tension between scaffolding and shepherding learners in these circumstances becomes complicated by teachers' needs to develop strategies for their own survival. The struggle to maintain standards against the odds becomes a source of frustration rather than a source of satisfaction, as one might reasonably expect. When this occurs, the combined effect of all the other insignificant structural inadequacies can be overwhelming. The relative insignificance of the following issue is intended to reinforce this point.

> During the break, Helen had spoken of the need to display some more of the kids' art work. When class resumed she sent one of the girls to the office for some 'Blu-tac' to attend to this issue. The report which came back was that the cupboard was bare. When the messenger asked if she would request some from another teacher, Helen responded rather despondently, 'No, I'll have to buy some'. (fieldnote 10/12/'90)

When discussing many of the irksome inconveniences to which Helen was exposed, she remarked that 'if teachers stopped subsidizing the system it would fall asunder' (fieldnote 10/12/'90). The general perspective to which she referred reinforces my earlier argument that the more successfully teachers develop coping strategies, the less incentive there is for management and policy-makers to alter existing structures. This results in a form of 'cooptation' of teachers by management which 'is a technique for survival . . . ultimately concerned less with change than with continuity', with preserving the status quo (Purpel, 1989, p. 142). In a climate where educational discourse is dominated increasingly by the 'new managerialism' and its demands for accountability, efficiency and enterprise, Helen and her colleagues may be exhorted to still greater effort so that all can pull themselves up by the boot straps. Such rhetoric tends to focus on the practitioner in 'splendid isolation', thus leading 'to incomplete accounts of school processes' because 'there is a tendency to exaggerate the latitude and freedom engaged by the teacher' as well as to 'underestimate the constraints bearing down on the teacher from the wider society' (Hargreaves and Woods, 1984, p. 8). Succinctly stated: '. . . the problems that pervade our schools go well beyond problems of curriculum' (Eisner, 1985, p. 72). Consequently, a more complete account of the tensions Helen experienced when attempting to both scaffold and shepherd her class requires that we 'understand the teaching community, the work culture of which that teacher is a part' (Hargreaves, 1992, p. 217).

This is particularly the case in the Irish context where tradition has placed an undue burden on the individual teacher without reference to colleagues or context. I am in agreement with the conclusion reached by Hargreaves and Woods (1984, p. 9) when they suggest that there is a 'need to link the closely observed world of teaching to changes in society and educational policy as a whole' to provide a complete account of classroom practices. Such an account has more potential also for increasing understanding of the problems and the possibilities for child-centredness by grounding them in the situated realities of practitioners rather than in the rhetorics of grand narratives.

Scaffolding and Shepherding: Practitioners

It is generally accepted in Ireland that there are 'relatively large areas' of the school curriculum which are 'still unresearched' (Ireland, 1985, p. 40) The limited amount of survey research which has been completed in the setting (to the virtual exclusion of qualitative studies), of its very nature ignores the contextual constraints which this study regards as essential to an adequate account of teaching. Focus on local constraints is not an attempt to deny that some teachers are better than others, however 'good' teaching might be defined, and that some may even be inefficient. However, the point is that practitioners play by very different sets of rules depending on the context in which they function. Research on structural inequalities in the Irish context suggests that:

> The additional funds from parents and the community, available to schools serving middle class clientele, and the disadvantages suffered by schools in run-down deprived areas . . . mean that the quality of education available to working class and middle class pupils is far from uniform. (Breen, Hannan, Rottman, and Whelan, 1990, p. 130)

Consequently, in the absence of adequate government policy and structures, networks of support at the local level become critical. In the Irish system where management and much of the funding for day-to-day running of schools is devolved to each management board working in isolation, the potential for fluctuation in support and resources is enormous. While there is justified concern in some research literature about the effects of these inequalities on learners, rarely, if ever, are structural inequalities discussed in relation to their negative impact on the morale of teachers and the quality of their teaching.

Helen's expectations were influenced by a lack of resources and the general lack of maintenance of the immediate environment. This had a demoralizing effect which rendered her more susceptible to internalize the despair and disillusionment of the immediate community. Internalization of these myriad influences increased her sense of the need to shepherd the learners. All of these factors heightened her sense of outrage that despite the enormity of these constraints which she strove to surmount, the standards by which her work and that of her class were judged were determined far away from her milieu. It was the frustration and demoralization of this vicious circle which Helen addressed in our conversation (Nias, 1989; Hargreaves and Tucker, 1991).

> The comments to which she wished to respond were in relation to the idea of creating small cognitive steps so that the learners would choose to attempt the challenge being provided rather than opting out or seeking help. There was frustration in Helen's voice as she spoke. Because the pace of progress was so slow, she remarked, 'I don't look too far ahead,' as it would be too depressing to do so. She continued, as if giving assent to the various contextual issues which contributed to demoralization, 'You begin to believe what other people are telling you about these kids'. As the daily grind becomes internalized in the teacher she became 'resigned in terms of expectations'. These comments are best understood from within an educational context where the dominant culture of schooling was didactic with an emphasis on the acquisition of factual information (OECD, 1991) and

the dominant measure of success was the number of learners who get into 'A' streams in high status, prestigious schools. These were, and in some cases still are, the criteria against which the status and success of teachers are measured, and by which teachers, in many instances, also measure themselves and one another. In this climate, teachers such as Helen and her colleagues who teach in similar contexts, became marginalized by a system which seemed to deny them status and recognition so that they began to lose confidence in their own ability and the value attached to the work they were doing. Helen expressed this kind of angst when she said, 'I don't think I could teach in a middle-class area'. Part of her reasoning for this was, she continued, 'I have not been stretched as much in my own general knowledge'. She recognized that a change in the context in which she taught would probably be desirable personally and professionally. However, the tradition of being employed by a particular school . . . reduced mobility to close to zero. It was for these reasons that Helen felt, 'I'll never get out of here'. (fieldnote 14/12/'90)

There is implicit recognition in Helen's comments that in the absence of a change in policy and/or structures that would materially alter conditions at the level of the school and classroom, the best possibility for professional growth and the avoidance of recidivism brought on by insuperable constraints is to move to another context. Her comments also convey an intuitive sense of how classroom practice is linked to issues of policy and structure.

Helen worked in isolation and this was the general pattern in Barrytown school, reflecting the dominance of a culture of individualism nationally. Neither was there any clearly defined support structure by way of specialist teachers or advisors with the exception of a remedial teacher. The system was also marked (at the time) by a virtual absence of structured support for ongoing professional development: internationally there is a growing expectation that school principals and their staffs take more responsibility for their own professional development. This broader environment posed a challenge to Helen and her colleagues 'to devise and enact, creatively and constructively a set of teaching strategies which [would] make life bearable, possible and even rewarding . . .' (Woods, 1984, p. 66). The strategies which they developed locally had particular significance for the tension between the need to scaffold and to shepherd learners in and through their classroom actions.

Developing a school plan through collegiality and collaboration within the school has become an accepted orthodoxy in recent years (Coolahan, 1994; Ireland, 1995). Barrytown school had a partially completed plan to which Helen never referred. She expressed concern on a number of occasions that such a document, if taken seriously as a form of 'contrived collegiality', could interfere with the autonomy she enjoyed in her own classroom (Hargreaves, 1992, 1994). This autonomy was an aspect of her work which she would relinquish with misgivings. In the absence of a school-wide support system in the form of a school plan and appropriate professional development structures, Helen and her colleagues developed their own informal support network.

This informal network was particularly important to them as they had long since abandoned discussion of their dilemmas with colleagues who worked in very different social contexts. They had found such conversations to be frustrating as they increased their feelings of isolation. This contextually determined ghettoization of Helen and her colleagues implicitly recognized the extent to which Barrytown influenced their intentions and actions. When such fracturing or balkanization occurs in a system, practitioners no longer have a shared understanding of policy which, in this instance, was child-centred. It may be that context had come to dominate their thinking so that Helen and her colleagues no longer derived any sustenance from a common vision of child-centredness. They intuitively recognized that standards set by the mainstream did not fit their particular circumstances and were a source of frustration rather than vindication. Yet they could not escape their influence. Within the structurally balkanized world of Barrytown, they created their own informal support network which attempted to generate a set of standards more appropriate to their context. Creating this informal local support enabled them to respond sensitively to learners' needs by creating their own norms while protecting themselves against feelings of professional inadequacy induced by reference to the mainstream.

In Barrytown, this informal support was a mixture of a 'morale-boosting' strategy achieved by 'rhetoric and laughter' (Woods, 1984, p. 60) and 'contrastive rhetoric'. Hargreaves describes contrastive rhetoric as:

> . . . *that interactional strategy whereby the boundaries of normal and acceptable practice are defined by institutionally and/or interactionally dominant individuals or groups through the introduction into discussion of alternative practices and social forms* . . . (Hargreaves, 1984a, p. 218)

The form of contrastive rhetoric, which Helen and her colleagues employed, differed in important ways from its classic manifestations outlined above, but the staffroom anamnesis[1], in which they engaged, had sufficient similarities to enable the term to apply to both. Reminiscing about the extremes of professional engagement became an effective means of recasting everyday experiences as quite normal in relation to the difficulties which were less frequently encountered. Mattingly (1991) captures the essence of this process:

> Experience is obviously an inconsistent teacher; it is perfectly possible to live through something and not learn much as a result. One motive for telling stories is to wrest meaning from experience especially powerful and disturbing ones. (p. 237)

In Barrytown's particular circumstances 'the individual is shaped by the situation and shapes the situation in the living out of the story and in the storying of the experience' (Clandinin and Connelly, 1991, p. 275). However, in the complex world of practice the form of contrastive rhetoric, in which Helen and her colleagues engaged, carries within it the conflicting need for amnesia as well as anamnesis. The process of remembering enabled them to construct local standards which facilitated their being responsive to learners' needs. However, this same process pushed the standards of others from their consciousness so that it also became a form of negation, of forgetting, thus enabling them to cope more readily. In the absence of adequate support for professional growth, they used contrastive rhetoric as a form of scaffolding and shepherding for themselves to confer meaning on their routines in place of quiet despair. The meaning-making process of their story-telling provided (temporary) amnesia against the standards of the mainstream; a form of contrastive rhetoric I described as 'circling the wagons'.

> They (Helen and three of her colleagues) continued to remind each other about individual learners and their parents who had proved particularly difficult to deal with in the past. This was also a kind of contrastive rhetoric where the most tragic cases were remembered, recalled and repositioned within the collective folklore and psyche of those staff who were party to this conversation. As I struggled to come to terms with the effect that this rhetoric had on their respective classroom actions, the metaphor which came to mind was that of 'Circling the Wagons' . . . the classroom became the last bastion of civilization surrounded by a sea of social disintegration over which the teachers, who toiled in this environment daily, had no control. These stories revealed the sense of heroism of teachers who had dealt with emotionally disturbed pupils, and who had intervened to find suitable places for severely stressed or sexually abused children. This collective anamnesis served a number of important functions in sustaining these practitioners. By citing some of the worst cases that they had had to deal with in their careers, there was a sense of triumph. They actually succeeded in making a difference even in the most extreme cases and under the most extreme provocation they somehow managed to rise above adversity. It reaffirmed their own humanity and made their contribution seem worthwhile. (fieldnote 14/12/'90)

This informal, even vicarious, support network increased Helen's capacity to cope. By creating local norms the tension between scaffolding and shepherding the learners was reduced. The flexibility these locally derived standards provided enabled her to apply greater sensitivity to individuals' needs and to provide a more balanced programme that catered for the full and harmonious development of the learners; commitment to care was reaffirmed and vindicated.

Helen agreed that exchanging stories with her colleagues did provide a 'sense of triumph', giving her and her colleagues a sense of 'sisterhood' (fieldnote 18/12/'90). However, this anamnesis carries within it an amnesia regarding structural inadequacies and inequalities. Consequently, though the primary purpose of this staffroom discourse was fulfilled by providing support, it had the inherent tendency to accept existing structures as immutable, thus making the prospect of 'getting out of here' the most likely means of change or renewal.[2] Such encounters suggest that without policy changes and structural alterations survival becomes the practitioner's primary concern, allowing little time or energy for even questioning existing teaching constructions or the constraints which shape them. There is a quiet despair about such situations that has a devastating effect on teacher morale.

> In the same way that members of the legal profession argue that 'hard cases' make 'poor law', the effect of staffroom anamnesis may be to protect a set of values and their attendant classroom actions which would be difficult to sustain without this collective rhetoric. The very criteria which sustained the practitioners in difficult circumstances, also formed a barrier to a more radical appraisal of the practice they constructed. (fieldnote 14/12/'90)

When I discussed with Helen the possibility of constructing a more radically conceived programme that would include an interrogation of issues such as poverty and unemployment, she rejected my suggestions because they would be likely, in the short term, to 'destabilize' or 'deskill' (Kilbourn, 1990c; Bennett *et al.*, 1991; Buchman and Floden, 1991). Radical change of practice is out of bounds for practitioners because the very notion of scaffolding learners requires a certain rigidity of structure, which is one of a programme's strengths (Kilbourn, 1990b). Collective staffroom anamnesis provides temporary respite from the standards of the mainstream, while in the isolation of the classroom traditional preoccupation with 'the basics' continues to influence the balance in teaching. Change must, therefore, be gradual in response to the nature of practice itself, its complexity and need for continuity, integrity and equilibrium. If standards of the mainstream are to be applied meaningfully to all schools, there is an obligation on policy-makers to alter existing structures so that expectations in relation to standards may be realistic: tinkering is not a substitute for structural reform (Apple, 1981; Aronowitz and Giroux, 1985).

Helen rejected my suggestions for a more radical pedagogy as potentially too destabilizing because one of her central concerns was that the girls 'be happy in school' (transcript 8). It might also negate a very powerful desire among primary teachers to care for, nurture or shepherd their learners (Noddings, 1992; Hargreaves and Tucker, 1991). Helen thought that such an approach would result in 'opening up the many conflicts in their lives and she would be very uncertain as to how these might be handled' (fieldnote 20/12/'90). She was conscious also that many of these learners would be early school leavers, some of whom would be teenage mothers. Helen was keen to break this vicious circle and one of the means at her disposal was to make school as positive an experience as possible. She reasoned that as young mothers they would be keen to send their children to school regularly if their own school experience had been positive. She was also more hopeful that an initial positive experience for these potential young mothers would keep the door of second chance education open for them. These were the more general concerns that influenced Helen's deliberations when dealing with the dilemma of scaffolding and shepherding the learners. It was through her responsiveness to these contextual details that she sought to resolve the inevitable tensions of individual needs, full and harmonious development, and society's demand for a good grounding in the basics. By responding to these dilemmas, Helen resolved, in consort with the deeply held conviction of many practitioners, 'to improve the lives or life-chances of children' (Nias, 1989, p. 32). However understandable, laudable even, the balkanized contrastive rhetoric of Helen and her colleagues and its importance as a survival strategy in difficult circumstances, it was ultimately self-defeating as it served also to legitimate the very structures, policies and constraints which confined and consigned them to a nether world of Nietzschean 'closed horizon' where they became cocooned by their own dilemmas and sought to cannibalize them for solutions without reference to mainstream influences or structured support, which was all but non-existent in any event (Gadamer, 1975, p. 304). When practitioners lack appropriate scaffolding and shepherding, their own grounded theories may reduce them to classroom automatons.

Policies, structures and a variety of professional supports are necessary to broaden practitioners' horizons and make qualitative improvements to their practices. The reflective collaborative process of interpretive inquiry indicates just how such supports can enable practitioners to reconstruct their practice.

Scaffolding and Shepherding: Research

The collaboration and the reflective dialogue, which the research process involved, underscores the importance of, and need for, sustained professional support at the level of the school so that professional isolation is overcome. Helen remarked that through the 'reflective turn' (Schön, 1991) of the research process, 'it was like beginning teaching all over again' (fieldnote 18/12/'90). As she became more aware that 'I'm having that kind of effect on the kids' when the fieldnotes identified social and cognitive benefits about which she was only tacitly aware, it gave her renewed 'enthusiasm to go back . . .' into the classroom and strive all the harder (fieldnote 21/12/'90). This feedback demonstrates in a very tangible way that even the temporary scaffolding and shepherding afforded by the research process was a sufficient structural alteration to enable Helen to understand her practice differently: proof positive that structural alterations have implications for practice, though the pervasive culture of individualism in the setting inhibited more collaborative action. Nevertheless, encouraged by the tenor of this conversation, I asked her if she was attracted by the concept of the 'reflective practitioner' (Schön, 1983). Her reply, and indirectly that of her colleagues, indicated the implausibility of this in their particular circumstances. Collectively, they concurred with the view expressed by Nias (1989, p. 208) that: '. . . primary teaching has a bottomless appetite for the investment of scarce personal resources such as time, interest and energy'.

> 'I'd love to, but when I go home I'm too tired,' [said Helen in reply]. In a conversation in the staffroom several of the teachers spoke of the need to 'wind down' after going home each day, 'to become human again,' while others looked forward to going into a totally quiet house after the noise of the school and found this 'therapeutic'. Because teachers are very busy people and do very demanding work, many are not capable of doing

the kind of reflection implied by Helen on their own without some outside assistance. (fieldnote 20/12/'90)

In the adverse circumstances of Barrytown, imagining new horizons of practice for Helen was heavily circumscribed and proportionately modest. She had already indicated that music was a discipline which had potential for the learners, as well as being an area in which she would like to develop additional expertise. However, she was immediately confronted by the issue of her knowledge and skill, and the structures which facilitated or inhibited their development. Our conversation indicated that reflection alone without professional support in the form of pedagogical and subject matter knowledge, was more likely to increase awareness of the limitations of existing teaching rather than to encourage its development in any significant way (Alexander *et al.*, 1989).

> She recognized that it would be difficult to extend the learners much beyond the point at which they had arrived. This was so because she was not too clear where she wanted to go. Through comments which she had made on previous fieldnotes, it is fair to say that she was recognizing, in the words of Stenhouse (1975, p. 83) that 'the improvement of practice rests on diagnosis . . .' and that 'there can be no educational development without teacher development'. (fieldnote 12/12/'90)

Without the necessary support structures the lion's share of individual practitioner's energy is channelled into developing survival strategies. Through participation in this inquiry, Helen indicated a willingness to take risks and to develop her professional expertise but she cannot do it alone. The tradition of schooling in Ireland has put 'the burden of virtue and vice totally on the *individual* while ignoring the larger social conditions in which human actions are embedded' (Sullivan, 1990, p. 140). The final vignette indicates very clearly that the context of classroom, school and community — including government policy and its implicit structures — are powerful influences alongside practitioners' intentions and actions, to the extent that:

> . . . the teacher is thus a crucial lynch pin in the wheels of causality that connects structural features of the society to interactional patterns in the classroom and back again, thereby helping to reproduce those structural arrangements. (Hargreaves, 1984a, p. 66)

As one of my interviewees remarked, '[practice] is where the rubber meets the road' (transcript 13).

There is an onus on practitioners also to take responsibility for their own development and to shed a 'culture of dependency' which the oppressive nature of traditional schooling engendered (Coolahan, 1994). However, if schools are to become 'learning communities' where teaching traditions are revisioned and revitalized, then time and space have to be created to facilitate professional dialogue (Barth,

1990). For practitioners to scaffold and shepherd learners adequately they too have to be challenged and supported: challenged to take greater responsibility for their own professional renewal, and supported in their endeavours by a variety of policy and structural changes.

Summary

This cultural theme of balance (more so than structure and communication), because it took a more wide-angled perspective on classroom processes, demonstrates that a practitioner's personal and professional biography, apprenticeship of observation and the contexts of her work, have more of a shaping influence on classroom actions than the rhetorics of grand narratives. Helen's decisions in relation to scaffolding and shepherding the learners in her classroom were shaped significantly by the social and economic realities of Barrytown, traditions of schooling in the setting, and the tensions and dilemmas to which they contributed within the confines of the classroom. Nevertheless, challenging learners while caring for them was a persistent dilemma of practice which, as it was played out in Helen's classroom, reflected local needs and circumstances as well as larger social forces. While balance is critically important to teaching and teachers, the manner in which practitioners challenge and care for learners and the breadth and depth of learning experiences they construct as part of that process are shaped by much larger social forces.

With horizons of practice circumscribed significantly, Helen and her colleagues appealed to a form of contrastive rhetoric which shepherded them against the application of the mainstream's standards to their situation, while simultaneously deriving a form of scaffolding from this rhetoric by appeal to the extremes of their experiences to give a normal appearance to everyday classroom encounters. The scaffolding and shepherding they derived from this rhetoric, in tandem with the prevailing culture of isolation and individualism within the school, meant that the selective anamnesis it created was ultimately self-defeating. Local circumstances, in competition with wider socio-cultural forces and teaching traditions, contrived to have them play a game of Sissyphaean proportions. Cut off from collective action within, and sustained support from without the school, teaching constructions were primarily influenced by the vicissitudes of everyday life without reference to a wider discourse on traditions of teaching. Nevertheless, aspects of these grand narratives were evident in the structures, communication routines and ongoing attempts to balance the social and cognitive needs of learners. In these circumstances, the research process itself became a form of scaffolding and shepherding for Helen whereby, through reflective dialogue stimulated by fieldnotes and teacher–researcher dialogue, she became re-energized to begin to think of her practice differently. It is clear, therefore, that the putting into practice of teaching ideologies is not a simple, linear task of following a series of preplanned implementation steps. Rather, teachers manipulate and are manipulated by prevailing ideological winds and in particular by tides of local circumstance. Harnessing the energies of winds and tides is the most surefooted means of charting a grounded and inclusive account of child-centred teaching.

Notes

1   Anamnesis and amnesia are two important terms which Voeglin (1966) uses in relation to the works of Plato and Aristotle. The former is particularly significant as it becomes a means of recovering meaning through story, thus providing for continuity and change. Voeglin's notion of remembering/story-telling connects in important ways with recent educational research, particularly the notion of 'Reflective Storytelling' (Mattingly, 1991) and 'Narrative and Story' (Clandinin and Connelly, 1991). Voeglin's term has the advantage of being comprehensive and succinct as it includes the notion of story and remembering.

2   Sullivan (1990, p. 124) supports this point when he suggests that 'human action must . . . be understood as being caused by social conditions over which the agent exerts no conscious or intentional control.' Apple (1981, p. 5), while drawing on the work of Williams (1961) and Gramsci (1971), indicates that hegemony functions 'to saturate our very consciousness' so that it becomes almost impossible to question 'commonsense interpretations of our world'.

Chapter 9

Reconstructing Teaching Traditions: Child-centred Perspectives

Introduction

This reconstruction of teaching traditions from a child-centred perspective is situated within the larger canvas of postmodernity, which 'means coming to terms with ambivalence, with the ambiguity of meanings and with the indeterminacy of the future' while recognizing that 'acceptance of ambivalence can be life-enhancing, especially when contrasted to the driven world of certitudes that modernity used to foster' (*The Polity Reader in Social Theory*, 1994, p. 349). In similar vein, Boyne and Rattansi (1990, p. 21) assert that 'the ambiguities of the postmodern condition are its most valuable features'. Grand narratives are therefore deconstructed to identify a plurality of perspectives. Lest such a position be interpreted as a retreat into or capitulation to relativism, it is precisely because of the conditions of postmodernity that the necessity arises to rethink, and to realign old verities; to reconstruct them in 'more inclusive and productive . . . ways' by bringing 'together the varied voices of . . . participants in shared dialogue and critical community' (Hargreaves, 1993, p. 1).

From the outset, I have taken the view that such a reconstructed vision of child-centred teaching should be grounded in the multiple realities of teachers' intentions, their classroom actions, and the contexts of their work. While documenting these details, care has been taken to connect the voices of practitioners with commonly held beliefs about the grand narratives of teaching. There is no intention on my part to privilege the voices of practitioners over the legitimate interests of others concerned with the project of teaching and learning. Rather, understanding of practitioners' perspectives has been sought with a view to unlocking the potential of their professional knowledge for constructing a more inclusive narrative on progressive teaching. I am conscious also that the voices of learners and parents (for example) have not been accorded the same status as teachers' voices in this narrative, and for this reason the account is inevitably partial.

It may appear to some readers that the inclusion and positioning of child-centred teaching in the title of this chapter is an attempt to invest progressive ideology with olympian superiority over traditional didacticism or the voices of teachers. The context in which the study has been conducted espouses child-centredness in official policy documents and it is endorsed overwhelmingly by those who work in the system. Such pervasiveness may lead to 'ideological corruption' (Callan, 1988) and there is a growing acceptance in the educational community that the rhetoric has become jaded and, in some instances, a barrier to more open dialogue (Alexander, 1992, Alexander *et al.*, 1989). Nevertheless, my experiences of versions of traditional teaching remain a distinct discouragement to revisiting its archetypal axioms on present or future learners. Child-centredness, in my view, is more in tune with postmodern sentiments and is preferable to the 'certainties' of traditional teaching which educational restorationists seek to reinscribe, reinstate, rehabilitate and restore, but not to reconstruct (Ball, 1994; Smyth, 1993; Lawton, 1992). It is important to distinguish between *looking back* in a critical manner in preparation for facing the future with greater purpose and coherence but this task is qualitatively different from *putting the clock back* which endeavours to imprison the future in the past (Sugrue, 1996a, 1996d). Putting the clock back is a cycloptic attempt to refashion the world of schooling in a fossilized image. The inquiry's detail indicates that influences on practice are not confined exclusively to a januform tension between traditions of teaching. Practitioners' struggles for equilibrium in their routines include school cultures, their apprenticeships of observation, espoused policies and the contexts of their work. However, to confine understandings of practice to the detail of everyday life in classrooms is to move unacceptably close to a Nietzschean 'closed horizon' where the insulation and isolation of routines and rituals become self-perpetuating and exculpatory.

The fieldwork and crafting of this study provide a certain 'vantage point' from which to communicate my sense of the problem: to envision new horizons of practice. A horizon is 'the range of vision that includes everything that can be seen from a particular vantage point' (Gadamer, 1975, p. 302). The promontory on which I stand provides an 'enlightened eye' rather than an 'immaculate perception' (Eisner, 1991). In moving beyond the boundaries of the study, it is appropriate to seek a new image which expands on the janus-face of current classroom routines. Practices need to be more diverse to reflect changing conditions and uncertainties of the society it serves, shapes, and by which it is fashioned. The complexity of classroom life and the multiple social realities in which, and for which, it is expected to educate future citizens suggests an equally complex image: the multi-headed Hydra seems more appropriate to the task than the inherent refraction of Janus. Reconstructing a more complex, diverse, yet inclusive, image of practice necessitates moving beyond the narrowed horizons of traditional and progressive ideology: embracing the very uncertainties which oppositional discourses have sought to deny and suppress.

From a methodological perspective, however, there are difficulties about moving beyond the 'boundaries of the case' but I agree with Stake (1988, p. 261) that 'the unique case can help us understand the more typical cases' and that the issue of generalization is a matter more for the reader than the researcher (Stake and Mabry, 1993). It is anticipated, therefore, that individuals will connect their own understanding of the problem with details of the inquiry and the following discussion of child-centredness, thus perpetuating the process of moving from the whole to the part in a continuous 'reflective turn' (Schön, 1991; Hunt, 1987, 1992; Gadamer, 1975). Such an approach resists the temptation to generate formal theory that would prescribe 'rules to-be-followed' and prefers the challenge of isolating 'points for discussion and consideration' (Kilbourn, 1988, p. 110). My intention to articulate a vision of teaching and learning which includes the voices of practitioners, as a means of lending some situated certainty and tentative coherence to the project, is modern rather than postmodern while remaining sensitive to the conditions in which these perspectives are communicated.

An exclusive emphasis on voices without vision would reduce practitioners' intentions and actions to a 'chaotic babble, where all voices are valid and where there are no means to arbitrate between them' (Hargreaves and Fullan, 1992, p. 5). Similarly, a vision which is not tempered by the voices of practitioners becomes sterile and moribund as 'there is no place for the practical judgement and wisdom of teachers . . .' (p. 6) resulting in 'a kind of Robinson Crusoe dream . . . of [the] . . . unattainable' (Gadamer, 1975, p. 304). My intent, therefore, is to avoid what Mannheim (1991, p. 86) has described as 'ideological distortion' which occurrs when 'new realities applying to a situation' are ignored. Articulating such a vision seeks coherence and inclusiveness, yet remains provisional and tentative, and invites the reader to come to terms with various dilemmas and the apparently irreconcilable so as to reground and revision them in his or her own context, whatever that might be (Sugrue, 1994). There is no pretence on my part that the issues discussed in this chapter provide an exhaustive account of all aspects of these multiple realities: that would be an impossible task. Rather, from the vantage point of the study, and within the social uncertainties of postmodernity, a series of emergent issues are discussed. With these caveats in place, the focus of attention shifts to the substance of this final chapter.

My comments are at three levels. The primary focus is on aspects of teaching and learning in classrooms which have emerged as germane to a revisioning of child-centredness. These concerns are nested within comments on school- and system-wide policies and structures. First, (at classroom level) there is a series of tensions around issues such as: prescription of content; integration and subject boundaries; social and cognitive development; classroom relationships; a broadly based programme and what is basic to primary content; and the very nature of teaching in its various manifestations — class, group and individualization — all of which contribute to a reconstructed vision of progressivism. Second, there is the issue of school planning and the tensions between teacher autonomy and the possibilities afforded by collaboration and collegiality. Additionally, use of time, as well as deployment and development of expertise are important school level issues which have significant impact on the nature and quality of classroom actions and the quality of child-centred teaching. Third, there are system-wide policies, structures and supports which inhibit or enable practitioners to deal with the dilemmas and tensions at classroom and school levels. This section seeks to reinforce the view that any vision of practice, and the voices of practitioners which shape it, are dependent on adequate provision of resources and, in particular, opportunities for practitioners to work and plan collaboratively, to reflect and to reconstruct themselves and their practices throughout their careers. Failure to make such provisions is tantamount to denying teachers a voice in the ongoing project of reconstructing teaching and learning in our schools and, it will be argued, when this occurs, visions are tarnished, voices are distorted and silenced, and the potential of students and practitioners is re-tarded: quality suffers.

The contextualized details of this study reveal the interdependence of class-room routines, school cultures and system-wide policies and structures. The image of the multi-headed Hydra seeks to capture this complexity and mutual dependence. It suggests also that a secateured, piecemeal, pruning of existing routines frequently results in more vigorous regrowth, thus perpetuating existing deeply embedded rou-tines of practice when a more organic, holistic approach, which respects and recog-nizes complexity and the interdependence of classroom actions, school communities and systems' policies, seems more appropriate. These considerations, and their guid-ing metaphor, suggest a more inclusive and more securely grounded reconstruction of child-centred teaching.

Classrooms

When discussing the ecology of classrooms it is important to recognize the chang-ing context in which teaching and learning takes place. In recent years, when work-ing with and supervising student teachers in classroom and micro-teaching situations, the extent to which even the youngest learners indicate their lack of interest and disengagement from topics presented by students and teachers has become more apparent. In subsequent conversations, more democratic parenting styles, decline of traditional family structures, influences of television, the absence of fear and the threat of corporal punishment, improved self-confidence and articulation, changing attitudes towards authority and authority figures, and lower boredom thresholds, are frequently cited as reasons for a creeping restlessness if not a growing anarchy in classrooms and schools which become more problematic with older learners (Sarason, 1990). Learners have suggested that it is 'good fun' to send up teachers when topics, methodologies or personalities do not appeal to them. Even in middle-class contexts, where greater congruence has existed between the values of schools and homes, there is growing evidence that McLaren's street corner state increasingly insinuates its way into classrooms: evidence, perhaps, that the rules, routines and rituals which were honed during periods of stability and continuity are increasingly being undermined, eroded, ignored and contested. It is tempting, in these circumstances, to entertain learners by providing them with what they want rather than to challenge them with material that is potentially more engaging and more meaningful. It is a very inad-equate resolution of this dilemma to allow the tyranny of subjects and syllabi to be replaced by the despotism of learners. In these (often trying) circumstances, practi-tioners are devoting more time and energy to establishing rapport and sustaining relationships with learners.

Relationships

The weight of evidence in this study indicates that perhaps the most significant, and the most firmly embedded, change in classroom routines in the Irish context is in the nature and quality of relationships. Informal, interpersonal exchanges are commonplace and characterized by humour, spontaneity, warmth, caring and nurturing, all of which implicitly recognize the individuality and personalities of learners. This generally positive classroom climate contrasts sharply with some interviewees' recollections of their apprenticeships of observation and this is confirmed by other studies (Sugrue, 1996a). These relationships have important implications for positive classroom climate and their significance is far from being cosmetic. It is important not only to acknowledge these gains, and to realize the extent to which they have supplanted the austerity and intimidating nature of many traditional classrooms, but to celebrate them also, to give due credit to teachers, to recognize that, far from taking them for granted, these relationships need to be reviewed, renewed, revitalized and developed. Because of shifting social sands which have significant impact on children's lives, it is likely that 'being there' for learners will become even more important in the foreseeable future. In contexts where ethnic, religious and cultural diversity is the norm in classrooms, there is an urgency and importance about the nature of relationship to avoid charges of racism, intolerance and cultural imperialism. Nested within this generally supportive and enabling environment, therefore, it is important to interrogate some features which appear to indicate aspects of traditional thinking in an unreconstructed form.

It would be simply naïve to imagine that in this positive climate 'the power of the teacher' is anything other than central to classroom processes (Sarason, 1990, p. 89). How this power is exercised is critical to reconstructing teaching traditions with a more child-centred face. Details of the study reveal that classroom rules and routines were very much the creation of practitioners and, having invented these rules in their own image, they entered into a process of 'selling' them to learners. These rules were interpreted flexibly, in most instances, to accommodate individual difference, and learners (for the most part) seemed content to 'buy into' teachers' rules. Nevertheless, they remained controlled by teachers rather than being empowered by them through participative dialogue on the rules and routines of classroom life. Tensions were created and, when this occurred, it was necessary to apply sanctions to reinforce rules. In these circumstances, relationships sometimes took on a contractual dimension where the rapport which had been cultivated between learners and teachers was used as a means of moral coercion: because you are my friend you must keep my rules. Of course, it is possible to argue that all relationships are predicated on shared understanding, but an inevitable inequality appears to exist in adult–child relationships, and there are risks attached to burdening learners with too much responsibility at too early an age, thus denying them their childhood (Winn, 1983). Differentiation is necessary but this needs to be balanced against an adult duty to educate for responsible citizenship and participatory democracy (Purpel, 1989). Such differentiation must be mindful of childhood as a distinct stage of development, but this should not be reduced to forms of infantilism.

Negotiation of rules is an exercise in democracy, while manipulating classroom relationships is a form of coercion no less attractive than more traditional use of force to impose an adult's will on those who are powerless to resist. Part of this process is learning to respect and tolerate difference, to listen and to actually hear others' points of view and to learn the art of compromise in the interest of cohesion and harmony. In the absence of these more elaborate procedures, learners intuitively recognize tensions and differences between mutual respect and imposition of predetermined conditions. Children regularly invent games and rules which govern their play. By contrast, the game of school, in its present form, in many instances necessitates playing exclusively by teachers' rules. Because the game of school is compulsory, it seems reasonable that those who play actually participate in the formulation of its rules in a manner appropriate to their age and level of maturity.

Too often in the past, learners' immaturity has been taken advantage of by teachers who interpret it as giving license to fashion rules that make life easy for them rather than promote responsibility and maturity in learners. More democratic rule-making has the potential to improve the quality of classroom relationships further while promoting independence among learners in ways that do not necessarily undermine the authority of teachers. Far from being a trivial issue, the nature and quality of classroom relationships have profound implications for all activities. For, as Noddings (1992, p. 36) suggests, '. . . students will do things for people they like and trust. This is a fact that we must acknowledge.' There is need for more widespread debate on the nature of these relationships and the rules, rituals and routines which govern them. Despite their importance, relationships are one aspect only of the classroom Hydra, and while they have important implications for the cognitive focus of classroom work, one must not be sacrificed to the detriment of the other.

Structuring

Details of the study reveal that cognitive structuring is a very necessary element of planning and mediating programme content. Traditionally, little attention was paid to structuring with an overriding emphasis on 'covering the course'. This preoccupation with content placed emphasis on teaching and engendered an unwarranted separation between teaching and learning, where the latter was the responsibility of learners. Failure to learn could then be attributed to the lack of effort, ability or a combination of both and teachers had fulfilled their obligations once content had been delivered, and the most efficient means of doing so was class teaching: teaching as telling. It is important, in the present climate, when the virtues of class teaching are being espoused by some researchers, to acknowledge that traditionally it had many shortcomings (Alexander, 1992; Mortimore *et al.*, 1988). It is necessary to recognize, however, that class teaching can be highly interactive as well as engendering passivity in learners.

Due to the intimacy of the relationship between teaching and learning, planning and structuring content must, of necessity, pay attention to pedagogy also. Evidence in the empirical chapters, and other research in the setting, shows that planning is focused almost exclusively on the selection of content: because it is assumed that practitioners know how to teach, the focus of deliberations on planning centre on selection of content only (INTO, 1990). Structuring content to challenge learners appropriately by maximizing the match between developmental level and difficulty of tasks, tends to be left to the privacy of individual classrooms. When this occurs, pedagogical variety and engagement of learners is the sole preserve of individual teachers. Consequently, it is difficult to ensure continuity from one year to the next as well as variety of tasks and learning experiences. As long as teachers continue to work in isolation, despite some developments in school planning, structuring of learning is likely to remain uncomfortably idiosyncratic, though care must be taken not to privilege collective engagement over the notion of teacher as artisan (Huberman, 1993; Fullan, 1995).

Structuring of content and learning tasks, the study indicates, gains in importance from its potential to challenge learners while encouraging independence and, as a Vygotskian perspective gains further credibility, greater attention is likely to be paid to the social dimension of learning and the attendant importance of teacher intervention and peer coaching: assisting learners in *'framing'* their worlds (Bruner, 1990). Vygotsky's work has done much to restore the central importance of language and interaction to the learning process, to the extent that 'understanding, however abstract it may eventually become, always begins as *praxis* in particular contexts in which the child is a *protagonist* — an agent, a victim, an accomplice' (Bruner, 1990, p. 85). It is important when planning and structuring this 'interactionist-dialectic', which also embraces the realms of abstract thought or higher cognitive functioning, that the learner is not coerced into being the 'victim' which was so often the case with traditional teaching (Cole *et al.*, 1978, p. 124). Because Vygotsky's work has kindled fresh awareness of the importance of language (and assistance) for cognitive development, there is renewed interest in, if not restorationist tendencies towards, class teaching. It is important therefore to give careful consideration to its implications; it is necessary to understand the role of learners as agents and accomplices to prevent them from being casualties of the teaching–learning process.

Those who have tutored learners individually, either in classrooms or elsewhere, will be aware that there is a very thin line between challenge and coercion. Learners, particularly those who lack social confidence and self-esteem, may accept the assistance of teachers or more able peers far too readily. Assistance and modelling may become teaching-as-telling with the result that the intent of fostering independence and cognitive growth can be reduced to dependence and procedural knowledge. It is critical, therefore, to recognize that understanding and development require negotiation, and while scaffolding learners by 'reducing the number of degrees of freedom that the child must manage in the task' is a necessary element of the process, in the complex world of classrooms this can become prescriptive and procedural rather than liberating and enabling (Wertsch, 1989, p. 29). If the latter outcome is to be avoided, teachers will need to become much more adept at diagnosis which goes against the grain of a long and deeply embedded tradition of providing ready-made routine answers. It is possible to agree with Edwards and Mercer (1987, p. 167) that 'a cognitive climbing frame — built by the children with their Vygotskian teacher . . . structures activity more systematically than the discovery sandpit of the Piagetian classroom . . .' while remaining alert to the dangers that this perspective may be used by some as a vindication of class teaching. Maximizing challenge without resorting to prescription, traditional didacticism, or coersive classroom relationships is the task of teachers. The developmental level of the learner and appropriate assistance are critical ingredients in balancing facets of the Hydra's complex persona. Emphasis on cognitive structuring and assisted learning pose important questions also for the integrity of disciplines and subjects.

Integration

Practitioners who were most committed to integration and theme teaching engaged in detailed planning on a daily basis, which also involved production and use of resource materials. Those who relied on textbooks had least need for planning as they were tempted to adhere to the selection and sequence of content as it appeared in texts. However, it is important to distinguish between those who adhere to textbooks slavishly, and those who regard them as an important resource to be used for the imaginative engagement of learners. Due to the absence of curriculum guidelines, such as those provided in Scotland and England for example, Irish primary teachers regard themselves as fortunate to enjoy a degree of professional autonomy which has been eroded elsewhere (Goodson and Hargreaves, 1996a; Smyth, 1993; Ball, 1994; Goodson, 1994; Lawton, 1992). It has been suggested that one of the reasons for a return to more centralized prescription in England is precisely because teachers did not honour the autonomy conferred on them by planning with sufficient rigour and coherence within schools (Hargreaves, 1989). Much of this freedom is relinquished, however, once textbooks are selected by schools and the meagre financial assistance available for the procurement of additional resource materials is such that selection of texts implicitly involves a degree of prescription which quickly erodes flexibility and variety. The study revealed that texts are much more likely to be used in the basics while practitioners felt much more at liberty to 'do their own thing' in other areas of the programme. Yet, little reliance on texts, when resources are inadequate, can be a recipe for a narrow programme that is reductionist rather than enriching. Such situations seem to reinforce a traditional culture which accords priority to versions of the 3Rs, while anything goes in relation to other subject matter areas. The majority of interviewees expressed a preference for 'incidental' integration, while art was the most frequently integrated subject with other areas of the programme. Incidental integration is largely fortuitous and unplanned and very dependent on opportunist teachers thinking on their feet, which is sometimes sparked by an incisive question or casual remark from a learner.

When planned thematically, subjects appeared to retain their traditional identities and time was allocated in a manner remarkably similar to those who taught subjects as discrete entities. In practice, therefore, discernible differences between those who claimed to be integrating material and those who were not did not emerge as particularly significant. However, a thematic approach did, in some instances, appear to facilitate greater conceptual development as learners made connections between disparate information, primarily because practitioners were aware of organizing themes and went to some lengths to point out similarities. Learners, too, on occasions, made these connections themselves and this can be attributed to the structuring of the material and the manner in which it was taught. There was a certain quality and excitement among learners particularly when these connections were 'discovered' without assistance from the teacher. This kind of 'communitas' has 'something magical about it' as it enables learners to move 'outside, above and beyond structure' in a manner which marks a moment of release when they demonstrate that they no longer need the support of the scaffolding and function outside its frame of reference (Woods, 1993b, p. 362). I agree with Woods (1993a) that more of these moments, critical incidents and events, should be an ongoing and recurring feature of work in classrooms; an integral element of a revisioned progressivism.

Despite these moments, the study's detail suggests that there was no diminution of time spent on 'the basics'. Theme planning had a deceptive informality which cloaked traditional subject divisions and teaching emphases. When this occurred, 'other' subject matter areas tended to be deployed as complimentary to, or light relief from, a focus on 'the basics'. Despite some tentative claims that there are cognitive gains which accrue when content is organized (more so than structured) thematically, it may have the less desirable consequence that 'other' areas of a programme are less visible with the result that their significance is diminished in the perceptions of learners, if not in fact. When subjects such as art and music are required to play a primarily supportive role within a theme, some additional undesirable consequences may accrue while inadequacies remain hidden.

'Other' subject matter areas frequently do not have structured differentiated programmes available to the same extent as pertains to 'core' subjects. In the absence of such guidelines and materials there is a greater burden of responsibility on practitioners to have sufficient expertise to plan a coherent developmental programme, individually and collectively. However, when these subjects are used consistently in supporting roles to enliven basic subjects, their importance derives from providing relief rather than developing learners' skills and potentials through those subjects in an appropriately challenging manner. Participants admitted to a lack of expertise in some of these subject matter areas and their deployment in supportive roles simply underscores the olympian position afforded traditional forms of literacy and, perhaps, (conveniently) cloaks some practitioners' lack of expertise. Taking integration seriously, therefore, makes assumptions about breadth and depth of subject matter knowledge as well as uncommon levels of planning acumen. Forced to make a choice, I would argue that developing expertise should rate more highly than integration though they are not mutually exclusive, while this, too, creates its own problems.

Broadly Based Programmes

Provision of a broadly based programme due to lack of subject matter expertise emerges as problematic. Perhaps it is time to question, therefore, as others have done, the practicality of generalist primary teachers actually delivering a broadly based programme, particularly at the senior end of primary schools (Alexander, 1992). Many practitioners with whom I have discussed this issue would welcome the provision of specialist teachers, while such arrangements would be particularly problematic in a system with so many small schools. Some practitioners expressed the view that if they were to rely on additional expertise they would no longer have sole responsibility for a particular class and that caring for the 'whole child' would be more difficult to achieve. However, while caring is important to progressives, it should not, as the study illustrates, be at the expense of challenging learners maximally. Caring cognitively, as well as personally, socially and morally, are additional facets of the Hydra.

As new social ills are identified there is virtually instant demand that schools add topics such as environment, health, media studies, technology, and sexuality, to mention but a few, to an already over-crowded programme; as Noddings (1992, p. 49) indicates, '. . . our standard approach is given a problem, add a course'. All of these recent developments bring into question the dominance of language and mathematics as the sole claimants to the accolade — 'basic' to primary education. It is possible to acknowledge that language, in particular, is such an enormous repository of culture that it cannot be ignored. But music, art, drama, dance, film, science and technology have legitimacy in this arena also. From teachers' perspectives, they are expected to deal with an ever increasing array of issues within the same time-frame. Fragmentation of content and time, intensification of teachers' work-loads inevitably mean that there is more surface learning in order to 'cover' an ever-expanding programme (Fullan, 1993; Hargreaves and Fullan, 1992). Restorationists then complain that standards are declining in 'the basics' because too much time is being spent on 'frills'. After cries of 'back to basics', some retrenchment is advocated by policy-makers, only to be followed by demands for new additions and the cycle begins anew!

Institutions which are rooted in the nineteenth century whose mission was 'concerned with basic skills of numeracy and literacy . . . for the children of the labouring poor' so that they would not get 'ideas above their station' and to 'reaffirm the existing system of social stratification', have difficulty adjusting to a more complex role (Eggleston, 1977, p. 31). However, arguments which support back to basics are not simply about a return to the values and structures of the last century. There is genuine concern also about standards; to ensure adequate levels of literacy and numeracy. It is necessary, this argument goes, to focus more on these subjects to the virtual exclusion of others. Evidence to support this argument is difficult to find but it does not prevent the case being made repeatedly. Breadth and depth can be accommodated only within limits of what is humanly possible and what resources will allow. Noddings (1992, p. 61) questions 'the morality of forcing material on people' but this needs to be balanced against a need to cultivate learners' interests.

There is an onus on practitioners to ensure that 'school knowledge builds upon the tacit knowledge derived from the cultural resources that students already possess' (Aronowitz and Giroux, 1991, p. 15). This is not a simplistic argument about relevance for some and rigour for others (Hargreaves, 1989). Rather, when content remains unconnected with learners' experience, rigour becomes an instrumental intellectual ritual. There is a need, therefore, to focus on real issues, real problems formulated by learners themselves. This will inevitably mean that different topics of interest will be pursued so that control, organization and expertise are immediately challenged in ways that encourage practitioners to resist such moves for fear of loosing control, while policy-makers resist such reforms because monitoring standards becomes much more difficult when programmes are diversified. Being practical about this dilemma, it is unlikely that literacy and numeracy as traditionally defined are going to loose their dominance in classrooms in the near future. Beyond this arena, there is scope for much interdisciplinary work that is driven by a desire to solve problems and not just to play intellectual games. Some specialist help would be beneficial to work alongside class teachers but not to replace them. By working collaboratively the knowledge and expertise of both will be enhanced. Specialist help does not always have to be provided in the form of additional teachers with particular expertise. There is a great untapped reservoir of talent and expertise in communities which schools need to utilize more, and to achieve this practitioners will have to overcome isolationist tendencies and feelings of professional inadequacy. In my experience, respect for teachers' work increases as other adults become more *au fait* with the complex roles they perform. With declining rolls, many classrooms are becoming vacant thus providing additional space for centres of interest. Beyond core literacy programmes, perhaps, it is time to look at the possibility of schools providing centres of excellence in different subject matter areas. If this were planned with coherence it would provide genuine (and not cosmetic) choices where programmes could be matched to individual bent. Care should be taken to ensure that such initiatives did not become sedimented on the basis of existing social structures, thus perpetuating and exacerbating existing inequalities of access and provision. More flexible registration requirements would enable learners to attend centres at more than one school.

This study indicated that learners' interests did not find clear expression in the programme content they pursued. Learners need to be brought into this planning process more than at present so that practitioners are not confined to accommodating individual needs and interests by dint of rapport, relationships and pedagogical sleight of hand, when negotiating content can potentially empower students by granting them more responsibility for shaping programmes than is presently the case. In a world that grows increasingly more complex, providing a broad, liberal education for everyone is neither sustainable, sensible or attainable (Noddings, 1992). While in principle it is difficult to disagree with the merits of a broad general education, I think that self-confidence and self-esteem are enhanced by being able to do some things really well rather than doing many things in a mediocre fashion. If this kind of mastery is attained, even in a rather narrow area, such achievements are much more likely to encourage learners to take up the challenge and the opportunity of lifelong learning, a phenomenon which is becoming more of a reality as well as a necessity. Another face of the Hydra, therefore, is the possibility of attending centres of interest in a number of locations, which would enable practitioners to develop additional expertise also.

Nineteenth-century British versions of 'the educated gentleman' continue to have profound implications for the nature and conduct of schooling despite being outmoded (Hirst and Peters, 1970). The educated person of the future is much more likely to be a lifelong learner, a perpetual student who was a somewhat despised individual until recently because he (usually he!) never quite grew up: an intellectual Peter Pan, while others had to do 'real' work. If learners can gain mastery over their lives by in-depth investigation of real problems, then they should be facilitated in that process (Sizer, 1984). Such an approach would be much more child-centred, in my view, than what prevails at present, and it would be a genuine attempt to meet learners' real needs while issues about breadth, depth and balance would become lifetime projects and not confined to periods of compulsory schooling. Fostering such excellence in learners requires that practitioners place much greater emphasis on diagnosis than is manifest in schools at present. One of the major barriers to shifting the education system in this direction is perceived (and probably actual) loss of control because national testing would become much more difficult, unfair and unsustainable in a differentiated system; it would be impossible to apply the same standard yardstick of achievement to all learners.

Standards

The rhetoric of 'new' right managerialism is replete with terms such as: accountability, transparency, efficiency, effectiveness, and quality control — to mention but some of an extensive repertoire. As part of this package, practitioners are expected to spend more time planning, testing learners and keeping records of their progress, as well as being much more *au fait* with a wider range of subjects, work collaboratively with colleagues, which is also very time-consuming, and be engaged in self-appraisal and professional renewal on an ongoing basis. Meanwhile learners are emerging into a much more uncertain job market where highly skilled, adaptable people are those most likely to find employment. While the dangers of taking a rather instrumental approach to education have been well documented, a more differentiated programme does not appear to be a very radical measure given future employment prospects (Coolahan, 1994; Hogan, 1995). National testing, especially when accompanied by league tables, seems like an attempt to impose control mechanisms forcing greater conformity in ways which are reminiscent of the payments by results era, when differentiation appears to be a more desirable and defensible response to present uncertainties.

This study revealed very graphically the demoralizing impact of imposed 'standards' on some teachers and learners. Even in contexts where learners came to school with cultural capital, pressure of entrance examinations ensured a degree of rigidity and uniformity which did not have benefits for every learner. Such impositions are like making it compulsory to compete in track and field events against those who have made such events their forte when your bent is in team games. The imposition of such standards is an elaborate selection mechanism with a pyramidic structure which has the effect, intended or otherwise, of labelling some as successful, while the majority inevitably become second rate if not downright failures. Small wonder, therefore, that a growing number of learners, particularly in the secondary sector, but increasingly at primary level also, are reluctant to participate in this game of selection.

Recent international comparative research, which has been analysed from an Irish perspective, indicates very clearly that primary schools in this country concentrate on basic skills (Martin and Morgan, 1994; La Pointe, Mead and Askew, 1992; Elley, 1992). It is reasonable to assume that the mind-set of practitioners and their classroom actions are still powerfully influenced by a combination of traditional perspectives on teaching which include national examinations, the scholarship syndrome, and robust inspection, in addition to large classes and poor resource provision (OECD, 1994, 1995). Importing a version of the new managerialism into such a context is a recipe for retrenchment when a different vision and mind-set is called for. If there is truth in the assertion that testing narrows the range of experiences as a consequence of 'teaching to the test', then testing should not be privileged over a system's other needs. It is necessary to acknowledge that testing is essentially behaviourist in orientation, and when tendencies towards selection and control are already embedded in a system, the benefits of testing must be weighted against the need for a more expansive and developmental approach to schooling (Woods, 1993b). It is necessary to 'provide an education system which can cater for the needs of individuals rather than one which reduces everyone to the lowest common denominator' and this requirement needs to be reinscribed into a revisioned version of child-centredness (Burgess, 1996, p. 18).

Student profiles have much to offer in this arena while available and sophisticated technology can be harnessed to find alternative means of recording learners' gains in the social, aesthetic, and moral areas, as well as documenting achievements in more conventional subject matter. More comprehensive record-keeping is likely to increase practitioners' awareness of the need to match the difficulty of tasks to learners' developmental levels. However, if record-keeping erodes a significant amount of teaching time, then it becomes counter-productive as it invades the central (teaching and learning) spaces in classrooms. It is important to recall that the birth of progressive education was, in many ways, a response to the rigidities of prevailing educational provisions, its preoccupation with selection, of providing rigour for some and relevance for others. It is necessary to recommit to rigour and relevance, and not to privilege one or the other. Imposing national criteria on all students regardless of interest or natural bent is putting the cart before the horse. The primary task assigned to teachers in classrooms is development of human potential and evaluation, assessment and testing need to be harnessed towards that end rather than dictating its shape and direction. In the global village and its economy, postmodernity provides possibilities and opportunities to recognize that there is potentially greater strength in diversity than uniformity and control. Coming to terms with this reality poses an enormous challenge to traditional cultures of schooling which continue to have a significant shaping influence on classroom practice. A reconstructed vision of child-centredness will have to grapple with these changing contexts and new realities without losing sight of the importance which it has traditionally attached to educating the 'whole child'. This study indicates clearly that privileging standards, in many instances, has serious negative consequences for learners' self-esteem and teachers' morale.

Social Development

It is apparent from this inquiry that the social and cognitive development of learners are inextricably linked. Where learners come to school with cultural capital, practitioners are more inclined to take social development for granted and to provide a challenging, more cognitively (and academically) oriented programme. Conversely, those who teach in disadvantaged contexts could not make any such assumptions and felt demoralized by lack of progress in the cognitive domain and, in such circumstances, lowering of expectations is not uncommon, while relevance can take precedence over rigour (Alexander *et al.*, 1989). Practitioners can become consumed by, rather than being concerned for, the welfare of learners (Hargreaves and Tucker, 1991). Another dimension of catering for the 'whole child' is the extent to which participants indicated that their first priority was for their pupils to be happy in school. This is a laudable intention, particularly when considered against the backdrop of fear and abuse that existed in many schools in the past. However, critics suggest that privileging happiness sentimentalizes childhood, thus attaching less significance to cognitive challenge. In the Irish context, where secularism and pluralism have gained significant toe-holds in civil society, with an attendant value flux which characterizes this postmodern condition, there is much greater need to be aware of social, civic and moral formation than heretofore, as the influence of institutional religion becomes less pervasive. In this context, there is a need for 'major rethinking, reform and renewal of education policy' and practice (Roche, 1992, p. 233). Roche asserts that 'in the education process the state "grows" its citizenry as much as young people "grow" themselves and their future identities' (p. 233). While it is obvious from this study that practitioners have taken seriously the need to care for and to nurture children — to look out for their welfare — there is a need to be much more proactive in educating them for citizenship.

Due to our particular historical inheritance there is probably greater need here, than perhaps exists elsewhere, to recognize that moral duties, for example, are not 'mere conformity to social norms' or derived from an 'ideal of altruism', but require characterization as 'enlightened self-interest' (Roche, 1992, p. 241). When value systems were much more homogeneous and widely shared, they were largely taken for granted: assimilated by a process of osmosis. Consequently, there is something of a social and moral vacuum in school programmes. From an international perspective, there is an urgent need to:

> . . . grasp the emerging *structural complexity* and the new post-industrial [postmodern] and post-national dynamics influencing social citizenship, from familial and local levels to the trans-national and the inter-generational sphere. (Roche, 1992, p. 244)

Teachers, therefore, can no longer confine their attentions in relation to social development of learners to the pastoral, and relatively passive, role of caring. Learners too must be taught systematically to become caring, responsible citizens (Noddings,

1992). Only then can practitioners legitimately claim to be educating the whole child. Learners need to be challenged to become good citizens in the same manner that they are expected to achieve appropriate levels of mastery in various disciplines. The need to care needs to proactively and systematically develop '*emotional intelligence*, which includes self-control, zeal, persistence, and the ability to motivate oneself' (Goleman, 1996, p. xii). An important dimension of this emergent revisioning of progressivism is a challenging of learners to care, and not just for practitioners to care for them. Commitment to care necessitates an approach to standards which encompasses the social and cognitive development of learners.

Teaching and Learning

The interdependence of teaching and learning emerged as important in this study. So much so, it would be extremely difficult to argue that teachers' primary responsibility is to teach while learners take responsibility for learning. This neat separation has enabled teachers, particularly those in a traditional mould, to give priority to teaching a programme where engagement was often of little concern. When content had been delivered, learners were instructed to learn, which frequently meant to memorize material in their own time and in private. These routines conveyed the very powerful message that learning was private and personal while teaching was conducted in a more public forum. Interactional dialogue played a peripheral role in this process. The potential of language and its capacity to provide structured assistance to learners as they sought to come to terms with content, to make sense of it, to take ownership of it through internalization, was frequently absent. The study indicates that scaffolding and structuring provide assisted learning where teaching and learning become part of a single process. Over-elaborate structuring is likely to foster dependence leading to procedural knowledge while appropriate structuring is expected to promote independence, understanding and principled knowledge. It is not merely a question, therefore, of providing cognitive challenge. How these teaching–learning interactions are constructed, how they are planned and executed, is critical to the development of higher cognitive processes. It is necessary to return to classroom praxis to articulate a vision of how this process might function as a further dimension of a reconstructed child-centredness. Restorationist approaches to teaching are likely to be conducted in a mentally moribund manner, while revisioned and reworked routines may provide the necessary structures, discourses, and spaces for imaginative and creative engagement. The rubber meets the road in the pedagogical spaces that teachers create *for* and *with* learners.

Class Teaching

Evidence from this inquiry suggests that commitment to class teaching has remained more steadfast in the setting than in other contexts (Alexander *et al.*, 1989;

Alexander, 1992; Mortimore *et al.*, 1988; Cuban, 1993; Galton and Williamson, 1992). Explanations for this are not difficult to find. Until relatively recently, Ireland was predominantly rural and conservative with a strong religious influence particularly in education and, these factors, along with a dearth of resources and relatively large classes, have meant that teachers strayed little from established routines (OECD, 1991, 1995). My knowledge of the system, and conversations with many practitioners, reveal a common belief that there is less variety in teaching methods today than in the mid-1970s when there was a younger teaching force and practitioners remained exercised by, and had enthusiasm for, progressive ideals. Literature on planned change and implementation suggests that the absence of consistent support in the form of sustained inservice programmes give rise to 'tissue rejection' so that changes do not become embedded in classroom routines (Hoyle, 1974). There was evidence in the study, however, that group teaching and group work occurred in classrooms and this was commonplace in English and mathematics. Alexander (1992, p. 67) argues that 'the strategy of grouping has become an end in itself rather than a device adopted for particular educational purposes'. So ingrained are group and class teaching in the system, he says, it is 'almost impertinent' to question their efficacy. Cuban (1993) summarizes the reasons for such continuity and stability as follows:

Cultural beliefs about the nature of knowledge, how teaching should occur, and how children should learn are so widespread and deeply rooted that they steer the thinking of policy makers, practitioners, parents and citizens toward certain forms of instruction. (Cuban, 1993 p. 14)

Not surprisingly, therefore, in a time of uncertainty and unprecedented change, some argue for a return to the certainties of traditional teaching: a combination of good, old-fashioned discipline and a grounding in the basics. Nostalgia and romanticism rarely provide the most appropriate basis for a secure and viable future.

One of the benefits of traditional teaching, according to Dearden (1984, p. 10), has been that 'it made clear to the teacher what he was supposed to do . . .'. Privileging content over pedagogical considerations, however, resulted in an overemphasis on memorization and accuracy to the detriment of understanding, imagination, creativity and social development. In a content-driven teacher-directed environment there were few spaces in which learners' minds could grow. Conversely, emphasizing process has, it is argued, lead to busy work and a trivializing of content (Bantock, 1980). It is appropriate to ask, in these circumstances, to what extent a reconstructed version of class teaching can broker a new synergy between these widely differing perspectives.

The conversational style of the major case study serves as an appropriate model of synthesis between framing and caring, thus providing appropriate assistance for cognitive growth. Additionally, it is necessary to combine these ingredients so that learners are *enabled* to develop both cognitively and socially. The teacher's role is more interventionist, therefore, than often envisaged in popular versions of child-centred ideology. Vygotsky makes this very point when he states:

> Precisely because . . . children, when left to themselves, will never achieve well-elaborated forms of abstract thought, the school should make every effort to push them in that direction and to develop in them what is intrinsically lacking in their own development. (Cole *et al.*, 1978, p. 89)

Progressive ideology, in opposition to traditional rhetoric, has emphasized the importance of teacher as facilitator of learning, as manager of resources, as organizer of learning environments and opportunities, and this perspective, harnessed to Piagetian stage theory, suggests that learners can be autodidacts. What this study reveals is that this vision remains inadequate until it gives a more prominent position to interactional dialogue: to identify more precisely the teaching responsibilities of practitioners. However, this is not a panacea. This conversational style, or what Gallimore and Goldenberg (1992, p. 208) describe as 'instructional conversations', must come to terms with 'the paradox of playful intention and responsive spontaneity' (p. 209). Failure to resolve this paradox can be a recipe for a return to traditional didacticism and prescription if learners are not allowed to become genuine partners in the dialogue. Even when this occurs, it is difficult to envisage how interactive instructional conversation can simultaneously accommodate the developmental needs (cognitive and social) of all participants from the brightest to the weakest in a typical classroom.

In large classes, in particular, there is a risk, despite the best intentions and efforts of practitioners, that the more extrovert, articulate, able and motivated learners gain the lion's share of teacher's attention because managerial issues such as pace of lessons, and maintaining (the illusion of) progress, frequently take precedence over educational concerns such as challenge and match (Bennett *et al.*, 1984; Bennett *et al.*, 1991). Nevertheless, if the notion of teaching as a form of assistance is taken seriously, and highly interactive exchanges, particularly when questions from learners are encouraged in addition to initiatives taken by practitioners, then classrooms can become learning communities where practitioner–learner, learner–practitioner, and learner–learner encounters provide the kind of scaffolded assistance which is necessary for cognitive dissonance which promotes development and fosters understanding. Such a dynamic process appears to resonate with notions of activity, in the sense of being participatory, and the scaffolding provided can be regarded as guided or directed discovery. However, this is not an unqualified endorsement of class teaching: far from it.

This study demonstrated that in the complex world of the classroom there are inevitable limitations to, and constraints on, any routine, particularly when it is over-used. On grounds of pedagogical variety alone, therefore, and the avoidance of monotony and boredom, a comprehensive repertoire of teaching strategies is necessary. Much more investigation is necessary into how different subject matter can be mediated effectively to various age groups. Impact of context has significance for adequate understanding of this issue also because teaching and learning will not occur without 'effort' on the part of learners and this is particularly significant in the case of disadvantaged children (Oeter, 1992). The pedagogical head of the Hydra requires significant differentiation. Group teaching is most frequently proposed as an effective means of dealing with the shortcomings of class teaching.

Group Teaching

The study reveals that group teaching with ability groups is most likely to be provided in language and mathematics with mixed ability groups being deployed when project-type work is being undertaken. This widespread practice suggests that practitioners are more conscious of match in the basics, whereas project work and discussion-type lessons such as history, geography and nature study are less structured so that the entire ability range in a classroom can be accommodated. This practice seems to provide further confirmation of a traditional distinction between 'the basics' and 'the other' areas of primary programmes. It may be indicative also of less rigour in approach to these subject matter areas.

When learners were taught in ability groups in the major case study, the routines in that context were remarkably consistent with the more general conversational style employed in class teaching. However, because these groups were significantly smaller than an entire class, it was possible to retain more informality. There was more interaction including elements of peer-coaching, active listening and individual attention, and these factors made the encounters more participative than class teaching. The relative homogeneity which exists in ability groups increases the possibility that the conversation of instruction will scaffold all the members and that the relative informality will facilitate and encourage participants to seek assistance. The teacher remained in control and though learners were more likely to ask questions than in a class situation, they were, nevertheless, cast in the role of responders for much of the time. Ability groups of this nature appear to have much in common with tutorials in university settings: there is structured and focused dialogue, feedback which is critically important, direct and indirect praise, as well as peer interaction and dialogue which creates a kind of intellectual excitement, while tutors must be careful that this does not become intellectual point-scoring (Dillon, 1994). It is necessary to distinguish between healthy disagreement and unhealthy competition which can have a destructive rather than an enabling effect.

More time appeared to be spent with less able ability groups where oral work, which had been done with the entire class, was repeated while the more able did seat work. However, there remained a preoccupation with a class standard so that the purpose of ability group teaching for the less able was to try to ensure that they kept up with the more able. Similarly, where additional work was assigned to the more able group(s), to keep them occupied, this work was largely at the same level, thus it often lacked the kind of challenge and differentiation that might be expected for this calibre of student. Despite the tutorial attractiveness, intimacy and other positive features of these ability groups, there seemed to be more concern for standard and keeping students loosely working on the same topics more or less at the same level than matching and challenging. In these circumstances, less able learners appear to gain more cognitively from ability grouping. This is group teaching as a form of remediation, which does not serve the more able very well as they are less likely to be adequately challenged. The overarching concern of practitioners, which seems to militate most against the more able, is a traditional preoccupation with reaching the required 'standard'. Ability group teaching's primary goal should be to enable learners to maximize their developmental potential, classroom management and organizational considerations not withstanding. If this form of group work is to become more child-centred, differentiation of task and maximization of challenge and match, rather than maintenance of standard and class homogenization, need to be its central focus.

One of the purposes of mixed ability grouping in the major case study was the assistance of less able learners by their more able peers. However, through division of labour, which was an integral part of these groups' responsibilities, learners appeared to reinvent ability groups. The more able learners took leadership roles, decided on content, (when designing books), and largely wrote the scripts (literally and metaphorically) while less able learners were invited to provide some illustrations and to do some 'colouring in'. Though these opportunities provided some peer-coaching for less able learners, these roles did not appear to rotate from one assignment to another, in part because the structure and content of tasks remained much the same. While it may be argued that this is how peer-coaching functions — where the more able provide assistance for the less able — if these roles become sedimented then experience becomes constrained and restricted rather than extended, and less able learners have their inadequacies confirmed by being consigned and confined to subordinate and peripheral roles by their more able peers. If mixed ability groups are to function more as teams and to foster genuine collaboration, then much greater attention will need to be paid to: a) identifying tasks which lend themselves to collaborative group work; b) building in variety to tasks thus facilitating rotation of roles, and; c) educating learners themselves about group dynamics so that they can be more self-conscious about how these groups are intended to function. Groups of this nature should not become an opportunity to reinvent behaviours which resemble some features of class teaching, where some learners dominate, very often at the expense of others. However, it is important to acknowledge that when mixed ability groups were created for subject areas such as art, the informal social exchanges, in addition to negotiations surrounding sharing of resources, had importance for personal and social development (Reid, Forrestal and Cook, 1982).

There were occasions during the major case when some students worked in pairs and collaboration was much more apparent while discussions were an integral element of task completion. However, to have an entire class working in pairs, rather than a much smaller number of groups, is a significant challenge to the planning, organizational and record-keeping skills of practitioners as well as to classroom resources. Even with small groups their benefits, Alexander (1992, p. 65) argues, would need to be 'set [against] the increased managerial challenges of having a larger number of groups', while others suggest that, in evaluating their merits, social and emotional benefits need to be considered in addition to cognitive outcomes (Galton, 1989; Galton and Williamson, 1992). As long as the prevailing culture in schools and classrooms is characterized by individualism and isolation, it will be extremely difficult for practitioners to develop more sophisticated routines around grouping that pay attention to social and cognitive development. A reconstructed vision of child-centred teaching requires more adequate understandings of pedagogical complexity and variety rather than bipolar advocacy of process or product.

Group Work

The preceding discussion strongly suggests that group teaching, as distinct from group work, was a prominent feature of classroom life in this study. However, where there was group teaching, group work existed also; when practitioners taught one group, another or others were typically assigned activities or (more commonly) seat work. Details of the inquiry concur with research findings internationally that a significant proportion of what is labelled group work is primarily a managerial mechanism whereby individuals are grouped for certain activities but work largely in isolation (Cuban, 1993; Galton, Simon and Croll, 1980; Bennett *et al.*, 1984; Alexander *et al.*, 1989). Frequently, when individuals (who constitute these groups) converse it is with their nearest neighbour and the nature of the communication is typically not task related. To all intents and purposes, therefore, these groups serve no cognitive or group (as distinct from useful) function. When these are ability groups, they can surreptitiously communicate to their memberships that certain expectations have been set for their achievements thus, potentially at least, fuelling a self-fulfilling prophecy. However, complexities in classrooms surrounding group work should not become a headlong avowal of more class teaching which, I suspect, is an element of recent cries of 'back to basics' in tandem with some effective schools literature (and time on task research) which has rediscovered, though not necessarily recon-structed, class teaching. It is necessary to pay more attention to the purposes of group teaching and group work rather than privileging issues surrounding management and organization, though these concerns constitute important constraints.

Group work is constrained significantly by group teaching. When practitioners are working in class teaching mode with a group of learners, they generally do not wish to be disrupted or interrupted by questioning or noise from groups doing seat work. Learners very quickly adapt to this requirement so that snatched social sound-bites and the occasional giggle are at the boundaries of teachers' tolerance, rather than sustained task-related dialogue which constitute peer-coaching or cognitive framing. Practitioners, in these circumstances, have no apparent intent that such groups actually collaborate and learners behave accordingly. Tasks, therefore, can-not be very challenging as neither teacher nor a more able peer are available to provide assistance.

Recent literature on restructuring teaching has extolled the virtues of less hierarchical structures in favour of a team approach, and this has led to renewed interest in group work: classrooms as 'learning communities' (Barth, 1990) and schools as 'learning organizations' (Fullan, 1993; Elmore and Associates, 1990; Shedd and Bacharach, 1991). However, it would be quite erroneous to suggest that this team approach, currently being promoted in industry, is comparable with mixed ability groups in classrooms (Handy, 1995). Such teams are frequently tightly knit, highly educated professionals whose backgrounds are in disparate disciplines. Teams are commonly formed to generate creative thinking, typically in the research and development end of the industrial complex, and are highly motivated, if not entirely driven, by competition and profit. Probably the most significant lesson to be learned from these developments is that if more sophisticated forms of group work are to become a reality in schools, teachers themselves will need to collaborate as a first step so that they can model such behavious for learners; teachers need to become learners also and need to be perceived as such by those they teach.

Class teaching, group teaching and group work are problematic. A conversational style may bring a welcome degree of interaction, structuring, and participation to class and group teaching, but much remains to be learned about a mix of tasks and pedagogies that will maximize variety of classroom experiences while simultaneously increasing cognitive challenge. Grouping and class teaching are deeply ingrained in primary consciousness and, as the foregoing analysis indicates, class teaching, at least in the Irish context, has a Lazarus-like capacity to reinvent itself. There is an ongoing need to interrogate current practice to find ways and means for its improvement, of building on traditions rather than seeking to ensure that one prevails over the other. As Sarason (1990, p. 88) reminds us: '. . . if the regularities of the classroom remain unexamined and unchanged . . . failure of . . . reforms is guaranteed.' Revisioning progressivism requires ongoing interrogation of practice rather than ideological commitment to particular classroom routines and actions. Identification of 'good' practice needs to move beyond the anecdotal — where documentation and dissemination are the norm for practitioners working in new alliances and partnerships with researchers — if uncritical re-enactment of routines and rituals are to be avoided, and critical revisioning of teaching traditions is to be embedded in the professional activities of practitioners.

Child-centred Teaching?

It may seem superfluous to comment directly on child-centred teaching after the foregoing discussion but I want to argue that the sum is greater than its constituent parts, that there is an indefinable quality that is central to the process of teaching and learning in this manner. Child-centred teaching retains an uncertainty, a tentativeness with allows the magic of childhood and the thrill of discovery to manifest itself in contrast with the predictability and certainty of finding right answers. It is unapologetically optimistic about human nature, but not in any sloppy sentimental sense. It seeks to face the future with confidence and recognizes that it is necessary to instil confidence in learners that is self-assured but not arrogant; it is task oriented but creates spaces for humour, spontaneity, dialogue and individual initiative, yet recognizes that social development is an investment in learners' and societies' futures also. It recognizes that paying attention to relationships is not merely an instrumental necessity for more effective cognitive development, but that they have educational importance in their own right, for moral formation and responsible citizenship.

An inclusive understanding of child-centred teaching recognizes the importance of standards but seeks to mobilize them in ways that develop potential and foster productive endeavour rather than merely measure and apportion success and failure. This reconstructed vision also acknowledges the importance of planning and structuring content but seeks to do it in a manner that creates spaces and allocates time for sustained imaginative and creative engagement; for participation of learners in the process of structuring so that individual bent and interests are recognized and fostered, while sterility and homogenization are avoided. It recognizes that there is strength in diversity which outweighs the seductive security proffered by conformity and uniformity. In pursuit of these goals, child-centred teaching casts its net widely over the cultural landscape to avoid over prescription and to acknowledge and to celebrate many modes of engaging with the world, not all of which need to be pursued by each and every learner. It promotes the idea that happiness is not an end in itself but that purposeful activities bring their own rewards.

This list is potentially endless. I make no apologies for its inherent optimism. However, in addition, it is necessary to recognize (and this has been a constant thread throughout this text), that the wider contexts in which practitioners function have a significant shaping influence on what happens in classrooms. How traditions of teaching are reconstructed, therefore, depends significantly on school cultures and general educational policies and structures.

Schools

Reconstructing an inclusive vision of child-centred practice is not something that can be achieved by practitioners working in the 'cellular' isolation of their classrooms (Lortie, 1975). The interdependence of classroom and school is articulated by Sarason (1972) as follows:

> . . . *schools are not created to foster the intellectual and professional growth of teachers. The assumption that teachers can create and maintain those conditions which make schools stimulating for children, without those same conditions existing for teachers, has no warrant in the history of man.* (quoted by Gallimore and Goldenberg, 1992, p. 218)

I agree wholeheartedly with Rosenholtz (1991, p. 205) when she states, 'What teaching is, how it is performed, and how it is changed cannot be divorced from the social organisation in which it occurs'. Almost all of the participants in this study worked alone in the privacy of their classrooms. Given the complexity of classroom life, and the pervasiveness of the culture of individualism, seeking assistance or collaborating with colleagues is often interpreted as a sign of weakness (Hargreaves, 1994). In these circumstances, rethinking teaching traditions may be too much of a burden. Shedd and Bacharach (1991) indicate the extent of this burden for the isolated practitioner.

> Teaching is such a demanding occupation, and learning to teach is so difficult, that many people count it a substantial achievement merely to master a limited number of techniques that appear to work reasonably well with their students. When teachers are given a choice of continuing to use those techniques or abandoning them and possibly 'losing' their students,

it is hardly surprising that many continue to do what they think will allow them to keep their heads above water. (p. 80)

Such practitioners are likely to 'lose' their students sooner rather than later because the teaching recipes they employ have a much shorter shelf-life than heretofore due to the accelerating pace of social change, and the consequent changing expectations and aspirations of parents and learners. Revisioning child-centred teaching is a challenge that is beyond the most committed teacher working in isolation and must, therefore, be taken up by the entire schools community.

In the context of the study, collaborative school planning has been espoused since the introduction of progressive policy, and this has been reiterated and reinforced in a number of subsequent publications (Ireland, 1995, Coolahan, 1994). It has been slow to take root but, as a consequence of regular whole school inspection and some inservice provision, most primary schools presently have a working document. However, details of the study reveal that while there are instances of 'bounded collaboration' (Hargreaves, 1992, 1994), the 'legendary autonomy' of class teachers continues to prevail (OECD, 1991). This 'masks teachers' evaluative apprehension' and serves 'as the rationale for excluding observers' (Hargreaves, 1993, p. 55). Altering these characteristics, which are deeply embedded in the collective psyche of practitioners and school cultures, will take time, commitment and resources. However, there is no magic formula, for in contexts where policies have been developed and generous resources allocated to these complex processes, teaching traditions have remained remarkably resistant to change also (Cuban, 1993). More complex structures are required to facilitate teachers' professional development needs in response to changing circumstances and greater complexity of classroom life.

Fostering a positive attitude towards change, risk-taking, and experimentation is obviously important (Fullan, 1993, 1995). There are a number of issues that arise from the study which may help to further this agenda. Allocation and use of time, as well as deployment of teaching expertise, have significance for learners and staff development. The tradition of one-class one-teacher militates against school-wide deployment of particular talents and expertise among staff which has implications also for development, continuity and diversity of programme provision. Within this reappraisal, serious consideration will need to be given to the possibility of specialist teachers. Some researchers have already suggested that 'the class teacher system makes impossible demands on the subject knowledge of the generalist primary teacher' (Alexander, 1993, p. 25). Some practitioners in the study were conscious of their limitations in particular subject areas. These details suggest that

> . . . it is no longer reasonable to expect class teachers to cope individually and unaided with the range of demands now being made on them, and that individual self-sufficiency is undesirable in any case in view of the importance of continuity of experience and reasonable consistency of approach from class to class within the school. (Richards, 1987, p. 194)

However, it is unrealistic to expect school staffs to undertake the task of restructuring within existing structures and constraints on time and personnel. Without adequate support such an undertaking is potentially demoralizing, disillusioning and devastating; thus escape rather than recommitment seems more attractive. It is necessary to recall that in the days of major curriculum development projects, teams of experts without any teaching responsibilities devoted their energies full time to the design and production of materials, while others sought to encourage practitioners to implement their programmes. It is very unrealistic to expect practitioners, many of whom are already over-committed just getting through the day, to be seduced by the rhetoric of decentralization — or Local Management of Schools (LMS), or Site-Based Management (SBM) — to carry a burden once shared by a much more extensive group of professionals. If schools are to become learning communities for teachers, time and space must be created away from the hectic routines of classroom life on a regular and ongoing basis. For, as Shedd and Bacharach (1991, p. 194) suggest, 'If schools are to *teach* creativity and problem solving and cooperation and involvement, they must *practice* them, not just in classrooms but at all levels of the system.' Revisioning child-centred practice is a task for the entire school community but teachers remain a non-renewable resource (or spent force) in the absence of structured, systematic, sustained and accessible support.

Policies: Structures and Supports

As the inquiry revealed, teachers, too, are in need of scaffolding and shepherding. During a time of unprecedented change, pressure for reform and restructuring and the anxieties induced by the uncertainties of the change process itself have led policy-makers internationally to advocate decentralization as a means of conferring more autonomy on schools to respond to the task of restructuring in the light of local expertise and circumstances. However, in the interest of engendering coherence, it is tempting for policy-makers to prescribe, to seek to dictate the shape of future educational provision. If and when policy becomes prescription, teachers unite against the common enemy. For example, on a recent visit to schools in England, heads and class teachers spoke of being 'advocates for children', to stave off, as they perceived it, the worst excesses of prescriptive reforms. While they may well be justified in this response, the more important point is that their energies become directed towards defending the status quo rather than rethinking traditions of teaching. This study sought to rehabilitate teachers' voices, but learners, too, should be heard in the restructuring debate, and documenting their perspectives is a further challenge which awaits attention from the research community.

Policy-makers must resist the temptation to dictate reforms and practice as well as espouse an interactional or transformational leadership style which seek to encourage but not coerce, to hasten but not to force, the process of restructuring. Such decisions, frequently determined by an ethic of practicality and relevance, are 'likely to promote a more limited conception of teaching and being a teacher than has hitherto been the case' (Day, 1993, p. 30). Nevertheless, leadership can be 'patterned and directional' as well as cultivating a 'robust and creative partnership' (Skilbeck, 1992, p. 6). In short, policy-makers have an obligation to scaffold practitioners and school principals by modelling behaviours that the former need to adopt. They need to be shepherded also with a range of policies which include, interalia, structural changes which create opportunities for dialogue and collaborative planning at school level, and professional support in the form of more comprehensive and sustained professional development opportunities which balance personal needs against the interests of schools and systems.

Not all of these initiatives can be taken at once. Partnership is an important and appropriate means of setting immediate and longer term priorities, of making provision for sustained development and reducing uncertainty. Without such policies and provisions 'the craft performance of skilled practitioners [becomes] heavier, less responsive, and more sluggish' (Nias, 1989, p. 201). In the Irish context, given the current serious underfunding of primary education, lack of mobility and career opportunities in a settled and ageing workforce, in addition to a history of inadequately resourced reforms in the past, practitioners are inclined to adopt a wait and see strategy; they are unwilling 'to give generously of their selves to their work' (Nias, 1989, p. 214).

Teachers need to shed a 'dependency culture' which has been engendered by more autocratic and dictatorial styles of leadership practised by bureaucrats, policy-makers and management in the past (Coolahan, 1994). In forging new partnerships inside and outside schools, teachers — through new networks and discourse communities —

> must expect and endure the pain that comes with ambitious rethinking and redesign of schools. To pretend that serious restructuring can be done without honest confrontation [of their own cherished practices and beliefs] is a cruel illusion. (Sizer, 1991, p. 34, quoted by Fullan, 1993, p. 79)

Teachers are the fulcrum of rethinking teaching traditions and the role of policy-makers is to create 'the basic conditions for professional development' which facilitate 'open discussion of . . . difficulties and complexities' which is one of the hallmarks of 'professional maturity rather than of professional weakness' (Alexander *et al.*, 1989, p. 297). It is necessary for both practitioners and policy-makers to realize that they are part of a single process, thus 'by collaborating selectively within the local and expanded community' it is possible to 'build scenarios . . . that may not come apart quite so readily . . .' (Huberman, 1993, p. 47). The metaphor of the Hydra facilitates emergence of additional facets to child-centredness and its continued refashioning in ways that avoid restorationist tendencies and to critically calibrate the growing complexities of teaching and learning.

Conclusion

Throughout this study, I have attempted to occupy the borderlands between the grand narratives of teaching in an attempt to find common ground on which to restructure a more inclusive account of these traditions, albeit from a child-centred perspective. This inquiry recognized that the oppositional discourses that these paradigms of teaching have been used (and abused) to create, have hidden the truth of their mutual dependency; it is impossible to understand one without recourse to the other. By acknowledging both traditions, as well as availing of the spaces and possibilities created by the social conditions of postmodernity, an inclusive dialogue was constructed and guided by a spirit of cross-fertilization rather than colonization. While charting a course, which sought to ground these traditions in the contextualized accounts of practitioners' intentions and classroom routines, the phrase 'too far east is west', repeatedly came to mind. This januform world view was rejected in favour of a more complex image — the Hydra — as a more inclusive and elaborate metaphor for characterizing complexity and diversity while striving to find some situated certainty; there is strength and unity in diversity in the same way that chaos theory belies patterns and continuities. Old tunes are revitalized when played in different registers and idioms, and teaching traditions are no exception. However, the cultural contexts in which these traditions are orchestrated will continue to play an important part in shaping their futures. For this, and other reasons, there is no definitive statement that can be made that neatly encapsulates a reconstructed vision of child-centred practice. However, it is hoped that the details of this study, and the emergent issues which have been discussed in this chapter, can form part of an agenda for debate. These issues will be reshaped, refashioned, recontextualized and reconstructed in very different way in a multiplicity of settings, and researchers will continue to identify and document their complexities, commonalities and differences.

While it was once axiomatic to declare, 'at the heart of the educational process lies the child', the head, heart and guiding hand of the teacher needs to be reinscribed in that process also. Without supportive and enabling policies and structures, teachers' hearts will not be in the task. Overly prescriptive policies are likely to ensure that practitioners intervene with a heavy hand with negative consequences for learners. Policy-makers and practitioners need to bear in mind that their task is to enable learners to imagine and construct their own futures and not to predetermine them. It is my hope that this text will enable practitioners to revision and revitalize child-centred practice in ways that empower learners to imagine and create better futures. My attempts to deconstruct, document, reconstruct and revision child-centred teaching will have been worthwhile if it contributes towards that end.

Appendix

Name	Age	Qualification	Length of Career (years)	No. of Schools	Teaching Level	School Type	School Size	Social Context
Aoife	50+	NT	30+	2	Jun. Inf.	Boys	15–20	Suburban Disadvantaged
Barry	36–40	NT, BEd	15+	1	6th. Class	Boys	15–20	Suburban Disadvantaged
Chris	21–25	BEd	2	1	1st. Class	Co-ed.	20+	Suburban Middle class
David	41–45	NT, BA, MEd	20+	2	3rd. Class	Co-ed.	15–20	Urban Working class
Emer	21–25	BEd	4+	3	3rd. Class	Co-ed.	15–20	Urban Middle class
Frank	31–35	NT	10+	1	5th./6th.	Co-ed.	15–20	Suburban Middle class
Gena	31–35	BEd	10+	1	5th. Class	Boys	15–20	Suburban Middle class

Helen**	36–40	NT, BEd	15+	2	4th. Class	Girls	15–20	Urban Disadvantaged
Ian*	41–45	BA (NT)	15+	1	2nd. Class	Co-ed.	20+	Urban Middle class
Jane*	26–30	BEd	5+	3	4th. Class	Girls	8	Village Rural
Kate	21–25	BEd, MEd	4+	2	1st. Class	Co-ed.	20+	Middle class Suburban
Laura	31–35	BEd	10+	1	3rd. Class	Co-ed.	15–20	Urban Disadvantaged
Mark	41–45	NT, BA	20+	2	6th. Class	Co-ed.	15–20	Urban Disadvantaged
Noel*	36–40	NT, BEd	15+	2	5th./6th.	Co-ed.	20+	Urban Middle class
Orla*	36–40	NT	15+	3	3rd./4th.	Girls	5	Village Rural
Paula*	31–35	BEd	10+	2	5th. Class	Co-ed.	9	Village Rural

*Participants in phase two: mini case studies
** Participant in phase three: major case study

The letters NT are abbreviations for National Teacher. Though a Diploma was awarded at the end of a two-year programme in teacher training colleges (discontinued in 1975), recipients are invariably referred to as NTs. A similar Diploma was awarded to graduates in the 1970s and the early 1980s who completed a one-year postgraduate Diploma which has been bracketed in the table above to distinguish it from the two-year qualification. Some NTs who participated in the research had completed BEds on a two-year part-time basis since 1985. All other BEd graduates who participated completed a three-year programme while one of these did so in a Froebel College. The longest serving teacher began as an untrained Junior Assistant Mistress (JAM) and, along with many others, was awarded a Teaching Diploma (NT) after completing a series of summer courses.

Bibliography

AITKIN, M., BENNETT, N. and HESKETH, J. (1981) 'Teaching styles and pupil progress: A reanalysis', *British Journal of Educational Psychology*, **51**, pp. 170–86.

ALEXANDER, R. (1984) *Primary Teaching*, London, Holt, Rinehart and Winston.

ALEXANDER, R. (1992) *Policy and Practice in Primary Education*, London, Routledge.

ALEXANDER, R., ROSE, J. and WOODHEAD, C. (1992) *Curriculum Organisation and Classroom Practice in Primary Schools: A discussion paper*, England, Department of Education and Science.

ALEXANDER, R., WILLCOCKS, J. and KINDER, K. (1989) *Changing Primary Practice*, London, Falmer Press.

ALEXANDER, R. (with contributions from WILLCOCKS, J., KINDER, K. and NELSON, N.) (1995) *Versions of Primary Education*, London, Routledge.

APPLE, M. (1981) *Ideology and Curriculum*, London, Routledge & Kegan Paul.

ARONOWITZ, S. and GIROUX, H. (eds) (1985) *Education Under Siege: The Conservative, Liberal, and Radical Debate Over Schooling*, Massachusetts, Bergin and Garvey Publishers, Inc.

ARONOWITZ, S. and GIROUX, H. (1991) *Postmodern Education: Politics, Culture, and Social Criticism*, Minneapolis, University of Minnesota Press.

ASHTON, P. (1975) *The Aims of Primary Education: A Study of Teachers' Opinions*, London, Macmillan Education Ltd.

BAKHTIN, M. (1981) *The Dialogic Imagination: Four Essays by M.M. Bakhtin* (M. Holquist (ed.); C. Emerson and M. Holquist (trans.)), Austin, University of Texas Press.

BALL, S. (ed.) (1990) *Foucault and Education: Disciplines and Knowledge*, London, Routledge.

BALL, S. (1994) *Education Reform: A Critical and Post-structural Approach*, Buckingham, Open University Press.

BALL, S. and GOODSON, I. (1985) *Teachers' Lives and Careers*, London, Falmer Press.

BANTOCK, G. (1980) *Dilemmas of the Curriculum*, Oxford, Martin Robertson.

BARKER-LUNN, J. (1982) 'Junior schools and their organisational policies', *Educational Research*, **24**, 4, pp. 250–61.

BARROW, R. (1984) *Giving Teaching Back to Teachers: A Critical Introduction to Curriculum Theory*, Sussex, Wheatsheaf Press.

BARTH, R. (1990) *Improving Schools from Within: Teachers, Parents, and Principals Can Make a Difference*, San Francisco, Jossey-Bass Publishers.

BASSEY, M. (1978) *Nine Hundred Primary School Teachers*, Slough, NFER.

BENNETT, N. (1976) *Teaching Styles and Pupil Progress*, London, Open Books.

BENNETT, N., DEFORGES, C., COCKBURN, A. and WILKINSON, B. (1984) *The Quality of Pupil Learning Experiences*, London, Lawrence Erlbaum Associates Publishers.

BENNETT, N. and JORDAN, J. (1975) 'A typology of teaching styles in primary schools', *British Journal of Educational Psychology*, **45**, pp. 20–8.

BENNETT, N., WRAGG, E.C., CARRÉ, C. and CARTER, D. (1991) 'A longitudinal study of primary teachers' perceived competence in, and concerns about, National Curriculum implementation', *Leverhulme Primary Project*, Exeter, University of Exeter.

BEN-PERETZ, M. (1996) 'Women as teachers: Teachers as women', in GOODSON, I.F. and HARGREAVES, A. (eds) *Teachers' Professional Lives* (pp. 178–86), London, Falmer Press.

BERLAK, A. and BERLAK, H. (1975) *The Dilemmas of Schooling*, London, Methuen.

BERLAK, A., BERLAK, H., TUSHNET BAGENTOS, N. and MIKEL, E. (1976) 'Teaching and learning in English primary schools', in HAMMERSLEY, M. and WOODS, P. (eds) *The Process of Schooling* (pp. 86–97), London, Routledge and Kegan Paul.

BERNSTEIN, B. (1971) *Class, Codes and Control, Vol. 1*, London, Routledge and Kegan Paul.

BERNSTEIN, B. (1976) *The Restructuring of Social and Political Theory*, New York, Harcourt Brace Jovanovich.

BLENKIN, G. and KELLY, A. (eds) (1981) *The Primary Curriculum*, London, Harper and Row Publishers.

BLENKIN, G. and KELLY, A. (eds) (1983) *The Primary Curriculum in Action: A Process Approach to Educational Practice*, London, Harper and Row Publishers.

BLYTH, W. (1965) *English Primary Education: A Sociological Description Vol. II: Background*, London, Routledge and Kegan Paul.

BOARD OF EDUCATION (1931) *Report of the Consultative Committee on the Primary School*, (Hadow Report), London, HMSO.

BOGDAN, R. and BIKLEN, S. (1982) *Qualitative Research for Education: An Introduction to Theory and Methods*, Boston, Allyn and Bacon.

BOLGER, D. (ed.) (1991) *Letters from the New Island*, Dublin, Raven Arts Press.

BOYD, W. (trans.) (1975) *Emile for Today: The Emile of Jean Jacques Rousseau*, London, Heinemann.

BOYDELL, D. (1975) 'Pupil behaviour in junior classrooms', *British Journal of Educational Psychology*, **45**, pp. 122–9.

BOYDELL, D. (1980) 'The organisation of junior classrooms: A follow up survey', *Educational Researcher*, **23**, pp. 14–19.

BOYNE, R. and RATTANSI, A. (eds) (1990) *Postmodernity and Society*, London, Macmillan Press.

BREEN, R., HANNAN, D., ROTTMAN, D. and WHELAN, C. (1990) *Understanding Contemporary Ireland: State, Class and Development in the Republic of Ireland*, Dublin, Gill and Macmillan.

BROWN, G. (1985) *Microteaching: A Programme of Teaching Skills*, London, Methuen.

BROWN, T. (1985) *Ireland: A Social and Cultural History 1922–1985*, London, Fontana Press.

BRUNER, J. (1989) 'Vygotsky: A historical and conceptual perspective', in WERTSCH, J.V. (ed.) *Culture, Communication, and Cognition: Vygotskian Perspectives*, Cambridge, Cambridge University Press.

BRUNER, J. (1990) *Acts of Meaning*, Massachusetts, Harvard University Press.

BUCHMAN, M. and FLODEN, R.E. (1991) 'Programme coherence in teacher education: A view from the USA', in COOLAHAN, J. (ed.) *Teacher Education in the Nineties: Towards a New Coherence* (pp. 107–18), Vol. 1, Papers from the 15th Annual Conference of the Association for Teacher Education in Europe (ATEE), Mary Immaculate College of Education, Limerick, Ireland, 1990.

BULLOUGH, R. (1992) 'Beginning teacher curriculum decision making: Personal metaphors and teacher education', *Teaching and Teacher Education*, **8**, 3, pp. 239–52.

BURGESS, D. (1996) 'State schools as they should be organised', *The Sunday Times*, **6**, p. 21, February 18th.

BURKE, A., DOBRICH, P. and SUGRUE, C. (1991) *Erziehungsraum Schule — Ein Internationaler Vergleich zur Schulwirklichkeit, Workshop Report 12*, Frankfurt am Main, Deutches Institut fur Internationale Padagogische Forschung.

BURKE, A., DOBRICH, P. and SUGRUE, C. (1992) *Time for School: An International Comparative Study*, Oideas, No. 38, Spring, pp. 5–40.

BURKE, A. and FONTES, P. (1986) 'Educational beliefs and practices of sixth class teachers in Irish primary schools', *Irish Journal of Education*, **20**, pp. 51–77.

CALLAGHAN, J. (1976) 'Towards a national debate', *Education*, **148**, 17.

CALLAN, E. (1988) *Autonomy and Schooling*, Kingston and Montreal, McGill-Queen's University Press.

CALLAN, T. and NOLAN, B. (1988) 'Family poverty in Ireland: a survey based analysis', in REYNOLDS, B. and HEALY, S.J. (eds) *Poverty and Family Income Policy*. Papers read at Social Policy Conference, 30th September, 1988, Dublin, Conference of Major Religious Superiors.

CAMPBELL, R. (1985) *Developing the Primary School Curriculum*, London, Holt, Rinehart and Winston.

CARLSON, J. (ed.) (1990) *Banned in Ireland: Censorship and the Irish Writer*, London, Routledge.

CARR, W. and KEMMIS, S. (1986) *Becoming Critical: Education, Knowledge and Action Research*, London, Falmer Press.

CENTRAL ADVISORY COUNCIL FOR EDUCATION (England) (1967) *Children and Their Primary Schools* (Plowden Report), London, HMSO.

CLANDININ, J. (1986) *Classroom Practice: Teacher Images in Action*, London, Falmer Press.

CLANDININ, J. and CONNELLY, M. (1991) 'Narrative and story in practice and research', in SCHÖN, D. (ed.) *The Reflective Turn* (pp. 258–82), New York, Teachers College Press.

CLANDININ, J. and CONNELLY, M. (1992) 'Teacher as curriculum maker', in JACKSON, P.W. (ed.) *Handbook of Research on Curriculum* (pp. 363–401), Washington DC, American Educational Research Association.

CLANDININ, J. and CONNELLY, M. (with CRAIG, C., DAVIES, C., FANG HE, M., HOGAN, P., HUBER, J., WHELAN, K. and YOUNG, R.) (1995) *Teachers' Professional Knowledge Landscapes*, New York, Teachers College Press.

CLARE, A. (1991) 'The mad Irish?' in KEANE, C. (ed.) *Mental Health in Ireland* (pp. 4–17), Dublin, Gill and Macmillan Ltd.

COBB, S. (1929) 'Concerning ourselves', *Progressive Education*, 6. Jan. Feb. March.

COLE, M., JOHN-STEINER, V., SCRIBNER, V. and SOUBERMAN, E. (eds) (1978) *L.S. Vygotsky Mind in Society: The Development of Higher Psychological Processes*, London, Harvard University Press.

COMBAT POVERTY AGENCY (1989) *Third Annual Report*, Dublin, Combat Poverty Agency.

COMBAT POVERTY AGENCY (1990) *Tackling Poverty in the Nineties: Policies for the Unemployed, Children, Women and Disadvantaged Communities*, Dublin, CPA.

CONFERENCE OF CONVENT PRIMARY SCHOOLS (1975) *Evaluation of the New Curriculum for Primary Schools*, Dublin, Folens.

CONNELL, R. (1985) *Teachers' Work*, London, Allen and Unwin.

CONNELLY, M. and CLANDININ, J. (1988) *Teachers as Curriculum Planners: Narratives of Experience*, Toronto, Ontario Institute for Studies in Education Press.

COOLAHAN, J. (1981) *Irish Education: History and Structure*, Dublin, Institute of Public Administration.

COOLAHAN, J. (ed.) (1994) *Report on the National Education Convention*, Dublin, Government Publications.

COOLAHAN, J. (ed.) (1995) *Issues and Strategies in the Implementation of Educational Policy* (Proceedings of a Bicentenary Conference Organised by the Education Department, St. Patrick's College, Maynooth), Maynooth: Cardinal Press.

COOLAHAN, J. and McGUINNESS, S. (1994) Report On The Roundtable Discussions in Dublin Castle on The Minister for Education's Position Paper 'Regional Education Councils', Dublin, Department of Education.

COUNTS, G. (1932) *Dare the School Build a New Social Order?* New York, John Day.

COX, B. and DYSON, A. (eds) (1969) *The Crisis in Education*, London, Critical Quarterly Society (Black Paper 2).

COX, B. and DYSON, A. (eds) (1970) *Goodbye Mr. Short*, London, Critical Quarterly Society (Black Paper 3).

COX, B. and DYSON, A. (eds) (1971) *The Black Papers on Education*, London, Davis-Poynter.

COX, B. and BOYSON, R. (eds) (1975) *Black Paper 1975: The Fight for Education*, London, Dent.

Cox, V. (1995) '"Concentration Camp" Playground Makes Residents See Red', *Evening Herald*, June 7th, p. 15, Dublin, Independent Newspapers Ltd.

Cuban, L. (1993) *How Teachers Taught: Constancy and Change in American Classrooms 1880–1990*, London, Teachers' College Press.

Cunningham, P. (1988) *Curriculum Change in the Primary School Since 1945: Dissemination of the Progressive Ideal*, London, Falmer Press.

Darling, J. (1994) *Child-Centred Education and Its Critics*, England, Chapman.

Day, C. (1993) 'Research and the continuing professional development of teachers', An inaugural lecture delivered at the University of Nottingham School of Education.

Dearden, R. (1984) *Theory and Practice in Education*, London, Routledge and Kegan Paul.

Delamont, S. (ed.) (1987) *The Primary School Teacher*, London, Falmer Press.

Denzin, N. and Lincoln, Y. (eds) (1994) *Handbook of Qualitative Research*, London, Sage Publications.

Department of Education and Science (1978) *Primary Education in England: A Survey by HM Inspectors of Schools*, London, Her Majesty's Stationery Office.

Dewey, J. (1902) *The Child and the Curriculum*, Chicago, University of Chicago Press.

Dewey, J. (1916) *Democracy and Education*, London, Collier Macmillan Publishers.

Dewey, J. (1928) 'Progressive education and the science of education', Address made at the Eighth Annual Conference of the Progressive Education Association, March 8th.

Dewey, J. (1938) *Experience and Education*, London, Collier Macmillan Publishers.

Dillon, J. (1988) *Questioning and Teaching: A Manual of Practice*, New York, Teachers' College Press.

Dillon, J. (1994) *Using Discussion in Classrooms*, Buckingham, Open University Press.

Doyle, R. (1988) *The Commitments*, London, Minerva.

Doyle, R. (1990) *The Snapper*, London, Minerva.

Doyle, R. (1991) *The Van*, London, Secker and Warburg.

Dunne, J. (1992) *Back to the Rough Ground: Phronesis and Techne in Modern Philosophy and in Aristotle*, Notre Dame, University of Notre Dame Press.

Edwards, D. and Mercer, N. (1987) *Common Knowledge: The Development of Understanding in the Classroom*, London, Methuen.

Egan, K. (1979) *Educational Development*, New York, Oxford University Press.

Egan, O. (1981) 'Informal teaching in the primary school: Characteristics and correlates', *Irish Journal of Education*, **XV**, 1, pp. 5–22.

Eggleston, J. (1977) *The Sociology of the School Curriculum*, London, Routledge and Kegan Paul.

Eisner, E. (1979) *The Educational Imagination: On the Design and Evaluation of School Programs*, London, Collier Macmillan Publishers.

Eisner, E. (1982) *Cognition and Curriculum: A Basis for Deciding What We Teach*, London, Longman Inc.

EISNER, E. (1985) *The Art of Educational Evaluation: A Personal View*, London, Falmer Press.

EISNER, E. (1988) 'The primacy of experience and the politics of method', *Educational Researcher*, **17**, 5, pp. 15–20, June–July.

EISNER, E. (1991a) 'What really counts in schools', *Educational Leadership*, **2**, 3, pp. 10–17.

EISNER, E. (1991b) *The Enlightened Eye: Qualitative Inquiry and the Enhancement of Educational Practice*, New York, Macmillan.

EISNER, E. (1996) 'What is education for?' A public lecture delivered at St. Patrick's College, Drumcondra to celebrate the 125th anniversary of the Irish National Teachers' Organisation, Dublin, INTO.

EISNER, E. and PESHKIN, A. (eds) (1990) *Qualitative Inquiry in Education: The Continuing Debate*, New York, Teachers College Press.

ELBAZ, F. (1983) *Teacher Thinking: A Study of Practical Knowledge*, London, Croom Helm.

ELLEY, W. (1992) *How in the World Do Students Read?* Hamburg, International Association for Evaluation of Educational Achievement.

ELLIS, T. (1976) *William Tyndale: The Teachers' Story*, London, Writers and Readers Cooperative.

ELMORE, R. AND ASSOCIATES (1990) *Restructuring Schools: The Next Generation of Educational Reform*, San Francisco, Jossey-Bass.

EMERSON, A. (1993) *Teaching Media in The Primary School*, London, Cassell.

ENTWISTLE, H. (1970) *Child-centred Education*, London, Methuen and Co. Ltd.

ERAUT, M. (1995) 'Schön shock: A case for reframing reflection-in-action?', *Teachers and Teaching Theory and Practice*, **1**, 1, pp. 9–22.

ERICKSON, F. (1986) 'Qualitative methods in research on teaching', in WHITROCK M.C. (ed.) *Handbook of Research on Teaching, Third Edition* (pp. 119–61), London, Collier Macmillan.

ERICKSON, F. and SCHULTZ, J. (1992) 'Students experience of the curriculum', in JACKSON, P. (ed.) *Handbook of Research on Curriculum. A Project of the American Research Association* (pp. 465–85), New York, Maxwell Macmillan International.

ERICKSON, G. (1988) 'Explorations in the field of reflection: Directions for future research agendas', in GRIMMET, P. and ERICKSON, G. (eds) *Reflection in Teacher Education* (pp. 195–206), London, Teachers College Press.

FITZGERALD, G. (1991) *All in a Life: Garret Fitzgerald, An Autobiography*, Dublin, Gill and Macmillan Ltd.

FITZGERALD, M. (1991) 'The child and the family', in KEANE, C. (ed.) *Mental Health in Ireland*, Dublin, Gill and Macmillan Ltd.

FONTES, P. and KELLAGHAN, T. (1977) 'The new primary school curriculum: Its implementation and effects', Dublin, Educational Research Centre (unpublished).

FORMAN, G. and TWOMEY FOSNOT, C. (1982) 'The use of Piaget's constructivism in early childhood education programs', in SPODEK, B. (ed.) *Handbook of Research in Early Childhood Education* (pp. 185–211), London, Collier Macmillan Publishers.

FOUCAULT, M. (1979) *Discipline and Punishment: The Birth of the Prison* (A. Sheridan, trans.), New York, Vintage Books.

FROEBEL, F. (1887) *The Education of Man*, London, Edward Arnold.

FULLAN, M. (1982) *The Meaning of Educational Change*, New York, Teachers College, Columbia University.

FULLAN, M. (1985) 'Change processes at the local level', *The Elementary School Journal*, **85**, 3. pp. 391–421.

FULLAN, M. (1991) *The New Meaning of Educational Change*, London, Cassell.

FULLAN, M. (1993) *Change Forces: Probing the Depths of Educational Reform*, London, Falmer Press.

FULLAN, M. (1995) 'Strategies for implementing large scale change' (Séamus Ó Súilleabáin Memorial Lecture) in COOLAHAN, J. (ed.) *Issues and Strategies in the Implementation of Educational Policy*, Maynooth, Cardinal Press.

FURTH, H. and WACHS, H. (1975) *Thinking Goes to School: Piaget's Theory in Practice*, London, Oxford University Press.

GADAMER, H. (1975) *Truth and Method*, London, Sheed and Ward.

GALLIMORE, R. and GOLDENBERG, C. (1992) 'Tracking the developmental path of teachers and learners: A Vygotskian perspective', in OSER, F., DICK, A., and PATRY, J.L. (eds) *Effective and Responsible Teaching: The New Synthesis* (pp. 203–21), San Francisco, Jossey-Bass Publishers.

GALTON, M. (1989) *Teaching in the Primary School*, London, David Fulton.

GALTON, M. and SIMON, B. (1980) *Progress and Performance in the Primary Classroom*, London, Routledge and Kegan Paul.

GALTON, M., SIMON, B. and CROLL, P. (1980) *Inside the Primary Classroom*, London, Routledge and Kegan Paul.

GALTON, M. and WILLIAMSON, J. (1992) *Group Work in the Primary Classroom*, London, Routledge.

GENET, J. (1991) *The Big House in Ireland: Reality and Representation*, Ireland, Brandon Book Publishers Ltd.

GIROUX, H. (1993) *Border Crossings: Cultural Workers and the Politics of Education*, New York, Routedge.

GIROUX, H. and SIMON, R. (1989) *Popular Culture, Schooling and Everyday Life*, Massachusetts, Bergin and Garvey Publishing Inc.

GLASER, B. (1978) *Theoretical Sensitivity: Advances in the Methodology of Grounded Theory*, California, The Sociology Press.

GLASER, B. and STRAUSS, A. (1967) *The Discovery of Grounded Theory: Strategies for Qualitative Research*, New York, Aldine de Gruyter.

GOETZ, J. and LeCOMPTE, M. (1984) *Ethnography and Qualitative Design in Educational Research*, New York, Academic Press.

GOLEMAN, D. (1996) *Emotional Intelligence*, Great Britain, Bloomsbury.

GOODSON, I. (1992a) 'Sponsoring the teacher's voice: Teachers' lives and teacher development', in HARGREAVES, A. and FULLAN, M. (eds) *Understanding Teacher Development* (pp. 110–21), London, Cassell.

GOODSON, I. (ed.) (1992b) *Studying Teachers' Lives*, London, Routledge and Kegan Paul.

GOODSON, I. (1994) *Studying Curriculum*, Buckingham, Open University.

GOODSON, I. (1996) '"Trendy theory" and teacher professionalism', *Journal of Education Teaching*.

GOODSON, I. and BALL, S. (eds) (1984) *Defining the Curriculum: Histories and Ethnographies*, London, Falmer Press.

GOODSON, I. and HARGREAVES, A. (eds) (1996a) *Teachers' Professional Lives*, London, Falmer Press.

GOODSON, I. and HARGREAVES, A. (1996b) 'Teachers' professional lives', in GOODSON, I. and HARGREAVES, A. (eds) *Teachers' Professional Lives*, London, Falmer Press.

GOODSON, I. and WALKER, R. (eds) (1991) *Biography, Identity and Schooling: Episodes in Educational Research*, London, Falmer Press.

GRACE, G. (1995) *School Leadership: Beyond Education Management*, London, Falmer Press.

GRACEY, H. (1974) *Curriculum or Craftmanship: Elementary Teachers in a Bureaucratic System*, Chicago, The University of Chicago Press.

GRAMSCI, A. (1971) *Selection from Prison Notebooks* (trans. and ed. by Q. HOARE, and G. SMITH), London, Lawrence and Wishart.

GRAY, J. and SATTERLY, D. (1976) 'A chapter of errors', *Educational Research*, **19**, 1, pp. 45–56.

GRAY, J. and SATTERLY, D. (1981) 'Formal or informal? A reassessment of the British evidence', *British Journal of Educational Psychology*, **51**, part 2, pp. 187–96.

GREANEY, V., BURKE, A. and McCANN, J. (1987) 'Entrants to primary teacher education in Ireland' *European Journal of Teacher Education*, **10**, 2, pp. 127–40.

GREEN, T. (1968) 'A topology of the teaching concept', in MACMILLAN, C. and NELSON, T. (eds) *Concepts of Teaching: Philosophical Essays*, Chicago, Rand MacNally.

GREENE, M. (1990) *Retrieving the Language of Compassion: The Education Professor in Search of Community*, Knoxville, University of Tennessee.

GRIMMETT, P. and ERICKSON, G. (eds) (1988) *Reflection in Teacher Education*, London, Teachers College Press.

GRUNDY, S. (1987) *Curriculum: Product or Praxis*, London, Falmer Press.

HAMMERSLEY, M. and ATKINSON, P. (1983) *Ethnography: Principles in Practice*, London, Tavistock Publications Ltd.

HAMMERSLEY, M. and WOODS, P. (eds) (1976) *The Process of Schooling: A Sociological Reader*, London, Routledge and Kegan Paul in association with the Open University.

HANDY, C. (1995) *The Empty Raincoat: Making Sense of The Future*, Great Britain, Arrow Books.

HANNAN, D. and SHORTALL, S. (1991) *The Quality of their Education: School Leavers' Views of Educational Objectives and Outcomes*, Dublin, The Economic and Social Research Institute.

HARGREAVES, A. (1984a) 'Constrastive rhetoric and extremist talk', in HARGREAVES,

A. and WOODS, P. (eds) *Classrooms and Staffrooms: The Sociology of Teachers and Teaching* (pp. 215–31), Milton Keynes, Open University Press.

HARGREAVES, A. (1984b) 'The significance of classroom coping strategies', in HARGREAVES, A. and WOODS, P. (eds) *Classrooms and Staffrooms: The Sociology of Teachers and Teaching* (pp. 64–85), Milton Keynes, Open University Press.

HARGREAVES, A. (1989) *Curriculum and Assessment Reform*, Milton Keynes, Open University Press.

HARGREAVES, A. (1992) 'Cultures of teaching: A focus for change', in HARGREAVES, A. and FULLAN, M. (eds) *Understanding Teacher Development* (pp. 216–40), London, Cassell.

HARGREAVES, A. (1993) 'Dissonant voices: Teachers and the multiple realities of restructuring', Paper presented at the International Invitational Symposium, St. Patrick's College, Drumcondra, Dublin, September.

HARGREAVES, A. (1994) *Changing Teachers, Changing Times*, London, Cassell.

HARGREAVES, A. and FULLAN, M. (1992) *Understanding Teacher Development*, London, Cassell.

HARGREAVES, A. and TUCKER, E. (1991) 'Teaching and guilt: Exploring the feelings of teaching', *Teaching and Teacher Education*, 7, 5–6, pp. 491–505.

HARGREAVES, A. and WOODS, P. (1984) *Classrooms and Staffrooms: The Sociology of Teachers and Teaching*, Buckingham, Open University Press.

HERNSTEIN, R.J. and MURRAY, C. (1994) *The Bell Curve: Reshaping of American Life by Differences in Intelligence*, New York, Free Press.

HIRST, P. (1974) *Knowledge and the Curriculum*, London, Routledge and Kegan Paul.

HIRST, P. and PETERS, R. (1970) *The Logic of Education*, London, Routledge and Kegan Paul.

HOGAN, P. (ed.) (1995) *Partnership and the Benefits of Learning: A Symposium on Philosophical Issues in Educational Policy*, Maynooth, Educational Studies Association of Ireland.

HOLLAND, S. (1979) *Rutland Street*, The Hague, Bernard Van Leer Foundation; and Oxford, Pergamon Press.

HOLMES, E. (1911) *What Is and What Might Be: A Study of Education in General and Elementary Education in Particular*, London, Constable and Company.

HOLT, J. (1970) *How Children Fail*, New York, Dell.

HOYLE, E. (1974) 'Professionality, professionalism and control in teaching', *London Educational Review*, 3, pp. 13–19.

HUBERMAN, M. (1993) 'The model of the independent artisan in teachers' professional relations', in WARREN LITTLE, J. and WALLIN MCLAUGHLIN, M. (eds) *Teachers' Work: Individuals, Colleagues and Contexts*, New York, Teachers College Press.

HUNT, D. (1987) *Beginning with Ourselves in Practice, Theory and Human Affairs*, Toronto, OISE, Press.

HUNT, D. (1992) *Renewal of Personal Energy*, Toronto, OISE Press.

IRELAND (1971) *The Primary Teacher's Handbooks*, Vols 1 and 2, Dublin, Government Publications Office.

IRELAND (1985) *Primary Education: A Curriculum and Examination Board Discussion Paper*, Dublin, Government Publications.

IRELAND (1987) 'The implementation of the principles of the primary school curriculum: Perceptions of teachers and inspectors' (Survey Report), Curriculum Unit, Dublin, Department of Education (unpublished).

IRELAND (1990a) *Report of the Review Body on the Primary Curriculum*, Dublin, Department of Education.

IRELAND (1990b) *Report of the Primary Education Review Body*, Dublin, Government Publications.

IRELAND (1992) *Education for a Changing World: Green Paper on Education*, Dublin, The Stationery Office.

IRELAND (1994) *Position Paper on the Governance of Schools, issued by Niamh Bhreathnach, T.D., Minister for Education*, Dublin, Department of Education.

IRELAND (1995) *Charting Our Education Future: White Paper on Education*, Dublin, Government Publications.

IRISH NATIONAL TEACHERS' ORGANISATION (1976) *Primary School Curriculum: Curriculum Questionnaire Analysis*, Dublin, INTO.

IRISH NATIONAL TEACHERS' ORGANISATION (1990) *School Plan: A Report by the Education Committee*, Dublin, INTO.

IRISH NATIONAL TEACHERS' ORGANISATION (1991) *The Place of Religious Education in the National School System: A Report by the INTO Education Committee*, Dublin, INTO.

IRISH NATIONAL TEACHERS' ORGANISATION (1993) *Professional Development of Teachers and Issues in Inservice Education*, Dublin, INTO.

IRISH NATIONAL TEACHERS' ORGANISATION (1994a) *A Career in Teaching: Develop—Recognise—Reward*, Dublin, INTO.

IRISH NATIONAL TEACHERS' ORGANISATION (1994b) *Poverty and Educational Disadvantage: Breaking the Cycle*, Dublin, INTO.

JACKSON, P. (ed.) (1992) *Handbook of Research on Curriculum*, Project of the American Research Association, New York, Macmillan.

JAEGER, R. (ed.) (1988) *Complementary Methods for Research in Education*, Washington, DC, American Educational Research Association.

JOHN-STEINER, V. and SOUBERMAN, E. (1978) 'Afterword', in COLE, M., JOHN-STEINER, V., SCRIBNER, S. and SOUBERMAN, E. (eds) *Mind in Society: The Development of Higher and Psychological Processes* (pp. 121–33), England, Harvard University Press.

JONES, D. (1990) 'The genealogy of the urban schoolteacher', in BALL, S. (ed.) *Foucault and Education: Disciplines and Knowledge* (pp. 56–77), London, Routledge and Kegan Paul.

KATZ, M. (1987) *Reconstructing American Education*, Cambridge, MA, Harvard University Press.

KEANE, C. (ed.) (1991) *Mental Health in Ireland*, Dublin, Gill and Macmillan Ltd.

KEARNEY, R. (ed.) (1985) *The Irish Mind: Exploring Intellectual Traditions*, Dublin, Wolfhound Press.

KEDDIE, N. (ed.) (1971) *Tinker, Tailor . . . The Myth of Cultural Deprivation*, London, Penguin Books.

KELLAGHAN, T., WEIR, S., ÓHUALLACHÁIN, S. and MORGAN, M. (1995) *Educational Disadvantage in Ireland*, Dublin, Educational Research Centre.

KELLY, A. (1977) *The Curriculum Theory and Practice*, London, Harper and Row Publishers.

KELLY, A. (1986) *Knowledge and Curriculum Planning*, London, Harper and Row Publishers.

KILBOURN, B. (1988) 'Reflecting on Vignettes of Teaching', in GRIMMET, P. and ERICKSON, G. (eds) *Reflection in Teacher Education* (pp. 91–112), London, Teachers College Press.

KILBOURN, B. (1990a) *Constructive Feedback: Learning the Art*, Toronto, OISE Press.

KILBOURN, B. (1990b) 'Pedagogical and subject-matter knowing: A case of history teaching', Paper presented at the American Educational Research Association, Boston.

KILBOURN, B. (1990c) 'Self-monitoring in teaching', Paper presented at the American Educational Research Association, Boston.

KING, R. (1978) *All Things Bright and Beautiful? A Sociological Study of Infants' Classrooms*, Chichester, John Wiley and Sons.

KUHN, T. (1970) *The Structure of Scientific Revolutions*, London, University of Chicago Press.

KUTNICK, P. (1988) *Relationships in the Primary School Classroom*, London, Paul Chapman Publishing Ltd.

LAKOFF, G. and JOHNSON, M. (1980) *Metaphors We Live By*, London, University of Chicago Press.

LANE, D. (1991) *Catholic Education and the School: Some Theological Reflections*, Dublin, Veritas.

LA POINTE, A., MEAD, N. and ASKEW, J. (1992) *Learning Mathematics*, Princeton, NJ, IAEP/Educational Testing Service.

LA POINTE, A., ASKEW, J. and MEAD, A. (1992) *Learning Science*, Princeton, NJ, IAEP/Educational Testing Service.

LAWTON, D. (1992) *Education and Politics in the 1990s: Conflict or Consensus?* London, Falmer Press.

LECOMPTE, M., MILLROY, W. and PREISSLE, J. (1992) *The Handbook of Qualitative Research in Education*, London, Academic Press.

LEE, J. (1989) *Ireland 1912–1985: Politics and Society*, Cambridge, Cambridge University Press.

LEITHWOOD, K. (ed.) (1987) *Planned Educational Change: A Manual of Curriculum Review, Development, and Implementation (CRDI) Concepts and Procedures*, Toronto, Ontario Institute for Studies in Education Press.

LE RIDER, J. (1993) *Modernity and Crises of Identity: Culture and Society in Fin-de-Siecle Vienna*, (R. MORRIS, trans.), Cambridge, Polity Press.

LIEBERMAN, A. (ed.) (1990) *Schools as Collaborative Cultures: Creating the Future Now*, London, Falmer Press.

LINCOLN, Y. and GUBA, E. (1985) *Naturalistic Inquiry*, London, Sage Publications.

LITTLE, J. and MCLAUGHLIN, M. (eds) (1993) *Teachers' Work: Individuals, Colleagues, and Contexts*, New York, Teachers College Press.

LORTIE, D. (1975) *Schoolteacher: A Sociological Study*, London, University of Chicago Press.

LOUDEN, W. (1991) 'Collegiality, curriculum and educational change', *The Curriculum Journal*, **2**, 3, pp. 361–37.

MACDONALD, A. (ed.) (1981) *Chambers Twentieth Century Dictionary*, Bath, Pitman Press.

MACMAHON, B. (1992) *The Master*, Dublin, Poolbeg Press.

MANNHEIM, K. (1991) (with a new preface by Bryan Turner) *Ideology and Utopia*, London, Routledge.

MARTIN, M. and MORGAN, M. (1994) 'Reading literacy in Irish schools: A comparative analysis', *Irish Journal of Education*, Special edition, **28**.

MATTINGLY, C. (1991) 'Narrative reflections on practical actions: Two learning experiments in reflective storytelling', in SCHÖN, D. (ed.) *The Reflective Turn: Case Studies In and On Educational Practice*, New York, Teachers College Press.

MCCARTHY, C. (1968) *The Distasteful Challenge*, Dublin, Institute of Public Administration.

MCDONAGH, K. (1969) *Reports on the Draft Curriculum for Primary Schools*, Dublin, no publisher credited.

MCGAHERN, J. (1965) *The Dark*, London, Faber and Faber.

MCLAREN, P. (1986) *Schooling as a Ritual Performance: Towards a Political Economy of Educational Symbols and Gestures*, London, Routledge.

MORTIMORE, P., SAMMONS, P., STOLL, L., LEWIS, D. and ECOB, R. (1988) *School Matters: The Junior Years*, Wells, Open Books.

NIAS, J. (1989) *Primary Teachers Talking: A Study of Teaching as Work*, London, Routledge and Kegan Paul.

NIAS, J., SOUTHWORTH, G. and CAMPBELL, P. (1992) *Whole School Curriculum Development in the Primary School*, London, Falmer Press.

NODDINGS, N. (1992) *The Challenge to Care in Schools: An Alternative Approach to Education*, New York, Teachers College Press.

O'BUACHALLA, S. (1988) *Educational Policy in Twentieth Century Ireland*, Dublin, Wolfhound Press.

O'DONNELL, J. (1990) *Word Gloss*, Dublin, Institute of Public Administration.

OETER, L. (1992) 'The zone of proximal development for learning and teaching', in OSER, F. *et al.* (eds) *Effective and Responsible Teaching: The New Synthesis*, San Francisco, Jossey-Bass Publishers.

ONTARIO MINISTRY OF EDUCATION (1990) 'The formative years consultation paper: Restructuring of education consultation phase 1', June, Toronto, Ministry of Education.

ORGANISATION FOR ECONOMIC COOPERATION AND DEVELOPMENT (1991) *Reviews of National Policies for Education*: Ireland, Paris, OECD.

ORGANISATION FOR ECONOMIC COOPERATION AND DEVELOPMENT (1994) *Education at a Glance: OECD Indicators*, Paris, OECD.

ORGANISATION FOR ECONOMIC COOPERATION AND DEVELOPMENT (1995) *Education at a Glance*, Paris, OECD.

OSER, F., DICK, A. and PATRY, J. (eds) (1992) *Effective and Responsible Teaching: The New Synthesis*, San Francisco, Jossey-Bass Publishers.

PERROTT, E. (1984) *Effective Teaching. A Practical Guide to Improving Your Teaching*, London, Longman.

PETERS, R. (1966) *Ethics and Education*, London, Allen & Unwin.

PETERS, R. (ed.) (1969) *Perspectives on Plowden*, London, Routledge and Kegan Paul.

PHENIX, R. (1964) *Realms of Meaning*, New York, McGraw Hill.

PIAGET, J. (1959) *The Language and Thought of the Child*, London, Routledge and Kegan Paul.

POLANYI, M. (1958) *Personal Knowledge: Towards a Post-Critical Philosophy*, London, Routledge and Kegan Paul.

The Polity Reader in Social Theory (1994). Cambridge, Polity Press.

POTTER, R. (1967) *The Stream of American Education*, New York, American Book Company.

PURKEY, S. and SMITH, M. (1983) 'Effective schools: A review', *The Elementary School Journal*, **83**, 4, pp. 427–52.

PURKEY, S. and SMITH, M. (1985) 'School reform: The district policy implications of the effective schools literature', *The Elementary School Journal*, **85**, 3, pp. 353–89.

PURPEL, D. (1989) *The Moral and Spiritual Crisis in Education: A Curriculum for Justice and Compassion in Education*, Massachusetts, Bergin and Garvey Publishers Inc.

REID, J., FORRESTAL, P. and COOK, J. (1982) *Small Group Work in the Classroom*, Language and Learning Project — Education Department, Western Australia.

REYNOLDS, B. and HEALY, S. (eds) (1988) *Policy and Family Income Policy*, Dublin, Conference of Major Religious Superiors.

RICHARDS, C. (1987) 'Primary education in England: An analysis of some recent issues and developments', in DELAMONT, S. (ed.) *The Primary School Teacher* (pp. 177–98), London, Falmer Press.

ROCHE, M. (1992) *Rethinking Citizenship: Welfare, Ideology and Change in Modern Society*, Cambridge, Polity Press.

RORTY, A. (1994) 'Habermas and Lyotard', in *The Polity Reader in Social Theory*, Cambridge, Polity Press.

ROSENHOLTZ, S. (1991) *Teachers' Workplace: The Social Organisation of Schools*, New York, Teachers College Press.

RUDDUCK, J. (1991) *Innovation and Change*, Milton Keynes, Open University Press.

RUSK, R. (1979) *The Doctrines of the Great Educators*, 5th edn, New York, St. Martin's Press.

RUSSELL, J., MILLS, I. and REIFF-MUSGROVE, P. (1990) 'The role of symmetrical and asymmetrical social conflict in cognitive change', *Journal of Experimental Child Psychology*, **49**, 1, pp. 58–78.

RUSSELL, T. and MUNBY, H. (eds) (1992) *Teachers and Teaching: From Classroom to Reflection*, London, Falmer Press.

RUTTER, M., MAUGHAN, B., MORTIMORE, P. and OUSTON, J. (1979) *15,000 Hours: Secondary Schools and their Effects on Children*, London, Open Books.

SAMUELOWICZ, K. and BAIN, J. (1992) 'Conceptions of teaching held by academic teachers', *Higher Education*, **24**, 1, pp. 93–111.

SARASON, S. (1972) *The Creation of Settings and the Future Societies*, San Francisco, Jossey-Bass.

SARASON, S. (1990) *The Predictable Failure of Educational Reform*, San Francisco, Jossey-Bass Publishers.

SARTRE, J.P. (1966) *Being and Nothingness*, (trans. by H. BARNES), New York, Washington Square Press.

SCHÖN, D. (1983) *The Reflective Practitioner: How Professionals Think in Action*, New York, Basic Books.

SCHÖN, D. (1987) *Educating the Reflective Practitioner: Toward a New Design for Teaching and Learning in the Professions*, London, Jossey-Bass Publishers.

SCHÖN, D. (ed.) (1991) *The Reflective Turn: Case Studies In and On Educational Practice*, London, Teachers College Press.

SCHWAB, J. (1969) 'The practical: A language for curriculum', *School Review*, **78**, pp. 1–24.

SHARP, R. and GREEN, A. (1975) *Education and Social Control: A Study in Progressive Primary Education*, London, Routledge and Kegan Paul.

SHEDD, J. and BACHARACH, S. (1991) *Tangled Hierarchies: Teachers as Professionals and the Management of Schools*, San Francisco, Jossey-Bass Publishers.

SHELDRAKE, R. (1990) *The Rebirth of Nature: The Greening of Science and God*, London, Century.

SHULMAN, L. (1988) 'The dangers of dichotomous thinking in education', in GRIMMETT, P. and ERICKSON, G. (eds) *Reflection in Teacher Education* (pp. 31–8), London, Teachers College Press.

SIMON, B. (1981) 'The primary school revolution: Myth or reality?' in SIMON, B. and WILLCOCKS, J. (eds) *Research and Practice in the Primary Classroom* (pp. 7–25), London, Routledge and Kegan Paul.

SIMON, B. and WILLCOCKS, J. (eds) (1981) *Research and Practice in the Primary Classroom*, London, Routledge and Kegan Paul.

SIMONS, H. and ELLIOTT, J. (eds) (1990) *Rethinking Appraisal and Assessment*, Buckingham, Open University Press.

SIZER, T. (1984) *Horace's Compromise: The Dilemma of the American High School*, Boston, Houghton Mifflin.

SIZER, T. (1991) 'No pain, no gain', *Educational Leadership*, **48**, 8, pp. 32–4.

SKILBECK, M. (ed.) (1984) *Readings in School-based Curriculum Development*, London, Harper and Row Publishers.

SKILBECK, M. (1992) 'School leadership and management for educational change', *Decision Maker*, 5, pp. 5–11.

SMITH, D. (ed.) (1992) *Understanding the Underclass*, London, Policy Studies Institute.

SMYTH, J. (ed.) (1993) *A Socially Critical View of the Self-Managing School*, London, Falmer Press.

SOUTHWORTH, G. (1995) *Looking into Primary Headship: A Research Based Interpretation*, London, Falmer Press.

SPARKS, A. (1994) *Tomorrow is Another Country: The Inside Story of South Africa's Negotiated Revolution*, Sandton, Struik Publishing.

SPODEK, B. (ed.) (1982) *Handbook of Research in Early Childhood Education*, London, Collier Macmillan Publishers.

SPODEK, B. (1989) 'Reflecting on individual differences in young children: Cognitive style and early education', *Early Child Development and Care*, **51**, pp. 157–74.

SPRADLEY, J. (1979) *The Ethnographic Interview*, London, Holt, Rinehart and Winston.

SPRADLEY, J. (1980) *Participant Observation*, London, Holt, Rinehart and Winston.

STAKE, R. (1988) 'Case study methods in educational research: Seeking Sweet Water', in JAEGER, R. (ed.) *Complementary Methods for Research in Education* (pp. 253–76), Washington, DC, American Educational Research Association.

STAKE, R. (1990) 'The evaluation of teaching', in SIMONS, H. and ELLIOTT, J. (eds) *Rethinking Appraisal and Assessment* (pp. 13–19), Buckingham, Open University Press.

STAKE, R. and MABRY, L. (1993) 'Case study for a deep understanding of teaching', Paper presented at the International Invitational Symposium, St. Patrick's College, Drumcondra, September.

STENHOUSE, L. (1975) *An Introduction to Curriculum Research and Development*, London, Heinemann.

SUGRUE, C. (1990) 'Child-centred Education in Ireland since 1971', *Oideas*, 35, Spring, pp. 5–21.

SUGRUE, C. (1992) 'Teachers constructions of child-centred teaching', Unpublished PhD Dissertation, OISE.

SUGRUE, C. (1994) 'Generating grounded theory and grounding grand theories in classroom inquiry', Paper presented at the International Sociology Association Conference, Bielefeld, July.

SUGRUE, C. (1996a) Student Teachers' Lay theories: Implications for Professional Development, in GOODSON I. and HARGREAVES, A. (eds) *Teachers' Professional Lives* (pp. 154–177), London, Falmer Press.

SUGRUE, C. (1996b) Primary Principals Perspectives on School Evaluation: Implications for professional development, *Irish Journal of Education*.

SUGRUE, C. (1996c) Reconstructing The Work Cultures of Teaching In The Irish Context, Dublin, INTO.

SUGRUE, C. (1996d) Change In Context: Back to the Future, in WILLIAMS, T. (ed.) *Primary Education in Lesotho: 2000 and Beyond*, Maseru, National University of Lesotho Press.

SULLIVAN, E. (1990) *Critical Psychology and Pedagogy: Interpretation of the Personal World*, Toronto, Ontario Institute for Studies in Education Press.

TANN, S. (1981) 'Grouping and group work', in SIMON, B. and WILLCOCKS, J.

(eds) *Research and Practice in the Primary Classroom* (pp. 43–54), London, Routledge and Kegan Paul.

THARP, R. and GALLIMORE, R. (1993) *Rousing Minds to Life: Teaching, Learning, and Schooling in Social Context*, Massachusetts, Cambridge University Press.

THOMPSON, J. (trans.) (1955) *The Ethics of Aristotle*, Harmondsworth, Penguin.

TOBIN, K. and MALONE, J. (1989) 'Differential participation in whole class activities', *Australian Journal of Education*, **33**, 3, pp. 320–31.

TÓIBÍN, C. (1991) 'Martyrs and metaphors', in BOLGER, D. (ed.) *Letters from the New Island* (pp. 44–55), Dublin, Raven Arts Press.

VAN DER EYKEN, W. (1982) *The Education of Three-to-Eight Year Olds in Europe in the Eighties*, Great Britain, NFER-Nelson.

VOEGLIN, E. (1966) *Plato*, Baton Rouge, Louisiana State University Press.

VYGOTSKY, L. (1989) *Thought and Language* (A. KOZULIN, ed. and trans.), Massachusetts, MIT Press.

WATSON, T. (1990) *Tests of Physical Fitness on Children from Irish National Schools*, Dublin, Cospóir Research Committee Report.

WATT, J. (1989) *Individualism and Educational Theory*, London, Kluwer Academic Publishers.

WERTSCH, J. (ed.) (1989) *Culture, Communication and Cognition: Vygotskian Perspectives*, New York, Cambridge University Press.

WERTSCH, J. (1991) *Voices of the Mind: A Sociocultural Approach to Mediated Action*, London, Harvester Wheatsheaf.

WHELAN, C., HANNAN, D. and CREIGHTON, S. (1991) *Unemployment, Poverty and Psychological Distress*, Dublin, Economic and Social Research Institute.

WHITEHEAD, A. (1962) *The Aims of Education and Other Essays*, London, Ernest Benn Limited.

WHITROCK, M. (ed.) (1986) *Handbook of Research on Teaching*, 3rd edn, London, Collier Macmillan.

WHITTY, G. (1985) *Sociology and School Knowledge*, London, Methuen.

WILLIAMS, K. (1995) 'Philosophy and curriculum policy', in HOGAN, P. (ed.) *Partnership and the Benefits of Learning*, Maynooth, Educational Studies Association of Ireland.

WILLIAMS, R. (1961) *Culture and Society 1780–1950*, London, Penguin Books Ltd.

WILLIAMS, T. (ed.) (1996) *Primary Education in Lesotho: 2000 and Beyond*, Maseru, University of Lesotho Press.

WILLIS, P. (1977) *Learning to Labour: How Working Class Kids Get Working Class Jobs*, Aldershot, Gower Publishing Company.

WINN, M. (1983) *Children Without Childhood*, London, Penguin Books.

WOLCOTT, H. (1992) 'Posturing in qualitative research', in LECOMPTE, M., MILLROY, W. and PREISSLE, J.J. (eds) *The Handbook of Qualitative Research in Education* (pp. 3–52), New York, Harcourt Brace and Company.

WOODS, P. (1984) 'Teaching for survival', in HARGREAVES, A. and WOODS, P. (eds) *Classrooms and Staffrooms: The Sociology of Teachers and Teaching* (pp. 48–63), Milton Keynes, Open University Press.

WOODS, P. (1993a) *Critical Events in Teaching and Learning*, London, Falmer Press.

WOODS, P. (1993b) 'Critical events in education', *British Journal of Sociology of Education*, **14**, 4, pp. 355–71.

WOODS, P. and JEFFREY, B. (1996) *Teachable Moments: The Art of Teaching in Primary Schools*, Buckingham, Open University Press.

YOUNG, M. (ed.) (1971) *Knowledge and Control*, London, Collier Macmillan.

ZILVERSMIT, A. (1993) *Changing Schools: Progressive Education Theory and Practice, 1930–1960*, Chicago, University of Chicago Press.

Index